ANOINTED PRAYERS TO PROVOKE YOUR DELIVERANCE AND BREAKTHROUGHS

A SPIRITUAL WARFARE & DELIVERANCE MANUAL

LADEJOLA ABIODUN

MESSAGE FROM THE AUTHOR

Dear valued reader,

I am Ladejola Abiodun, a pastor and author, and I hope you will find this book to be a powerful and transformative read. If the book has made a positive impact on your life, I would be so grateful if you could leave a review on Amazon. Your positive feedback will help others discover this work and will encourage me in my writing journey.

Your review doesn't have to be long or detailed. Even a few words about what you liked or what resonated with you can make a big difference. By sharing your thoughts with others, you'll be helping to spread the message of hope and inspiration contained within the pages of this book.

If you have any suggestions for improvement or constructive criticism, I would also love to hear from you. Your input will not only help me grow, but it will also benefit future readers.

Once again, thank you for taking the time to read this book. Your support and encouragement mean the world to me, and I am grateful for the impact that this book will make in your life.

Best regards,

Ladejola Abiodun

TABLE OF CONTENTS

CHAPTER ONE

Disgracing
Witchcraft Powers

Witchcraft is a leading power that has wrecked havoc in our world today. It is called public enemy number one. Everybody, one way or another has been affected by the operations of witchcraft powers. Therefore, whoever you are and wherever you are, you need to pray. Before I delve deeply into the topic, I want to remind you of our duty as believers, because many believers easily forget that we have a duty to God as people saved and washed by the precious blood of Jesus Christ. Our duty as children of God, who believe that we are going to meet God face to face is that we will give account of what we do with our lives here on earth. The life that we have is a gift, and if you read the Bible well, you would discover that we are called stewards. A steward is somebody whose responsibility is to take care of other people's property.

The Believer's Responsibility

The believer's responsibilities can be categorized into two. I call them the two Ss:

1. Soul Winning: This is making the world hear about Jesus. If actually it is true that you are saved, you are born again, it is your responsibility to win souls to the kingdom of God. Every child of God must be part of this assignment. This will determine whether you will be commended and rewarded or you will be queried and rebuked. This assignment will determine whether you will be commended or condemned. Please, don't forget that we are in the world to make our God known. We must endeavour to share His goodness with our friends, neighbours, colleagues, brothers and sisters and everyone we come across. It is a duty that we must keep doing otherwise, the blood of many souls will be required from us.

The Bible says he that wins souls is wise (Proverbs 11: 30). Meaning that he that does not win souls is foolish. The question is, if everything comes to an end now, what can you say that you have done for Jesus that will earn you a reward? Assuming that everything comes to a standstill now, what will you tell Jesus? What have you done? There are many people around you who need Jesus in their lives. You don't need to be a great preacher before you can preach to them. If you don't know how to preach, invite them to church so that they can hear the word of God. It was Apostle Paul who said, **"I am not ashamed of the gospel of Christ because it is the power of God to save souls."** Unfortunately, many believers are ashamed of the gospel. When they are going to church, they hide their Bibles inside their bags so that nobody will know that they are going to church. They are not even bold enough to tell people where they are going. Some people are only Christians in the city, when they go to their villages, they keep their mouths shut; they cannot preach the gospel to anybody.

2. Service: The second S stands for service. Another responsibility of believers that is also very important is serving in the house of God. People come to church; they take delight in coming to church but don't care how the house of God is doing. God saved you so you can save others, otherwise there is nothing stopping God from taking you away to heaven the day you got born again. But because we must serve, that is why He keeps us here on earth.

What is Witchcraft?

Witchcraft is the most combatant of the army of satan. The arsenal of witchcraft is the most effective and most used in the army of satan. Witchcraft is satan's executive power. The power carrying out satan's wish fully is witchcraft. Anywhere you see witchcraft, there would be carcasses and destinies that have been turned upside down. Witchcraft powers work with all the intelligence forces in the army of satan and with sophisticated equipment that have been developed to waste lives and destinies. The strength of witchcraft is the capacity to work without being detected. The capacity to work in secrecy and to hide their identity is what makes witchcraft very successful. They walk and you will never be able to trace their footsteps. They do evil and push the blame on somebody else. But thank God for His word in **Psalm 27:2: "When the wicked, even mine enemies and my foes came upon me to eat up my flesh, they stumbled and fell."**

Witchcraft powers are eaters of flesh and drinkers of blood. They have perfected the work of damaging peoples' lives and leaving no trace to them. No matter the classification people give to witchcraft, it does no good. People have classified it as white witchcraft and black witchcraft. They say one is kind while the other is wicked, but that is not what the Bible says about it. The Bible says, "Suffer not a witch to live." Meaning, kill them wherever you find them. Witchcraft is evil whether black, white, red or blue. All of them are evil and very destructive, they waste lives and destinies. Witchcraft is the highest level of wickedness and evil that you can imagine. It is merciless and inconsiderate. Whether you believe in the existence of witchcraft or not, it is inconsequential.

The first time I heard a witch confess was many years ago, it was a certain girl of about 10 years, who was so thin that she looked like a skeleton and of stunted growth. Nobody knew she was behind the series of calamities befalling her family until a revivalist came to the town. The man of God was so powerful that anywhere he appeared in a service, the witches and wizards there would come out and be confessing without him calling anybody to come out. This skeletal 10 year old girl attended the meeting and there, she confessed that all the cars, houses and money her family was supposed to have were inside her stomach. I looked at the stomach and it was very flat as if nothing was inside. But inside that stomach that looked like an egg were houses, cars, money, destinies and the goodness of her family members.

Many years ago, I read a book about a town in one of the African countries. In that town was a notorious witch, who was dealing with people. She specialized in wasting the destiny of people. Eventually, she started confessing. They asked her how she was able to remove people's brains and replace them with the brain of animals. To answer their question, she told to them to bring a big pawpaw fruit and put it on a table to prove to them that it was possible and they did. All that she did was to stare at the pawpaw and asked them to cut it open. By the time they cut the pawpaw open, all the flesh inside it had disappeared, nothing was found there. That is witchcraft technology to reverse people's destinies, to pull people down and to kill people. You might be wondering why this level of wickedness. But that is the world we are living in.

Two men were contesting for a chieftaincy title and one of them said to the other, "I will show you." By the following day, the one that was threatened woke up to find a coffin in his sitting room, without anyone breaking into the house. Which technology was used to achieve that feat? It is called witchcraft. When the man saw the coffin, although he was going to church, he changed his mind and went to get a native doctor to remove it. That was another complication.

If you are a pastor and you are not talking about deliverance, or praying for people to be healed, then you need to go for more training. There are churches now, if you tell them that you are being oppressed in the dream, they would say it is malaria, you should go and see a doctor. They don't understand anything about spiritual warfare. Such churches don't talk about the devil because they believe it is not necessary. They don't talk about witches, they just come to church, lift up their hands, do worship, read one scripture and everybody goes home. The devil does not have any problem

6

with such churches, in fact, he is happy with them because they are easy meat for him but they do not understand. Sometimes, when some people hear these things, they say it is impossible. But it is possible because the devil is able to perform some terrible wonders with witchcraft technology. Evil men and women can remove a woman's womb and replace it with a stone and there is no scanning machine that can detect the hand of witches, only fire prayers can detect and cut them off.

There was a man of God who did not believe in witchcraft; he only came to the pulpit and spoke good English. His church was full of witches but he didn't know until they messed him up. From that day, his eyes opened and he quickly believed that there is a wicked power called witchcraft. Witchcraft makes intelligent men and women useless. Some families, instead of producing geniuses, are producing mad men due to the activities of witchcraft. I pray that any witchcraft power that will not allow you to become the man or woman that God created you to be shall leave you alone and die, in the name of Jesus.

A certain man of God was in a conference where he was telling some pastors the importance of warfare prayers. He said, one man and his wife were praying in their house one night, and all of a sudden they heard a big bang on the roof. When they checked what it was, they saw a stranger standing in one of the rooms. It was a man, who was very angry and the man was accusing them of making him to crash land through their prayers. He said to the couple, "If I knew there would fire prayers going on here, I would not pass here at all. Now you must give me transport fare to go back to where I came from because I didn't plan to go by road." This is the kind of thing we are talking about. Witchcraft powers go about in the night to do evil when people are sleeping. Make your habitation too hot for witches to fly over, and if they try it, they die. Don't allow this power to overcome you rather, overcome them with the power in the blood of Jesus.

1 Peters 2:2 says, "As newborn babes, desire the sincere milk of the word that ye may grow thereby." It so important that you grow as a child of God. Don't just remain as a baby. You must grow, develop and mature. Your journey as a Christian starts the day you give your life to Jesus. When you give your life to Christ, you are like a new born baby. But as you study and grow in word of God with prayers, you begin to mature. **2 Peter 3:18 says, "But grow in grace, and in the knowledge of our Lord and Saviour Jesus Christ. To him be glory both now and for ever. Amen."**

If you come to church only on Sundays, you will not grow. It is akin to feeding or eating only once a week. But we eat food every time to maintain our well-being. It is the same thing with our spiritual growth. We keep eating and eating. And what do we eat? We eat the word of God and prayers. When you grow, you become eternity conscious. When you grow, you forgive people easily. When you grow, you rest in the Lord, you are no longer afraid, and your mind is at rest, no matter what is going on around you. A Christian that is not growing will be shaken at any little thing. When you grow, you are generous to God, and not stingy towards Him. Those that are growing in the Lord understand that anything they have is given to them by God. When you grow, you become powerful in the Lord. To deal with witchcraft powers, you must be spiritually strong and powerful.

Witchcraft powers are the most combatant in the army of satan and they are recording success. You can find them everywhere: household witchcraft, domestic witchcraft, environmental witchcraft, family witchcraft, sibling witchcraft etc. You can find witchcraft in every aspect of human life. Hardly would you see someone who has not suffered witchcraft attack in one area or another in his or her life. There is no witch that is good. Any love or care witches show to you is to help them capture and deal with you very well. They feed people very well in order to make them sumptuous Christmas goats. Witches don't understand relationship, the closer they are, the more wicked they become.

Galatians 5:12 says, "I would they were even cut off which trouble you." Micah 5:12 says, "And I will cut off witchcrafts out of thine hand; and thou shalt have no more soothsayers." Psalm 27:2 says, "When the wicked, even my enemies and my foes, came upon me to eat up my flesh, they stumbled and fell." In Exodus 22:18, the Bible says, "Thou shalt not suffer a witch to live." Leviticus 20:27 says, "A man also or woman that hath a familiar spirit, or that is a wizard, shall surely be put to death: they shall stone them with stones: their blood shall be upon them."

You can see that scriptures do not joke with the issues of witchcraft. Witchcraft has done a lot of havoc to families, communities and cities, and they have penetrated everywhere. There are blind witches, enfant witches, ancient witches, academic witches, illiterate witches, educated witches etc. They operate on the land, tree, water, air, everywhere. There are civilized and uncivilized witches, dormant and active witches, terrestrial witches, and conscious and unconscious witches. Whatever name they bear, they are still the same thing. They are all killers, wasters and destroyers.

Many years ago, there was a crusade somewhere, and a lady

who was using a wheelchair begged her sister to assist her to the crusade ground, and she agreed to help her. She wheeled her to the crusade ground for the three days the programme lasted. However, as programme came to an end on the third day, suddenly the power of God came down and her sister who was assisting her to the crusade ground started confessing to witchcraft. She said she was the one that put her on that wheelchair. They asked her why and she said she did it because she wanted to collect everything that belonged to her. As long as she was in that wheelchair, marriage and so many of her dreams cannot happen. That was how the lady received her deliverance.

Some people get attacked by witches in the night but they never find out until they get to the bathroom and see the marks on their bodies. When they pour water on their body, they have a peppery feeling. They inflict marks on the bodies of their victims, which they notice only when they wake up in the morning. The marks are to show that they visited you. They have done destructive works in the lives of many people. No wonder Apostle Paul said, "We wrestle not against flesh and blood but against principalities and powers, against the rulers of darkness of this world, and against spiritual wickedness in high places." Our battles are not physical but spiritual. The powers we are fighting reside in the heavenlies. They don't have physical bodies, they are invisible to the

11

naked eyes. They operate in the cosmic atmosphere. In **1 Corinthians 15:32, Paul said, "I have fought with beasts at Ephesus."** Paul was fighting forces of darkness, powers that were resisting the establishment of the church. I pray that every work of witches in your life shall be damaged, in the name of Jesus.

What makes people easy targets for witchcraft powers?

1.   **Abuse:** People that have been abused one way or another and they have not been healed from the abuse become easy targets for witches.

2.   **Anger:** Those who have uncontrollable anger are easy targets.

3.   **Careless eating:** Those who eat food anywhere and anyhow; in any restaurant or party. Some people would enter a restaurant and see charms hanging on the door or in a corner, yet they will still sit down there and eat.

4.   **Sexual immorality:** Those that are sexually loose are easy targets.

5.   **Excessive sleep:** Those who sleep too much will easily become victims of witchcraft.

6.   **Spirit of fear:** If fear is in your life, it would open door for all kinds of evil spirits to enter into your life. Job 3:25 says, "For the thing which I greatly feared is come upon me, and that which I was afraid of is come unto

me."

7. **Loneliness:** Those who feel lonely are easy targets.
8. **Low self-esteem:** Those who believe that they are ugly, or not good enough.
9. **Those who move about in the night:** Particularly those who always attend night parties.
10. **Unforgiving spirit:** Those who was once offended and they feel that they must revenge the offence. Some of them will be given the power to revenge by witches.
11. **Laziness:** Those who are lazy in spiritual things or those who cannot pray.
12. **Incomplete deliverance:** Those whose deliverance are not complete.
13. **Seeking help from Egypt:** Those who roam around strange places for spiritual help.

Potent weapons against witchcraft powers
1. Blood of Jesus (Revelation 12:11).
2. Fire of God (Hebrews 12: 29).
3. Praises (Psalm 149).
4. The word of God (Hebrews 4:12).
5. The name of the Lord (Philippians 2: 9-11).
6. Angels of God (Psalm 103:20).
7. Speaking in tongues (Acts 2:4).

Prayer Points

1. I cover my spirit, soul and body with the blood of Jesus, in the name of Jesus.
2. Witchcraft quota of suffering in my life and family, expire, in the name of Jesus.
3. Witchcraft powers waging war against my destiny, scatter, in the name of Jesus.
4. Powers gathered in my environment against my destiny, scatter, in the name of Jesus.
5. The work of witchcraft in my life and family, come to an end, in the name of Jesus.
6. Every witchcraft practice against me in the land, water and firmament, scatter, in the name of Jesus.
7. Every environmental coven that is troubling my life, wherever you are, catch fire, in the name of Jesus.
8. The hand of witches and wizards on my divine project, wither, in the name of Jesus.
9. Owners of evil load in my life, carry your load, in the name of Jesus.
10. Every chain of witchcraft tying me down, break, in the name of Jesus.
11. I pursue, I overtake and I recover all by the power in the blood of Jesus, in the name of Jesus.
12. Every conspiracy of darkness against my life in the heavenlies, scatter, in the name of Jesus.
13. Powers scattering what I am gathering, die, in the name of

Jesus.

14. Powers reporting me to the coven, O God, arise and scatter them, in the name of Jesus.

15. Garment of affliction assigned against me this year, catch fire, in the name of Jesus.

16. Powers sending satanic creatures to me at night, die by fire, in the name of Jesus.

17. Invisible walls surrounding my destiny, collapse by fire, in the name of Jesus.

18. Any power that wants to rubbish my destiny, you are a failure, die, in the name of Jesus.

19. I cover my spirit, soul and body with the blood of Jesus, in the name of Jesus.

20. I pursue, overtake and recover all, in the name of Jesus.

21. For every shame I have suffered, I receive double blessing, in the name of Jesus.

22. Forces and powers that have gathered together against me in the heavenlies, scatter, in the name of Jesus.

CHAPTER TWO

The Mystery of Satanic Arrows

Psalm 11:2 says, "For, lo, the wicked bend their bow, they make ready their arrow upon the string that they may privily shoot at the upright in the heart." From this passage of the Bible, you can see that the wicked have an assignment and the assignment is to distribute evil arrows. They send the arrows to people who are more righteous than them.

What is an Arrow?
1. An arrow is a device with a sharp point that can be shot at a person.
2. An arrow is a missile of darkness shot from a bow with a pointed or sharp end.
3. An arrow is sent to follow a direction.
4. An arrow has damaging effects.

5.   An arrow moves faithfully.
6.   An arrow moves fast and quick.
7.   An arrow is always directed at a particular target.
8.   An arrow has a source and a destination.
9.   There is someone operating every arrow.
10. An arrow does not manufacture or operate itself.
11. An arrow is made by someone.
12. An arrow is a weapon manufactured, produced, orchestrated and devised against a person.

Therefore, a satanic arrow is a device satanically prepared to oppress, possess and obsess. It can be described as an instrument of oppression, possession and obsession. Satanic arrows are specifically prepared to steal, kill and destroy. Satanic arrows are not fired for fun but to cause havoc in the lives of their targets. An arrow is the most potent and common weapon in the custody of satan.

Ephesians 6:16 says, "Above all, taking the shield of faith, wherewith ye shall be able to quench all the fiery darts of the wicked."

Heaven has provided an armoury for believers with which we can clothe ourselves such as the helmet of salvation and the sword of the Spirit, which is the word of God. As long as you wear these materials, you are well protected because the enemy cannot penetrate them to get to you. They are there to protect you against flying arrows, attacks from hell and arrows that are shot at you from the dark places of the earth. Arrows are produced in dark places of the world. What they do is destruction. The Bible calls them the dark places of the earth. Evil arrows are fired from there against those who are in the light. They fire arrows at those who are prospering in their careers, and those who are aspiring to make it in life. They fire arrows at anyone who wants to fulfill his destiny or who wants to rise in life. They can fire an arrow at somebody and it incubates in the life of the person for as long as they wish until the time it is assigned to begin to function. When the time comes for the arrow to begin to work, it starts to work. Some people are already dead although they are moving about. There are lots of walking corpses on the streets. Although they look well without any sign that something is wrong with them, there are many things already hidden in their hearts and other organs of their bodies yet to manifest. The arrows are already there waiting for the day of manifestation.

Psalm 91:5 says, "Thou shalt not be afraid for the terror by night; nor for the arrow that flieth by day." Arrows fly about but it takes an open eye to see them. Arrows are flying all over the place, moving from one location to another. All kinds of things are moving in the air but if God doesn't open your eyes, you can't see them. How do you explain the situation of someone who went for an exam, arrived in the exam hall, but immediately he was given the question paper to start writing, he slept off. That is the work of an evil arrow. There was a young man, who visited his sister in his car. He did this regularly. That day, he drove into her compound and parked his car in the usual place, only for him to get missing between the car park and his sister's house. He was not seen for two years. The car was where he parked it, but he was nowhere to be found. By the time they found him, he said he parked the car and something said to him, "Move away." He started roaming around and they couldn't find him until after two years. It is not normal; an arrow was fired at him which resulted in that predicament.

Children of God have divine protection that is why the arrows of the enemy cannot harm them. However, the moment a child of God starts sinning against God, the hedge of protection will be removed and the serpent will bite the person. The bite of the serpent is not good because the person bitten may never recover from it for life.

A husband and wife were sleeping on the bed, an arrow came, and the wife woke up, removed her clothes and started walking out naked. Somewhere along the way that night, she suddenly came to her senses. She looked at herself and discovered she was naked. She said to herself, "How come I'm naked on the street at this hour of the night?" It was then she went back home. If she didn't come to herself, she would have ran mad just like that. Many people slept in the night but they never woke up. They did not live to tell what they passed through in the night before they died. Many people encountered some strange powers, which were stronger than them but they didn't live to tell the story.

In **Isaiah 54:17, the Bible says, "No weapon that is formed against thee shall prosper; and every tongue that shall rise against thee in judgment thou shalt condemn. This is the heritage of the servants of the Lord, and their righteousness is of me, saith the Lord."**

The enemy does not form the same weapon for everybody; they look at your prayer life, your lifestyle and consider many things before they arrive at a particular weapon that will suit you. And if you are weak, they will get you. I want you to know that the whole world lies in wickedness according to **I John 5:19: "And we know that we are of God, and the whole world lieth in wickedness."**

The world is full of evil and wicked people. They are already here with us. People who drink and suck blood are mixed up with us. Unfortunately, it is not written on anyone's face, so don't be deceived by the looks of people and the way they dress. Many people you see on the street dressed in three-piece suits are witch doctors. Don't be carried away by the grammar they speak, some of them have their altars inside their stomachs. If they change to the realm of incantation, you would be amazed that they belong to the other side. If they tell you the places they have been to, you won't believe it. Some of them with their big SUVs visit evil spirits in the forests. Now we see all kinds of competition in corporate organizations. People are ready to kill one another because of position. That is the extent of the evil now. In many offices, many people are dabbling into fetish things to achieve what they want. That is why as a Christian, you have to empower yourself to be able to withstand the evil that is going on now. There are people who are still moving around but they have been shared out already by wicked people. Those that will pick the different body organs for consumption have already collected them. They are simply waiting for the person to pack up.

The Bible says that all the imaginations of the wicked are evil. **Proverbs 4:16-17: "For they sleep not, except they have done mischief; and their sleep is taken away, unless they cause some to fall. For they eat the bread of wickedness, and drink the wine of violence."**

These powers and those they possess are evil, they do wicked things. **Psalm 7:13 says, "He hath also prepared for him the** instruments of death; he ordaineth his arrows against the persecutors."** The arrow here is an instrument of death, they use it to kill people. So, if you don't want to die before your time, you need to pray against them. When this arrow hits some people, they will not wake up. It is an instrument of death. It has destroyed many lives and has wasted many glorious destinies.

In **Ezekiel 21:21**, we are told that there are people who have the capacity to see into people's liver. They project evil into people's liver and that is why at the hospital, you see all kinds of sicknesses that cannot be explained medically. The wicked have images that they project as human beings. When they want to attack a person, they will mention the person's name and say, "You this image, you are representing this person." Then they stick a pin-like object into the eyes of the image representing the person to puncture the eyes. And wherever the person is, he or she may become blind or wounded in the eyes.

Different Types Of Arrows
There are different types of arrows:
- Arrow of paralysis.
- Arrow of confusion.
- Arrow that makes people to lose good things.
- Arrow that wastes resources.

- Arrow of affliction.
- Arrow of torment.
- Arrow of manipulation.
- Devouring arrow.
- Arrow in the blood.
- Arrow of evil smell.
- Arrow of spiritual slumber.
- Arrow of suicide.
- Arrow of poverty.
- Arrow of aimlessness.
- Poisonous arrow.
- Peppery arrow.
- Burning arrow.
- Occult arrow.
- Arrow of infirmity.

Every fired arrow has a source and also a destination. An arrow is made by someone. **Psalm 45:3-5 says, "Gird thy sword upon thy thigh, O most mighty, with thy glory and thy majesty. And in thy majesty ride prosperously because of truth and meekness and righteousness; and thy right hand shall teach thee terrible things. Thine arrows are sharp in the heart of the king's enemies; whereby the people fall under thee."**

Arrows are specially made instruments of wickedness. They

are the most common weapon the enemy uses from time to time. In Ephesians 6, the Bible described an arrow as an instrument in the hand of the wicked. Arrows can pierce. It has wounding power, and can hide in the body. **Psalm 74:20 says, "Have respect unto the covenant: for the dark places of the earth are full of the habitations of cruelty."** The Bible says the wicked hide in dark places from where they shoot arrows at the upright. Every arrow is made by someone, targeting someone. That is why the Bible says in **Psalm 7:13: "He hath also prepared for him the instruments of death; he ordaineth his arrows against the persecutors."** There is an example of somebody in the Bible who was killed by evil arrows. The son of the widow, whom she gave birth to in her old age was killed by an arrow of death, which was shot at him. The boy fell and died. He was shouting, "My head, my head!" and gave up. Strange arrows were fired at him. The evil arrow fashioned and released against the boy was an arrow from the demonic world to terminate his life. I pray that every arrow looking for you shall go back to the sender, in Jesus' name.

Some people are going through some problems that are unbelievable. But when you see them, they carry on as if all is well but all is not well at all. There was a lady, who was a director in an organization with good working conditions. But she had a spiritual problem that nobody could understand or explain. Her problem was that when she walked on the road, an unseen wall would block her both in front and at the back and she would stay in the middle. She would be trapped there, struggling with the wall that did not exist. She was a director in an office, but see what the enemy was doing to her publicly. Many times, motorists would curse and boo her because they did not understand her problem. She could be there for ten minutes before the wall would disappear for her to move. That is a strange attack, a strange battle and a strange evil load of darkness that cannot be explained by any human being. I pray that any strange arrow deployed against you shall go back to the sender, in Jesus' name. Anyone devising for you to fall, they will not stand, themselves, in the name of Jesus.

Some arrows can make somebody to harm himself, and start regretting later. If a vehicle knocks down somebody on the road and the person dies, nobody will know what the person was going through before the calamity, or how long he or she was under the torment of the evil arrow. A certain man in the Bible was cutting himself with stones. Blood was gushing out but he could not stop. He could not help himself. That couldn't be normal, it was an arrow.

One day, a man who was working in a very big company as managing director with a good salary came to the office and tendered his resignation letter. They asked him if anyone offended him and he said no. They asked if he had got another job and he said, no. Then the company accepted his resignation letter. After they have accepted for him to go, he came to himself and started asking for the job he had resigned from. The company now said, "Mr. Man, we didn't chase you away, you resigned by yourself. So, go away." There are many people like that who lost good chances because of the evil arrows fired at them.

There was a boy, who was the only light in the family. He was the one taking care of his mother and siblings. One day, the evil group that the mother belonged said she had to donate one of her children, but instead of her donating the ones that were not so useful, she donated the only light in the family. In the spiritual realm, they put the boy in a pot, put the pot on fire and were cooking him. That was how the boy started having problems, and they were taking him from one place to another. He complained about heat in the body, head etc. The doctors sent him for scan and nothing was found to be wrong with him. Eventually, the boy died. After his death, his mother said it was not her fault but the group she belonged said they didn't need anyone else but the one she donated.

One brother gave a testimony of how witches descended on him and shared his body parts. At that point, he was brought for prayers. Flies were already perching on his body and his case appeared hopeless. He was prayed for and in the night,

Jesus appeared in the houses of all the witches that were in charge of his case. He said to one, "You are the one they gave his heart to, vomit it." And to another one, He said, "You are the one they gave his lungs to, vomit them." That was how He collected all his organs back and the man recovered mysteriously.

When an arrow is fired, two things can happen: The arrow might or might not prosper. But it may interest you to know that there are people, who the enemy fires arrows at and it returns to the enemy. The arrows the enemy fires at them boomerangs on the enemy. There are people, you mention their names and there would be an explosion. If you bring something to represent them, fire will answer on their behalf. That is the kind of person you should be. But for you to get to that point, you must take your life seriously. You must not live a careless life. Others may be drinking alcohol but you must not join them. Anyone that wants the presence of God around him and anyone that wants to carry the glory of God around him doesn't live carelessly. The reason is that the enemies are waiting for you to make mistakes, or do something that will remove the hedge around you. They will make attempts to penetrate but they will not succeed because there is a hedge of fire around you. That hedge of fire is what makes it difficult for them to penetrate otherwise, you will sleep and they will mess

27

you up. So, you must not allow it to be removed, and your prayer life must be strong.

Isaiah 59:1-2 says, "Behold, the Lord's hand is not shortened, that it cannot save; neither his ear heavy that it cannot hear: But your iniquities have separated between you and your God, and your sins have hid his face from you, that he will not hear." When you live in sin, defiling your body through immorality and harbouring evil thoughts, the Holy Spirit will leave you. The Holy Spirit cannot stay in an unholy place. Drunkenness, gambling, evil thoughts, and all kinds of evil things would make the presence of God to depart from a person's life. **Ecclesiastes 10:8 says, "He that diggeth a pit shall fall into it; and whoso breaketh an hedge, a serpent shall bite him."**

What to do
1.   Repent of all your sins.
2.   Pray back to sender prayers (Proverbs 26:27, Proverbs 28:10).

Prayer Points
1.   Evil arrows in any part of my body, go back to your senders, in the name of Jesus.
2.   Arrows from occult powers, go back to your senders, in the

name of Jesus.

3. Arrows of evil wind, go back to your sender, in the name of Jesus.

4. Arrow of wasted resources, go back to your sender, in the name of Jesus.

5. Arrow of evil smell, go back to your sender, in the name of Jesus.

6. Arrow of evil summon, go back to your sender, in the name of Jesus.

7. Arrow of the dropout, go back to the sender, in the name of Jesus.

8. My life, shall not be a dumping ground for evil arrows, in the name of Jesus.

9. Anywhere my name is mentioned for evil arrows, Holy Ghost fire, answer on my behalf, in the name of Jesus.

10. Arrow of use and dump, come out of my life, in the name of Jesus.

11. Evil arrows drinking the blood of my success, come out and die, in the name of Jesus.

12. Arrows assigned to kill good things in my life, die, in the name of Jesus.

13. Arrows attracting strange battles into my life, backfire, in the name of Jesus.

14. Arrows assigned to detain me in captivity, backfire, in the name of Jesus.

29

15. Oh God of possibility, answer your name in my life, in the name of Jesus.

16. Rain of favour, fall upon me, in the name of Jesus.

17. I send evil arrows back to the sender, in the name of Jesus.

18. Arrow of brain damage, go back to your sender, in the name of Jesus.

19. Arrow of poverty, go back to your sender, in the name of Jesus.

20. Arrow of exchange of blessings, go back to your sender, in the name of Jesus.

21. Blood of Jesus, purge my body of evil arrows, in the name of Jesus.

22. I fire back any arrow fired against my brain from an evil altar, in the name of Jesus.

23. Arrows fired to delay my celebration, backfire, in the name of Jesus.

24. Arrows of mockery and shame fired against me, backfire, in the name of Jesus.

25. Arrows of environmental and territorial bondage, break and release me, in the name of Jesus.

26. Arrows fired into my body, waiting for a particular time to strike, die, in the name of Jesus.

27. Any arrow hiding in my body, dry up, in the name of Jesus.

28. Holy Ghost, overshadow my life with miracles, signs and wonders, in the name of Jesus.

29. Every serpent hiding in my foundation, I chase you out, in

the name of Jesus.

30. Every handwriting of failure against my destiny, clear away, in the name of Jesus.

31. Poison of darkness in my blood, be flushed out, in the name of Jesus.

32. Every evil hand touching me, wither, in the name of Jesus.

CHAPTER THREE

Breaking the Foundation
of Stubborn Bondage

Proverbs 23:18 says, "For surely there is an end; and thine expectation shall not be cut off." Perhaps you have been asking God when your problem will be over, when the attack will cease or when you will have peace of mind? Believe that God is going to dry up the foundation of that problem and that His power will consume the problem. Isaiah 22:25 says, "In that day, saith the Lord of hosts, shall the nail that is fastened in the sure place be removed, and be cut down, and fall; and the burden that was upon it shall be cut off: for the Lord hath spoken it." Micah 5:9 says, "Thine hand shall be lifted up upon thine adversaries, and all thine enemies shall be cut off." Galatians 5:12 says, "I would they were even cut off which trouble you." Micah 5:12 says, "And I will cut off witchcrafts out of thine hand; and thou shalt have no more soothsayers."

What makes a problem stubborn? How do you explain a

stubborn problem? What are the features of stubborn problems? What is the description of a stubborn problem?

When we say stubborn problems, we mean problems that are complicated; problems that are not easily solved. It means difficult problems. Some problems can be easily solved, taken out, or dealt with, while some are unbendable, unrepentant and adamant but God is stronger than them. When we talk about stubborn problems, we are talking about problems that defy solution.

Stubborn problems are problems that refuse to let you go.

Stubborn problems are pretentious problems.

Stubborn problems are life-threatening problems.

Stubborn problems are problems that do not want you to exist.

Stubborn problems are problems that do not want you to have a breathing space.

Stubborn problems are problems that are after your healing and survival.

Stubborn problems are problems with multiple sources and tentacles. They have different branches; as you deal with one, another one is still somewhere.

Wicked Alliance

There are enemies who agree together for the purpose of dealing with their common enemy. We have a good example in the Bible, where Pilate and Herod who were not friends at all came together because they had a common goal of killing

Jesus; they reconciled for a moment. Likewise there are problems that conspire to kill or punish a person.

Isaiah 8:9-10 says, "Associate yourselves, O ye people, and ye shall be broken in pieces; and give ear, all ye of far countries: gird yourselves, and ye shall be broken in pieces; gird yourselves, and ye shall be broken in pieces. Take counsel together, and it shall come to nought; speak the word, and it shall not stand: for God is with us."

The mighty hand of God to deliver is not in doubt for He has done it for several people. There is nothing that can be compared to your peace and freedom. Any price you pay to secure your freedom is worth it. It is when you begin to enjoy freedom that you will understand that there is nothing to be compared with freedom. Unfortunately, there are many children of God who are in one bondage or another. They are being tossed up and down by their enemies. There are so many children of God that are battling with deep rooted problems. There so many too, whose deliverance is incomplete. There are many, who need a second touch of power. That is why Jesus came to give liberty, freedom, to set the captives free and to break yokes.

The strongest of witchcraft powers is called familiar spirit. If the whole of your life is cleared of the rubbish of familiar spirit, you will be amazed at what will happen to your life.

Familiar spirit is a terrible spirit. **Deuteronomy 18:10-11 says, "There shall not be found among you any one that maketh his son or his daughter to pass through the fire, or that useth divination, or an observer of times, or an enchanter, or a witch, or a charmer, or a consulter with familiar spirits, or a wizard, or a necromancer."**

Once you belong to God, you have no business with familiar spirits. The last sin that King Saul committed was consultation with familiar spirits, with the witch in Endor. The witch in Endor used her satanic powers to call out Samuel and that was the end of King Saul. In Africa, people believe in ancestral spirits. Thank God for churches and the work of the Lord in the land for the past forty years. There was so much idolatry, wickedness, and witchcraft activities before the coming of the missionaries who planted churches. They believed in their ancestors and their tradition such that when a child is born, they don't have anything to do with that child until they have taken him to a chief priest. It was the priest that would give a name to the child. They consulted evil spirits and sought help from them. In times of war, they went to satan to collect power to appear and disappear. Those were the things they relied upon. Many of our fathers believed that the spirit of their ancestors is guiding them even up till now. Some people believe that they can receive blessings from their ancestors.

You see people pouring libation, making sacrifices and doing rituals. Thank God for Christianity. I grew up seeing people eating things sacrificed to idols especially when they give birth to twins. They believed that the twins would die if the rituals were not done. The romance and consultation with dark powers are the reasons many lives are in trouble today. Eating of special beans and bean cakes is also part of it.

Burial is another ritual through which many people enter into captivity of darkness. The Bible says, the dead has nothing to do with the living but it is a problem to Africa because of the way burials are done in this part of the world. Marriage is also another way through which people get into big problem. The marriage ceremonies entail a lot of rituals. There is a number of certain items such as yams, kola nuts etc. that a suitor must produce, the washing of feet, face etc. are the reasons why so many things are not working.

Many people are in trouble also because of the names they were given. For example, Nnenna, Babatunde, Onwubiko, Nwosu etc. Many of these names are demonic; they are ancestral names. There are terribly wicked spirits attached to these names which pretend to be friendly but they lure the bearers into making covenants with them. And as soon as the covenant is formed, their lives are controlled by these evil spirits. Before some people can be totally free, they will need to direct the sword of their prayers towards familiar spirits, ancestral spirits, and the spirit of their forefathers. These are closely connected with the spirits of witchcraft, soothsaying, divination, sorcery, and mediums. These are satanic powers, that is why children of witch doctors and those involved in these things don't find life easy because these spirits go after them. But any victim that runs to Jesus Christ and trusts God, will receive deliverance.

Familiar spirits are the spirits that satan plants in a family to carry out his will. They are the spirits in charge of the family. They are the spirits planted in the family by satan to fulfill John 10:10. Familiar spirits are in every family and they don't die. They ensure that the will of satan is enforced in the family. Familiar spirits are the spirits that know everything about you. They know your history, the events happening in the family, and the mistakes that have been made in the past so they are ready to work on those mistakes to punish all the children in the family. Anywhere you see poverty, affliction and sicknesses being transferred from one generation to another, know that familiar spirits are at work. They ensure that the bondage in the family remains there. They ensure that the troubles in the family remain there. They are the ones that promote curses and ensure that the curses in the family are propagated. In **Isaiah 8:19, the Bible says, "And when they shall say unto you, Seek unto them that have familiar spirits, and unto wizards that peep, and that mutter: should not a people seek unto their God? For the living to the dead?"**

Familiar spirits are the spirits that speak death, affliction, failure, diseases, poverty, oppression, confusion etc. Anytime good things are coming, they speak and say the person will not have it. Familiar spirits check the files of every member of the family and apportion punishment as they deem fit. Familiar spirits monitor, and transmit information from one place to another. Familiar spirits are behind fake and counterfeit prophecies. In Acts 16:16, a damsel was following Paul and the other disciples around, declaring that they were the servants of the Most High. But Apostle Paul discovered that the spirit in her was a familiar spirit and he quickly cast the evil spirit out of the girl. The girl was saying the correct thing but with a wrong spirit that was not from God. Immediately Paul cast out the spirit, the girl's ability to see visions and to prophesy ceased.

Micah 5:9 says, "Thine hand shall be lifted up upon thine adversaries, and all thine enemies shall be cut off."

Micah 5:12: "And I will cut off witchcrafts out of thine hand; and thou shalt have no more soothsayers."

Jeremiah 1:10: "See, I have this day set thee over the nations and over the kingdoms, to root out, and to pull down, and to destroy, and to throw down, to build, and to plant."

In **Galatians 5:12, the Bible says, "I would they were even cut off which trouble you."** It means that all the powers that are troubling you, whether they are witches, wizards or household wickedness, all of them will be cut off.

Deliverance is not by power or by might but by the Spirit of God. It is the Spirit of God that does the work. **Isaiah 59:19 says, "So shall they fear the name of the Lord from the west, and his glory from the rising of the sun. When the enemy shall come in like a flood, the Spirit of the Lord shall lift up a standard against him." Luke 5:17 says, "And it came to pass on a certain day, as he was teaching, that there were Pharisees and doctors of the law sitting by, which were come out of every town of Galilee, and Judaea, and Jerusalem: and the power of the Lord was present to heal them."** The Bible says that Jesus was ministering, but the power of God was present to heal them. So, they are invisible but you cannot deny their operations.

In the African culture, there is belief in familiar spirits. Many people would hardly do anything without making consultations with these spirits. Most of the worship revolves around familiar spirits. People go to altars, shrines, etc. to make consultations. They are told to offer sacrifices, put things at road junctions or in rivers. These are what we call familiar spirits. Familiar spirits mean household servants. They have been in the family for generations. Many people are being held down by these spirits; that is why if you go to any of their prophets, they would deceive you. They know every information about you and you think they are genuine but they are fake. They have sourced the information using the spirit of the devil.

Familiar spirits transfer problems from the older generation to the younger generation. They enforce sicknesses and make sure the problem of an old man is also seen in the life of the younger ones. If a father was a drunkard, the children would also follow the same pattern. If the father was a polygamist, the children would also follow suit. That is wickedness of the highest order. You look at the children and see the same trend in their lives. Some of the things we see today did not just start, they have been in operation for many years.

There are people who have the wicked power to call up

people's spirits like in the case of Saul and the witch of Endor. There was a lady who was working as a cleaner in one organization. She got information that there was going to be a retrenchment exercise in her company. She discussed it with her friend, who promised to take her somewhere, so she would not be affected. The purpose for which she went there was to retain her job but when she got there, the man brought out a mirror and asked her who would compile the names of those to be retrenched? She mentioned the name of the person. The man said, "Take this mirror in your hand. I will call her name and she will come out in the mirror. As soon as you see her appear in the mirror, make sure you hit her." The lady said, "No, I didn't come here to kill anybody but to retain my job." The friend that took her there said to her, "Obey his instructions and do not slack." She insisted that she did not come there to kill and would not be part of it. The man said, "It's too late. However, if you don't want to kill her just target her eyes and hit her there." As the argument was going on, she accepted as she was instructed by the man and that was it. The woman that was to compile the list of those to be retrenched came to work one early morning, not knowing what was going on. As she sat on her chair, something like pin came from nowhere and entered into her eyes and she started shouting and crying. As she was shouting, it was the same cleaner who was in charge of her case that came to help her to blow the thing out of her eyes. It was the same person who took her name to the evil man that was blowing breeze into her eyes. That was how the lady that was supposed to compile the list was taken out of the company.

Familiar spirits are responsible for like-father-like-son and like-mother-like-daughter problems. The cycle of hereditary problems and afflictions that continue in the family, such as high blood pressure, hypertension, asthma, alcoholism etc. are the handiwork of familiar spirits. Familiar spirits manipulate their victims. They make them to come under a strange power and manipulation. When somebody is under the influence of familiar spirits, he won't know what he is doing. He would be acting like someone under a spell. He would see correction as abnormal. There was a certain young man, who was said to be smoking seven packets of cigarettes every day. One day, a man of God preached to him and he said to the man of God, "I was smoking seven packets of cigarettes in a day but for coming to preach to me, I will increase it to nine packets a day." That is the work of familiar spirits. The person will not see anything wrong in what he is doing. The same money that some people have used to build a house, somebody else will be using it to smoke and he won't see anything wrong with it. When you see people doing the wrong thing and you talk to them about it and they become angry and say, "Why are you talking to me?" It is the work of familiar spirits. Such a person may discover his problem when it is too late and nobody can help him. These spirits are also behind so many suicide cases. They are also called medium spirits; these are the spirits that mediate between men and other spirits. They cause people to move from one place to another, seeking help.

Many children don't know how they came about. Many don't know what their parents went through. Some people were searching for a particular sex and got into trouble along the line. For example, people who were having female children may want male children or vice versa and then they go somewhere, where they are given something to use, eat or cast into the river. Now the child is born and he or she doesn't know that he or she is connected to a river.

People use all kinds of things to fight their courses. A certain woman was promoted to the post of a regional manager in the bank and before they knew it, she started urinating uncontrollably. Initially she was managing it by using disposable nappies, but after sometime, people started noticing the stench in her office, and she had to resign from the job. That is why you must be careful where you go. They put things on people's chairs, under their seats and do all sorts

43

of things.

Familiar spirits hate righteousness and they don't want it. If you want to live a holy life, they will fight against you. They don't want you to serve God. They will do everything to discourage you from the path of righteousness. The level of manipulation of families today is unprecedented. Look at the kind of sins that are ravaging families today. There are fathers having carnal knowledge of their daughters, sons sleeping with their mothers, etc. That is the extent to which things are going on now.

Familiar spirits are good record keepers; they keep record of past mistakes. Familiar spirit is the counterfeit of the Holy Spirit. That is why when prayers are hot, you see some people manifesting very strangely. You see some people shouting and shaking. They will cease to be normal human beings. You see normal people behaving strangely because these spirits are inside them. I saw a family, where all the four boys were mad. That is the work of ancestral spirits. There are familiar spirits manifesting in children particularly, when you see excessive stubbornness. Children who would not be at peace until they see blood. They go out, break somebody's head, hit somebody and blood would be gushing out. All these are the handiwork of familiar spirits. There are also children, whose problem is constant sickness. You see deformed children who come to waste the wealth of the family through sickness. The assignment of these strange children is to trouble the family. Some children are possessed by the spirit of anger; the anger inside them is worse than the devil's. I know a boy, who anytime his teacher was talking, he would go to the teacher, interrupt him and say, "I know what you are teaching more than you." Then he would slap the teacher. He was dismissed from the school because of his bad behaviour. There are teachers who discipline their students during the day and in the night, it would be the turn of the children to visit them and flog them on the bed. These kinds of children go into crime and don't mix up with people. They just want to be alone. Also, they can eat anything.

One little girl was brought for prayer after she had been taken to a white garment prophet. When the white garment prophet saw her, he prostrated for her and said, "This is our mother." The parents of the girl started crying and said to the prophet, "We brought this girl for you to deliver her and you are calling her your mother." The prophet said to the mother that her daughter is their senior. The girl had ruined her family, spoilt their business and the family was already tired. But before the girl was brought to the church, they decided to kill her, not by hand but by taking her to one big forest where she would not be able to trace her way back home and leave her there. When they got home, to their shock, it was the girl that came to open the door for them, and she had eaten the little food they had in the kitchen. It was at that level they knew they needed to go to a higher level to look for solution.

When a child that has not seen life is talking about suicide, or when you see children that are notorious for stealing, they enter into a house and the spirit inside them tells them where the things they really want are kept and they go there straight, it is these powers. Some of these children are lazy in everything. They don't want prayers. Anytime you say, "Let us pray," they would pretend to be sleeping. It is deception; there is a spirit in them that doesn't like prayer. Some of them cry or shout from their sleep or talk to an invisible being or put their legs up while sleeping.

How do people get possessed by familiar spirits?
1. Through child dedication.
2. By attending uniform churches such as white, red, green etc. garment churches.
3. Eating from the dining table of darkness.
4. Reading of occult books.
5. Watching satanic films like horror films.
6. Going to the cemetery for spiritual help.
7. Through incisions and drinking of concoctions.

Prayer Points

1. Holy Ghost fire, set me free, in the name of Jesus.
2. Any problem in my life that is older than me, die, in the name of Jesus.
3. Hammer of the Almighty, dismantle the altar of familiar spirits, in the name of Jesus.
4. Wind of the Holy Ghost, blow away the poison of familiar spirits in my body, in the name of Jesus.
5. I withdraw my prosperity from the hands of familiar spirits, in the name of Jesus.
6. I destroy any image representing me on any familiar spirit altar, in the name of Jesus.
7. I command any problem created in my life by familiar spirits to die, in the name of Jesus.
8. Familiar spirits battle limiting my progress, die, in the name of Jesus.
9. Every internal coffin planted by familiar spirits, catch fire, in the name of Jesus.
10. Strangers living in my house, the fire of God is against you, die, in the name of Jesus.
11. Whatsoever the Almighty God did not plant in my life, catch fire, in the name of Jesus.
12. Cage of familiar spirits, release me by fire, in the name of Jesus.

47

13. Every veil of familiar spirits shielding me away from my helpers, burn to ashes, in the name of Jesus.

14. Every yoke of familiar spirits that has refused to let me go, break, in the name of Jesus.

15. Familiar spirits assigned to destroy my faith in God and make me a liar, die, in the name of Jesus.

16. Any man or woman that is flying in any basket against my destiny, crash land, in the name of Jesus.

17. I shoot down the army of familiar spirits shooting at me, in the name of Jesus.

18. Every internal coffin planted in my body by familiar spirits, catch fire, in the name of Jesus.

19. Holy Ghost fire, set me free, in the name of Jesus.

CHAPTER FOUR

Disgracing Environmental Wickedness

Every environment has its peculiar challenges and problems. We know that satan is not omnipresent, omniscient or omnipotent but he has his agents located in strategic places, working for him and carrying out his will, plans and evil purposes. That is why we see that every environment has its own problems, peculiar challenges and troubles.

If you are from the riverine area, you cannot escape being troubled by marine witchcraft and marine attacks in your marriage, health, business and destiny as a whole. It is an environmental challenge. However, there is no environment that is free; every environment has its own peculiar problems. 1 John 5:19 says, "And we know that we are of God, and the

whole world lieth in wickedness. *"* The meaning of that is that there is wickedness going on everywhere. It is not a problem of Africa alone or America alone or Europe alone but everywhere. Everywhere has its own share of wickedness.

The enemy is very wicked, they attack without mercy. There is nothing like mercy in the dictionary of the enemy. The enemy rejoices when you are ignorant of his methods of attack. The enemy rejoices when you don't know that he is the one attacking you and you are blaming what he is doing on another person. The enemy rejoices when you are completely ignorant that he is the one attacking you and you think that it is something else going on. That is why we must not be ignorant of the devices of the enemy.

In Ephesians 6:12, it is written, **"For we wrestle not against flesh and blood, but against principalities, against powers, against the rulers of the darkness of this world, against spiritual wickedness in high places."** So, wickedness is real, environmental wickedness is also real. Witches and wizards are real. Demonic oppression is real. When the enemy enters your house and begins to press you down to kill you; that is real. Someone that is going through oppression may lose his senses. The Bible says that oppression makes a wise man mad. The realm of the occult is real. People that gather together somewhere through astral travel in the night, to hold meetings on how to destroy, to kill people, to bury people, to use people for sacrifice, to make money, etc. are all real. You may still be arguing that there is nothing like that but as far as the Bible is concerned, they are real. Casting of spell, voodoo, witchcraft power, enchantment, divination, sorcery and manipulation are all real. You better wake up and fight the battle of life.

Isaiah 58:6 says, "Is not this the fast that I have chosen? To loose the bands of wickedness, to undo the heavy burdens, and to let the oppressed go free, and that ye break every yoke?" There is something called the band of wickedness. The enemy uses it to bind people and such people would go from one level of suffering to another.

Types of Bands of Wickedness

There are different bands of wickedness described in the Scriptures:

1. Psalm 10:15 says, "Break thou the arm of the wicked and the evil man: seek out his wickedness till thou find none."
2. Psalm 37:17: "For the arms of the wicked shall be broken: but the Lord upholdeth the righteous."
3. Psalm 75:10: "All the horns of the wicked also will I cut off; but the horns of the righteous shall be exalted." The

Bible is talking about the horn of the wicked. Some people would tell you that in their dream, they saw a cow chasing them around. That is the horn of the wicked. In the book of Zechariah 1:21, the Bible talks about the horn that scatters Judah; the horn that stops people from moving forward and the horn that hinders people from rising up to great heights in life.

4. Psalm 125:3: **"For the rod of the wicked shall not rest upon the lot of the righteous; lest the righteous put forth their hands unto iniquity."** There is something called the rod of the wicked. It is the rod of torment, the rod of affliction and the rod to cause trouble in the lives of people. Whoever this rod comes upon begins to suffer. When they lay this rod upon a person, maybe on his head, he will go to the hospital to waste his money and there will be no improvement until the rod is broken or set on fire.

5. **Psalm 129:4: "The Lord is righteous: he hath cut asunder the cords of the wicked."**

6. **Isaiah 14:5: "The Lord hath broken the staff of the wicked, and the sceptre of the rulers."**

7. **Psalm 119:61: "The bands of the wicked have robbed me: but I have not forgotten thy law."**

When the band of the wicked is upon a person, it would rob the person of his or her peace, joy, prosperity, and good health.

Various Bands

1.   Evil spell: Many people are under a spell. Such people have their eyes open but are blind spiritually. They have their eyes open but they are not able to see th midst of plenty and abundance but are isolated. They work very hard but have nothing to show for it. They are loving e opportunities and favours around them. They exist in theand kind but are not appreciated. The enemy ensures that their good character is misinterpreted; and people see the opposite of what they are really. A lot of people in the street are under a spell. The enemy has cast a spell on them; over their spirit, soul and body, and they cannot gain prominence; they are covered. Finding favour in life becomes very difficult. Isaiah 25:7 says, **"And he will destroy in this mountain the face of the covering cast over all people, and the vail that is spread over all nations."** The enemy has cast something over people so they are unable to see well.

2.   Evil Marks: **Galatians 6:17 says, "From henceforth let no man trouble me: for I bear in my body the marks of the Lord Jesus."** Evil marks are weapons of oppression, attack, initiation and death. When the enemy puts a mark on a person, no matter where the person runs to, he would be easily identified and dealt with. The mark actually is for

identification. The mark is for ownership. Trademarks and logos are used to identify companies or products. When the enemy puts a mark on you, it is a sign that they own you, it is a sign they can use to easily identify you. They can use the mark to punish a person, plant sickness or cause problems.

Types of Marks

Marks vary. There is a mark of death, mark of destruction, mark of rejection, mark of failure, and mark of limitation. I pray that any mark of the enemy on you will be removed, in the name of Jesus. All the marks of poverty, unfruitfulness, and disfavour, the Almighty God shall remove them, in the name of Jesus. Every mark that is identifying you with poverty, the Almighty God shall destroy it today, in the mighty name of Jesus. Other types of evil marks are:

1. Witchcraft mark.
2. Marine witchcraft mark.
3. Occult mark.
4. Familiar spirit mark.
5. Mark of slavery.
6. Mark of seduction.
7. Mark of sickness.
8. Mark of diseases.
9. Mark of misfortune.
10. Mark of disgrace and reproach.

At this juncture, I would like you to take these prayer points:

1. Mark of failure in my life, go back to your sender, in the name of Jesus.
2. Let the mark of Jesus remove every negative mark on my body, in the name of Jesus.
3. Holy Ghost fire, burn off every evil mark on my body, in the name of Jesus.

There are instruments, which the enemy uses to tie people down. In the book of Mark 11, we see where Jesus sent His disciples to go to a particular road junction, where a colt was tied down. He commanded them to bring it to Him.

Devices used by the enemy to tie people down:

1. Sickness.
2. Failure.
3. Reproach.
4. Delay.

3. Padlock: This is also an instrument for tying people down. The job of padlock is to hold, to hinder, to oppress, to cage, to frustrate and to bury. I pray that any evil padlock used to tie you down shall be broken, in the name of Jesus. There are people who have been tied down with padlocks and the padlocks were thrown into a flowing river, which took the padlocks away. When a person is tied down, he would discover that he cannot move anytime he wants to move.

There would be accident, failure and poverty. A particular exam would become a barrier to him, sickness would show up, or one thing or another would happen. It is a sign that the person has been tied down.

4. Buried charm: There are charms used to tie people down. There are charms that hinder people's progress, there are charms that stop people, there are charms that waylay people, there are charms that put afflictions on people's lives, and there are charms that put people down. **Psalm 10:8 says, "He sitteth in the lurking places of the villages: in the secret places doth he murder the innocent: his eyes are privily set against the poor."** There are secret places on the earth where great evil is done against many people. Charms carry evil powers. There are spirits attached to charms. They may be pieces of cloth, sticks etc. The materials used to make charms are nothing, what empowers them are the evil spirits summoned to make the charms potent. The evil spirits make the charms powerful. Charms always carry evil spirits employed to deal with the person the charm is meant for. A charm can close doors of favour against a person. **Ezekiel 21:21 says, "For the king of Babylon stood at the parting of the way, at the head of the two ways, to use divination: he made his arrows bright, he consulted with images, he looked in the liver."** Psalm 140:11 says, "Let not an evil

56

speaker be established in the earth: evil shall hunt the violent man to overthrow him." Evil speakers are those speaking evil words against your life, they are those making charms, pronouncing evil words and casting spell on you.

Prayer Points

1. Every voice of impossibility speaking against my breakthrough, be silenced, in the name of Jesus.
2. Rain of favour, fall upon me, in the name of Jesus.
3. Spirit of failure at the edge of miracle, lose your hold upon my life, in the name of Jesus.
4. Angel of my divine intervention, what are you waiting for? Appear, in the name of Jesus.
5. Spirit of delay in every department of my life, die, in the name of Jesus.
6. I shall not eat the food of sorrow, in the name of Jesus.
7. Spirit of rejection, lose your hold upon my life, in the name of Jesus.
8. Miracles that will advertise the power of God in my life, manifest, in the name of Jesus.
9. Prison of darkness, release my brain, in the name of Jesus.
10. I command every power that is holding unto my prayer to die, in the name of Jesus.
11. Blood of Jesus, kill every infirmity in my blood, in the name of Jesus.
12. Spirit of toiling and struggling without result, die, in the

name of Jesus.

13. The cage and prison of the enemy, release me, in the mighty name of Jesus.

14. (Mention your name and say) you shall be lifted and located with favour, in the name of Jesus.

15. Every satanic communal effort to bring me down, fail, in the name of Jesus.

16. My glory, my glory, my glory, hear the word of the Lord, arise and shine, in the name of Jesus.

17. Every satanic lion barking at my progress be silenced, in the name of Jesus.

18. The rage of the waters against my destiny, be silenced, in the mighty name of Jesus.

19. Evil covering over my head, catch fire, in the name of Jesus.

20. Every veil of poverty and hardship covering me, be roasted, in the mighty name of Jesus.

21. Every dark power claiming that they own me, you are a liar, die, in the name of Jesus.

22. Every magical covering of wickedness over my life, be roasted, in the name of Jesus.

23. Garment of shame and disgrace, I tear you up, in the name of Jesus.

24. Owners of evil covering in my life, carry your covering, in the name of Jesus.

25. You garment of suffering, I set you ablaze, in the name of

Jesus.

26. Evil prophets and priests divining evil against my star, fall down and die, in the name of Jesus.

27. Any power speaking evil against my destiny on any evil altar, shut up, in the name of Jesus.

28. Any evil thing that has been done on my picture in secret places, expire, in the name of Jesus.

29. Evil mouth speaking against my star, be silenced, in the mighty name of Jesus.

30. Angels of the living God, exhume all the evil things buried for my sake, in the name of Jesus.

31. Any demonic personality searching for my star in their evil mirror, fall down and die, in the name of Jesus.

32. O God, arise and trouble those that are troubling me, in the name of Jesus.

33. Every mark of rejection and failure in my body, clear away, in the name of Jesus.

34. Every evil river troubling my life, dry up, in the mighty name of Jesus.

35. Every demonic perfume that the enemies have put on me, to make me to be rejected, clear away, in the name of Jesus.

36. Blood of Jesus, remove rottenness from my body, in the name of Jesus.

37. Angel of my breakthrough, appear by fire, in the name of

Jesus.

38. Messenger of death assigned against me, go away with your message of death, in the name of Jesus.

39. Arrows of failure and defeat, go back to your sender, in the name of Jesus.

40. Every evil mark scaring good people away from me, be removed, in the name of Jesus.

41. Mark of poverty, be removed, in the name of Jesus.

42. Mark of prosperity, appear, in the mighty name of Jesus.

43. Mark of death in my life, clear away, in the name of Jesus.

CHAPTER FIVE

My Eagle Must Fly

S amson walked into the trap of his enemies and they caged him. Why did they cage Samson? They caged him because Samson was too dangerous for them; they knew the kind of man he was. With a jaw bone, he killed a thousand men so, they organized to cage him. But even when he had been caged, Samson realized that he had made mistakes and he repented. He said to God, "Give me back my strength," and God gave him back his strength. But unfortunately, he didn't know how to pray the correct prayers. The prayer he prayed was, "Let me die with all my enemies." If he had prayed, "O Lord, give me deliverance from this people," it would have been a different matter. But the beauty of it was that Samson's hair grew again.

Revelation 12:13-14 says, "And when the dragon saw that

he was cast unto the earth, he persecuted the woman which brought forth the man child. And to the woman were given two wings of a great eagle that she might fly into the wilderness, into her place, where she is nourished for a time, and times, and half a time, from the face of the serpent."

In the passage above, there was a serpent that wanted to harm a woman and her children, but heaven came to her rescue. Heaven gave her new wings of eagle. The job of the wings was to help her fly away from her enemies. Whatever has happened to somebody before can still happen again. Did the enemy steal or remove your wings? There is nothing God cannot do; God can bring back those wings, and your eagle will fly.

I want you to know that God always uses several things to teach us lessons. The lessons that heaven is teaching us about the eagle can be seen in the features of the eagle. The eagle is brave, strong and powerful. The eagle is a high flyer bird. It is a bird of power, freedom, endurance, tenacity, beauty, courage, honour, determination, boldness, vigilance, vitality, achievement and courage. The eagle is sharp, fearless, pure, productive and a long distance runner. The eagle has strength, strong vision and soars. However, the same eagle can be caged.

62

What are the things the enemy uses to cage the eagle?

1.   Fear: Many people know where God wants them to be but the fear to take steps or move forward has caged them. Many people are not aware that the things they are afraid of are also afraid of them. For each day, God is saying, "Fear not, don't fear the enemy, don't fear opposition, and don't fear risks. Just believe God, and don't be afraid." The Bible says that God has not given us the spirit of fear but of love, of power and of a sound mind but fear has caged a lot of people.

2.   Comfort: A lot of people get carried away with comfort, and they forget that no one gets to their place of destiny without some discomfort. There are times you may need to go through rough situations or times in order to get to where God is taking you.

3.   Ignorance: Many people don't know what they are supposed to know and so the enemy uses ignorance to keep them down.

4.   False Contentment: There are many people who are just contented with nothing, and the enemy has used it to cage them.

There was a certain brother, whose business was doing well.

63

He was so happy but then he had issues with some people and one of them said to him, "I will make sure that you start begging to eat." When the brother heard that, his mind went to his bank account balance, which he considered to be quite much so he didn't think much of the threat. But he did not know that those were not just ordinary words; they were curses backed up by demonic powers. The major weapon of evil people are evil words, words that are charged with charms and demonically employed to render their victims useless. The brother had a delivery bus for supplying goods to his customers. One day, as he was going to do his supplies, the bus went up in flames and burnt to ashes. And before he knew it, his business started going down. He started moving from one problem to another. Gradually, he started selling his properties and within a space of five years, everything was gone. After some time, he decided to use his only car for transportation business. But to his greatest amazement, people were not boarding the car but rather, they were going to the cars in front or at his back. You can see how he was rendered useless with curses, demonic words.

Lamentation 4:1-2 says, "How is the gold become dim! How is the most fine gold changed! The stones of the sanctuary are poured out in the top of every street. The precious sons of Zion, comparable to fine gold, how are they esteemed as

earthen pitchers, the work of the hands of the potter!"
The gold that is described in the passage above are the children of God. The children of God that are born with beauty and colourful destiny have become hewers of wood and drawers of water. How come the precious stones have become ordinary stones that can be found everywhere? How come a king has become a slave? It is an error. It is not supposed to be like that. That is why, when you don't fulfill your destiny, heaven weeps because you have lost your attractiveness. As a plus to the kingdom of God, you were sent to the world to fight on behalf of heaven. God sent you to the planet earth to represent Him, so when you are unable to represent heaven well, when you lose your colour, heaven will weep. It is just like the case of Samson, who was sent as a deliverer but the same Samson got caged and heaven wept over him. The people that Samson was supposed to deal with were the ones that captured him. I pray that any power that wants to put you in a permanent cage and render you valueless, useless and irrelevant shall be buried, in the name of Jesus.

Please don't go to the grave with your potential. It is often said that the cemetery is the greatest treasure on earth because many dead people there did not fulfill their destiny. They never manifested, so they died and were buried with their potential. They carried all those things back to the grave untapped. There are many celebrities, talented and gifted people who are frustrated. They were born great but are frustrated. Many who are supposed to be the head have been relocated to the tail. The intelligent die nameless and nobody will ever hear their names. The pacesetters are relocated to obscurity. Somebody so talented and gifted can die unnoticed. The superior can be ruled by the inferior. If you don't take your place, you will be replaced. The man or woman that is supposed to be on top can be found at the bottom. The man destined for the top may never smell that position till he dies, and a man of honour can die shamefully, without any relevance, if care is not taken. There is a dungeon that wastes destinies. There is a dust bin that wastes glorious destinies and render people useless and irrelevant. But the good news is that your eagle can fly again.

What to do to make your Eagle fly again

1. Pray inquiry prayers: You must ask the Lord why He sent you to the earth. God told Jeremiah that he was a prophet to the nations, ordained right from the womb to be a prophet of the whole nation; he carried the power of God, but Jeremiah did not know. There are many people, whose agenda of heaven for their lives is to feed many people

66

and pay the schools fees of some. There are people who are suffering because they are not doing what heaven has sent them to do. Some people are meant to be employers of labour but now they are going about seeking employment. Men who are supposed to be bread distributors are looking for bread to eat. What an error? I pray that any power that wants to relocate you to irrelevance shall die, in the name of Jesus. Your key of honour and relevance that has been taken away by the enemy, you shall recover it, in the name of Jesus. The ground shall open up and swallow the powers that are making you invisible to people ordained by God to help you, in the name of Jesus. The time has come for you to be dissatisfied with your situation and begin to ask, "Father, what is wrong with me? Sort me out. I need to leave this my present position and become better."

2. Cut off the evil chain that is tying you down: A lot of people are being tied down by the enemy. The enemy has seen that they are capable of flying high so the only thing they can do to prevent them from flying is to use a rope and tie them down. The problem is that the length of the rope with which an eagle is tied down determines the level of its freedom. Any time the eagles makes effort to

67

move, it cannot move beyond the length of the rope; the rope stops it. The danger is that after sometime, it will stop making attempts, conditions its mind and adjusts to the condition, and it remains like that for the rest of its life.

How to break Chains

How can you break the chains tying you down? You can break them through intimacy with God. Intimacy with God means more prayer. To be intimate with God, you need to take your prayer to a higher level. The enemy can only refuse to leave you alone if they are still able to endure your fire power. When they can no longer endure it, they will flee. Don't give up praying. Perhaps, you are very close to your breakthrough, don't give up reading the word of God. Don't give up going for fellowship because you never know, maybe out of ten chains, you have broken eight and at the next prayer meeting, the remaining two may be broken. Don't allow the enemy to divert you from that one prayer meeting, where the two chains will be broken. Don't give the enemy time to come back and start repairing the chains that you have broken off and before you know it, the ten chains are back again. Anytime you get discouraged and stop praying, the bondage increases. When the bondage becomes stronger, you would be wondering what is happening to you.

Prayer Points

1. Holy Ghost, lead me and order my steps to my place of blessing, in the name of Jesus.
2. Every collective captivity under which I am labouring, break and release me, in the name of Jesus.
3. Altar of foundational strongman blocking my path to greatness, catch fire, in the name of Jesus.
4. Heavenly bulldozer, unseat anyone sitting where I am supposed to seat, in the name of Jesus.
5. By the power of the Holy Ghost, I will sing my song and dance my dance, in the name of Jesus.
6. This year, I will not fall, I will not miscalculate, in the name of Jesus.
7. Arrows of manipulation and isolation from my place of blessing, backfire, in the name of Jesus.
8. Arrows of delay and denial fired against the works of my hands, backfire, in the name of Jesus.
9. Isaac saw the end of famine; I will see the end of all my problems by the power in the blood of Jesus, in the name of Jesus.
10. David saw the end of Goliath; I will see the end of all my enemies, in the name of Jesus.
11. After all is said and done, my head shall wear my crown, in the name of Jesus.
12. O God of wonders, arise and make a way for me, where

there is no way, in the name of Jesus.

13. Anything within me and anything around me blocking my blessings, what are you waiting for? Die, in the name of Jesus.

14. The word of an enchanter and the word of a diviner working against my greatness, expire, in the name of Jesus.

15. The word of the enemy shall not prevail over my life, in the name of Jesus.

16. Every spell and enchantment made to write me off, expire, in the name of Jesus.

17. My destiny shall not be devoured by evil words, in the name of Jesus.

18. Anything done in the night under the body of water that is affecting me now, be cancelled, in the name of Jesus.

19. Demonic words sweeping away my blessings, be arrested, in the name of Jesus.

20. Anything done to my picture in the hour of the night, be reversed now, in the name of Jesus.

21. Powers assigned to turn my fruitfulness to emptiness, expire, in the name of Jesus.

22. Battles of faded glory assigned against my life, fail, in the name of Jesus.

23. Powers hiding the key of my treasure house, release it to me, die, in the name of Jesus.

24. Jesus Christ, you are the story changer, change my story,

in the name of Jesus.

25. My glory, arise and shine at the right time, in the name of Jesus.

26. My destiny, you shall not be devoured by the lion of darkness, in the name of Jesus.

27. O Lord, thou art my glory and lifter of my head, arise and lift my head, in the name of Jesus.

28. Personal problems that came into my life by personal invitation, die, in the name of Jesus.

29. Powers that want me to gain some and lose all, die, in the name of Jesus.

30. My enemy will be sorrowful and I will rejoice because this is the time of my joy, in the name of Jesus.

31. Powers attacking me in the dream, die, in the name of Jesus.

32. My day of joy, this is the time for you take place, manifest, in the name of Jesus.

CHAPTER SIX

Deliverance from Marine Spirits

Revelation 12:11 says, "And they overcame him by the blood of the Lamb, and by the word of their testimony; and they loved not their lives unto the death."

From the scripture in the foregoing, we are told that the blood of Jesus is the reason we overcome principalities and powers: marine powers, witchcraft powers, serpentine powers and any kind of enemy, and have victory. The victory is already purchased for us, it is now our responsibility to declare to the enemy what we already have.

Revelation 12:12: "Therefore rejoice, ye heavens, and ye that dwell in them. Woe to the inhabiters of the earth and of the sea! for the devil is come down unto you, having great wrath, because he knoweth that he hath but a short time."

Before the statement in the foregoing came up, there was war in heaven. Rebellion was found in Lucifer and he was thrust out with his cohorts to the earth and that is the reason the world is no longer rejoicing in the presence of heaven. He came down to the earth and the sea that is why there is so much trouble. Water spirit is the most violent, aggressive, troublesome, difficult, stubborn, proud and wicked spirit.

The Bible says, my people perish not because they don't go to church, sing praises, or read their Bibles but because of lack of knowledge. A lot of people are in captivity today simply because of lack of knowledge. Ignorance is when you lack knowledge and it has made a lot of people to suffer. Ignorance is when you don't know what to do to get out of your problems. Ignorance is when you are encouraging your problems and you are not aware. That is, you are supplying your enemy strength to harm you. You are so ignorant that you are not aware that the things you do harm you. The enemy is living close to you, but you are not aware.

We live in a generation, where we run to the people we should run away from. The things we are supposed to run away from are the things we run to and the things we are supposed to embrace are the things we run away from. Ignorance is when you are using the wrong method that does not favour you. It is an ignorant act when you direct your prayers in the wrong

73

way.

Psalm 24:1 says, "The earth is the Lord's, and the fulness thereof; the world, and they that dwell therein. For he hath founded it upon the seas, and established it upon the floods." Marine spirits are so cocky because they believe they are older than any other spirit. **Genesis 1:1-2: "In the beginning God created the heaven and the earth. And the earth was without form, and void; and darkness was upon the face of the deep. And the Spirit of God moved upon the face of the waters."** God called forth the earth from the water so they believe that they are the oldest.

One of the creatures that claimed the power of the water is called Leviathan. Leviathan is a dangerous animal that lives inside the water. Our ancient fathers believe that water has a lot of potential that they can tap from, and many of them entered into a covenant with powers from the water. Some of them bear names after rivers. They would tell you that there are people living inside the river. At a particular time, the spirit in the form of a woman that lives in the river would come out of the river, and they would worship it and do all kinds of sacrifices to appease it. There are rivers, where you see fish touching your legs but you can't touch them because the people believe they are sacred. If by mistake, you take any of the fish home, maybe while fetching water, if you get home and you see the fish inside your water, you will quickly return it to the river where you took it from. Somewhere in Nigeria, there is a river, where it is believed that a rock came out from and a snake lives inside it. The villagers believe that the snake is not an ordinary snake. They believe in the snake and worship it. This snake comes out once in a while and vomits stones. New brides are often encouraged to fetch the water and stones because it is believed that the number of the stones they pick will determine the number of children they will have.

There are some places in the western part, where there are notable yearly sacrifices done in the rivers and people come from all over the world to participate in the ceremony. People with one need or another go there to table their requests: those looking for riches, children, power and all kind of things. Although people do not go there in large numbers anymore due to the increased awareness of Christianity, but the effect of those things are still troubling many people.

There are many children suffering, not because of what they have done, but because they were born into a shrine or an evil altar. And since nobody is worshipping these altars, the altars are demanding for worship, going after the children to deal with them.

75

A certain man, who was one of the founders of Lagos, was so powerful to the extent that he used to disappear and appear. We heard that he had many pots, and anytime he wanted to go hunting, he would turn into a snake and enter into one of the pots and when he was coming back with so many animals that he had killed, he would come back through another pot. That was how he lived and nobody dared touch those pots. A time came, the children got tired of what their father was doing. One day, he turned to his normal snake, entered through one of the pots and went hunting and the children went to the pot and broke it into pieces. When he came back to enter into the pot and turn into a human being as usual, he couldn't find the pot. That was how he crawled back into the bush to date.

These are people who have evil powers; they have eaten and slept with the devil. Now their children are paying for those things. I pray that the Almighty God with His mighty hands will set us free and break the yoke, in Jesus' name.

Isaiah 27:1 says, "In that day the Lord with his sore and great and strong sword shall punish leviathan the piercing serpent, even leviathan that crooked serpent; and he shall slay the dragon that is in the sea." The marine world believes that other realms came out from it. Certainly, you know that water is very important to the survival of mankind. It is believed that seventy per cent of the human body is water.

Living things have one thing or the other to do with water so, you can't avoid contact with water. You need water for drinking, cooking, bathing, washing etc. In 1 John 5:8, the Bible says that there are three that bear record on earth: the spirit, the water and the blood and these three agree.

Most cities of the world are built around water. Communities, villages, states, towns, and countries, one way or the other have connection with water. A lot of people believe that the power of the waters is for evil purpose. There are people who worship water. You see them wear white, and do all kinds of ceremonies; they believe that they can get whatever they want from the river.

There are musicians who go to water priests and priestesses for fame, popularity and inspiration. They want to sing with satanic power so they go there to seek help. We have heard about politicians who drove a whole vehicle into the river as a sacrifice. People throw money, food, clothes and all kinds of items into the river as sacrifice to the gods in the water. People call them queen of the coast, yemoja, ogbanje, olokun etc. Many countries of the world have their names connected to the water. In the days of Pharaoh of Egypt, he operated with power from the river. No wonder every morning, Pharaoh would go to the river even though he lived in a very expensive mansion where there was enough water. He had to go and renew the covenant in the river. This was a way to worship the water demons. In the Bible too, we see dagon, a water goddess which appeared in the form of half-human, half-fish.

I heard the story of a man who was having problems in his business. So, he complained to a friend who seemed to be doing well. His friend said to him, "Well, if you are willing to do what we are doing, you too will bounce back." The man said he was ready to do anything. The friend told him to meet him at a certain place by 12midnight. He met him there as agreed and before he knew it, they were going into a big deep river where they found themselves inside a large hall. They saw people who were coming to do business and all kinds of things were taking place. The moment they saw the man who was a new person, they asked him what he wanted, if he wanted to do business with them and if he came with money. He told them that he didn't come with anything. They gave him a form to fill, after which they told him to go. Two weeks later, his friend that introduced him called him to tell him that his goods had arrived. He asked which goods? To his surprise, his friend said he would give him some of his shops to display the goods. To cut the long story short, in a short time, he made a lot of money. But in that excitement, his first son died and he was expecting his friend to sympathize with him. His friend said to him, "Well, you still have other children, do a proper burial for this one that is dead." Few days later, they went to the river again and the people were busy doing their work. In that place, he saw his first son that died and shouted the name of the boy but to his surprise, his friend that took him there shouted at him and said, "We don't talk like that here, face the business you came for."

This is a wicked world that is why, if you want to be a Christian, be a Christian. But if you are going to have one leg in and one leg out, there would be no chance for you. The world is not going to get better; that is the truth. People are going deeper into evil because of money. People are doing a lot of ungodly things to acquire powers, wealth, fame, children etc.

Anytime you begin to dream constantly about water, don't let anyone deceive you, it means that water spirits are harassing you. It means that you have been initiated into the marine kingdom. If you have thrown things into the river as sacrifice, although you did it so many years ago, there is a covenant between you and the river. The marine world is very organized. Most of the inspiration for fashion, commerce, wealth, music etc. come from the water.

Marine spirits control the seat of power anywhere in the

world. Prime Ministers, presidents, mayors etc. are controlled directly or indirectly by the marine spirits around them. Marine spirits use wealth and power to entice men and women who are ready to serve them in exchange for their souls. You cannot enjoy your Christian life until you learn how to secure your victory from marine powers. As a Christian, if you don't pray yourself out of these things, you cannot be free. They could sit on your head, health, marriage and finances, unless you are ready to battle them. Any Christian that desires breakthrough and progress in life must not spare marine spirits. I know of a lady who anytime she got pregnant and dreamt of seeing herself swimming in her village river, she would have a miscarriage. She was not free until she prayed deliverance prayers.

Many people's breakthroughs and blessings are held in the water, not because they lack vision or because they are lazy. All the great men in the Bible dealt with water spirits. For example, Elijah, Moses and even the children of Israel. For their breakthroughs to emerge, they had to confront water spirits. Marine spirits cause all kinds of defilement. Swimming in the river and feeding in the dream are their handiwork. They do it for evil intentions. Food in the dream does not serve any good purpose. It is meant to defile, introduce sickness, heaviness, prayerlessness and emptiness into the victims' lives. No matter how spiritually buoyant they may be, after a particular dream, everything will quench especially their prayer life, which will just go down. Marine powers are behind strange diseases. They promote sexual perversion. They are the ones behind all kinds of sexual problems you see in our world today such as masturbation, rape, pornography, adultery, prostitution, lesbianism, nudity, looseness and recklessness.

Facts about Marine Spirits

1.   **The marine kingdom is a real:** There is another world apart from the physical world called, the marine world. Most of the beautiful architectural designs we see are from the marine world. It is real and people have discovered that if you want money, position, or any other thing, you can get them from there. I want you to know that the marine world is real.

2.   **The marine world is well organized:** It controls business, commerce and merchandise.

3.   **Marine spirits control the seat of power all over the world:** They control the government of nations, presidents, prime ministers, mayors and governors. They control and influence them.

4.   Marine spirits give wealth to those who worship them: Ezekiel 27:33 says, **"When thy wares went forth out of the seas, thou filledst many people; thou didst enrich the kings of the earth with the multitude of thy riches and of thy merchandise."**

5. **You must learn to deal with marine spirits:** You cannot enjoy your Christian life if you have not learnt to deal with these spirits and get your things from them. It is not enough to say, "I am born again, it is written, the Lord has given me power over all these spirits," you have to enforce it. The Lord has indeed given you power over marine spirits, but what effort are you making to ensure that the victory is enforced. Jesus has indeed won the battle for us. He spoilt principalities and powers, and made a show of them openly. He disgraced and tore them into pieces. But now as a child of God, what effort are you making to ensure that these things do not attack or hinder you? Many people are being harassed by these spirits including those who are born again. These powers have messed up so many things in their lives. If they die, they go to heaven, but then they would have lived a miserable life on earth. All the people that were able to do well in the Bible had to confront water spirits. Where do you think Pharaoh got his power from? It was from the river Nile. A king of his calibre

would have to go to the river every morning to bathe and renew his covenant with the water even though he had all kinds of water cisterns at home. He had to go to the river Nile with his daughter every day to bathe. For Moses to move forward, he had to contend and deal with these spirits including the river Nile. What I am saying is that as a child of God, you must know your right. A lot of Christians are suffering because of lack of understanding.

6. Marine spirits cause all kinds of problems: Eating and having sex in the dream is not in your interest. They are all meant for evil purpose. They are designed to harm or attack you. Sex in the dream doesn't serve God's purpose or yours. Anytime you have sex in the dream, your spirit is being polluted. Those who have these dreams constantly cannot enjoy a good spiritual life and growth.

7. Marine spirits promote sexual perversion: Today, we are living in a sexualized world, where everything is about sex: pornography, adultery, prostitution, rape, incest etc. These marine spirits are the ones behind them including lesbianism, homosexuality, addiction, drunkenness, alcohol, nudity etc. We have entered into another generation of ladies that don't want to wear clothes. They like to expose their bodies with all the fashion that doesn't glorify God. These clothes are designed to expose their private parts. Marine powers are promoting these things.

8. Marine spirits are swallowers of prosperity and wealth: There is so much wealth that belongs to the children of God in the waters. Job 20:15 says, **"He hath swallowed down riches, and he shall vomit them up again: God shall cast them out of his belly."**

9. The marine world controls fashion.

10. The marine world hates the environment of prayers: They don't want you to be serious with God or to be prayerful. They don't want you to go deep into the things of God. Therefore, they have introduced all kinds of things to discourage people from serving God. That is why most of the people that are delivered from the marine world, who come to the church are unable to cope, except they pray seriously. Marine powers are the ones corrupting the word of God; they send their agents to pollute believers and the church. Many churches that started well, along the line got infiltrated with the agents of the marine kingdom. They don't want anything that has to do with prayer. Prayer is no longer on the agenda of the church. Many churches have been converted to just preaching centres. They don't pray because they don't like prayer. They don't want an environment that is soaked with prayers. They don't want an environment of continuous praying. That is why they hate prayer warriors.

11. Marine spirits supervise dark covenants: The terms of these covenants are not known. It is their job to ensure that families are held down by these dark covenants that have been formed. They put a mark on all the family members to make sure that all of them suffer the same problems.

12. Marine spirits hate marriage: They enter into marriage to punish their innocent partners. If they go into a family, all the wealth in the family gets ruined. Indigenes of villages that are located in riverine areas are not usually serious about life; many of them are drunkards, and divorce cases are rampant. They don't have respect for marriage in these areas. Their men wake up in the morning and start drinking till night. It is the influence of marine spirits.

13. Marine spirits are planters: They plant strange materials into people's bodies to serve their purpose. The things introduced, may be moving about in the body. They are usually materials such as stones, pins, rings or needles. Things like beads, crowns, diamond etc. are used to represent them.

Prayer Points

1. Blood of Jesus, destroy the marine spirit troubling my life, in Jesus' name.

2. Holy Ghost fire, pass through my body, in the name of Jesus.

3. I break every covenant with marine powers, in Jesus' name.

4. Fire of God, consume every material planted into my body by marine powers, in Jesus' name.

5. Every inherited yoke of marine power, I destroy you, in Jesus' name.

6. Every anti-prosperity yoke of marine powers, break and release me, in the name of Jesus.

7. Every unexplainable problem from marine powers, release me, in Jesus' name.

8. Every stubborn chain holding me down to any body of water, break by fire, in Jesus' name.

9. Every leaking pocket and financial embarrassment from marine powers, lose your hold, in Jesus' name.

10. Every activity of dream criminals in my life, cease, in Jesus' name.

11. Every marine gadget monitoring my life, catch fire, in Jesus' name.

12. Arrows of marine spirit in my life, catch fire, in Jesus' name.

13. Every marine agent on assignment to recruit me, fail, in Jesus' name.

14. Any covenant between me and any marine agent, I break it now, in Jesus' name.

15. Witchcraft projects and activities in any body of water against my life, health and marriage, catch fire, in Jesus' name.

16. I fire back every arrow of marine power fired against my destiny, in Jesus' name.

17. I fire back every arrow of wickedness fired against me, in Jesus' name.

18. Every pot of evil concoction burning against me, catch fire, in Jesus' name.

19. Every image representing me in the body of water, be destroyed, in Jesus' name.

20. Every charm buried in the ocean against me, expire, in Jesus' name.

21. Marine spirits, hear the word of the Lord, my life and glory are not for exchange, in Jesus' name.

22. Power of amputation assigned against me, break and release me, in Jesus' name.

23. Marine powers attacking the glory of my Moses, die, in Jesus' name.

24. Blood of Jesus, erase evil marks of marine powers on my body, in Jesus' name.

25. Poison of serpents in my body, come out of your hiding

place, in Jesus' name.

26. I break the head of the leviathan assigned against my destiny, in Jesus' name.

27. Holy Ghost fire, burn the property of marine powers in my custody, in Jesus' name.

28. Holy Ghost fire, enter into my foundation, in the name of Jesus.

29. O Lord, you are a shield for me and the lifter of my head. Arise and lift my head, in Jesus' name.

30. My positive change, what are you waiting for? Manifest by fire, in the name of Jesus.

31. The work of the enemy in my life, come to an end, in the name of Jesus.

32. Wind of the Holy Ghost, blow every sickness out of my body, in the name of Jesus.

33. Holy Ghost fire, break every marine yoke troubling my life, in the name of Jesus.

34. Any problem of suffering brought into my life, expire, in the name of Jesus.

35. Every material and article of marine spirits in my life, I set you ablaze, in the name of Jesus.

36. Every marine cage holding me down, break, in the name of Jesus.

37. Multiple curses energized by marine powers, troubling my life, break, in the name of Jesus.

38. Finger of the Lord, arise and set me free, in the name of

Jesus.

39. Marine wickedness targeted against my destiny, I break your power, in the name of Jesus.

40. I pull down every stronghold of marine bewitchment; I pull you down, in the name of Jesus.

41. Holy Ghost fire, fill my spirit, soul and body, in the name of Jesus.

42. Fire of God, enter into my foundation and deliver me, in the name of Jesus.

43. I pull down every stronghold of darkness militating against my life, in the name of Jesus.

44. Wherever the good thing I have been expecting has been tied down, be released, in the name of Jesus.

45. Satanic womb that has swallowed my blessings, release them now, in the name of Jesus.

46. Holy Ghost fire, pass through my body and release me, in the name of Jesus.

CHAPTER SEVEN

Breaking
Unprofitable Covenants

The popular Isaiah 10:27 says, "And it shall come to pass in that day, that his burden shall be taken away from off thy shoulder, and his yoke from off thy neck, and the yoke shall be destroyed because of the anointing."

Every good reader of the Bible would understand that Christianity is also a covenant. In fact, the day you surrender your life to the Lord Jesus Christ, you enter into a covenant with God. Once you accept Him as your Lord and Saviour, you enjoy a covenant with Him.

What is a Covenant?

A covenant is a formal agreement that is legally binding on two or more persons. In the world, people enter into covenants every day. You may call it a business contract or a marriage covenant. It is a normal thing for mutual benefits. Two or more people could come together to reach an agreement. When a man and a woman get married, they stand before the congregation and take a marriage vow, they form a covenant to become one.

A covenant is a bond.

A covenant is a contract.

A covenant is a treaty.

A covenant is a bargain.

A covenant is an undertaking.

A covenant is a vow.

A covenant is a promise.

A covenant is an oath.

Usually, after elections, a day is set aside for swearing-in. The Chief Judge of the State will administer an oath to whoever will be the next governor or president as the case may be. They would be asked to read and accept to uphold the constitution of the state or country. However, many of them, after reading these things, they start their executive job and forget the oath they took and start misbehaving. They forget that the oath, which they took is a binding covenant or agreement. They bound themselves for a mutual benefit, for the protection of life and amelioration of human conditions. That is, promising to provide the necessary basic needs, good roads, water, good schools, security of lives and properties etc. It is binding. The government fulfills its own side of the agreement while the citizens fulfill their own side by paying their taxes, doing environmental sanitation, voting when it is time to vote etc. That is a social contract. But when the citizens fulfill their own part of the contract and the government neglects its own part, there would be crisis. Problems arise because somebody is breaking his own side of the covenant.

There are covenants that have brought pain to man. These covenants are responsible for many people's inability to rise. There are people today whose problems cannot be traced to their own making. The fact that they are not doing well does not mean that they are not working hard. In the Bible, there are people who made covenants on friendly basis, for example, David and Jonathan. **1 Samuel 18:3: "Then Jonathan and David made a covenant, because he loved him as his own soul."** David and Jonathan made a covenant and even after the death of Jonathan, David still remembered the covenant between him and Jonathan. Many years after the death of Jonathan, in 2 Samuel 9, David was made a king. He woke up one day and decided to show favour to anyone in Saul's lineage because of the covenant he formed with Jonathan many years ago. David reactivated the covenant by doing a special favour to Mephibosheth, Jonathan's son.

Laban and Jacob came together and formed a covenant. However, Jacob left the house of Laban without a formal notice to Laban, so Laban pursued him and eventually caught up with him. When he met Jacob, he agreed with him that he would not marry another woman apart from his daughters and Jacob agreed. They entered in to a covenant on that. Not only that, they also entered into a covenant of protection (Genesis 31:43). These were treaties that were made in the Bible.

Solomon also made a covenant with Hiram in 1 Kings 5:1-11. It was a covenant on commerce. Joshua entered into a covenant with the tribe of Gibeon. The Gibeonites were afraid of being destroyed by Joshua and his men on their way to the Promised Land, like they were destroying other nations to take over their lands. Seeing that God was with the Israelites, the leaders of the Gibeonites lied to Joshua that they were from a faraway country in order to enter into a covenant with them so that they would not be destroyed. The covenant was already made before Joshua and his men discovered that they had been deceived by the Gibeonites. That notwithstanding, the covenant remained binding on the two parties. Joshua said, "Why did you people deceive us? You forced us to make covenant with you which we would not have done." Because of what the Gibeonites did, Joshua laid a curse on them and said they would become hewers of wood and drawers of water. That was how the Gibeonites became slaves to the children of Israel.

Many years later, when Saul became the king of Israel, he enquired about the Gibeonites and was told that Joshua made a covenant to protect them. However, Saul refused to abide by that covenant and he killed them. After the death of Saul, and David became king, there was famine in the land. When they enquired of the Lord, it was revealed that the famine was the consequence of what Saul did to the Gibeonites (**2 Samuel 21:1-14**).

Are you experiencing famine today? Does it seem like some invisible powers are pushing you to the back? Does it appear as if you are not measuring up with your colleagues or people that you are even better than? The people you are more qualified than seem to be doing better than you. This could be the reason. If you read from verses 2 to 6 of 2 Samuel 21, you will see the price that was paid by the family of Saul for what he did to the Gibeonites. David gave the Gibeonites seven sons of Saul to the Gibeonites to atone for the sin that Saul committed against them. They hanged them immediately and the famine disappeared because it had been atoned and there was peace.

You need to pray because every covenant is binding, it doesn't matter whether you know or not. A covenant has binding power and unless you atone for it, it will continue to work until

94

somebody terminates it. Anytime a covenant is formed, spirits are involved, forces are involved and demons are involved. It is these forces that perpetuate wickedness in families. Things like barrenness, sickness, poverty, torment or insanity are signs that there is a covenant in place somewhere.

A covenant cannot be terminated by one person. If you entered into a covenant with a person, you can't just wake up one day and say you don't want it to continue. It can only happen when the two parties involved agree to do away with it. A covenant continues to work until it is broken. When there is a breach, there would be a penalty just as we see in the case of David and King Saul. It was King Saul who perpetuated the wickedness but it was King David that was suffering it.

Many people who have left uniform churches where they ate sugarcane and prayed all sorts of prayers with candles of different colours will not stop seeing water in their dreams because taking specials in the water is a usual remedy for everything in those kinds of places. Although they have been born again for ten years, one way or the other, they still see themselves in the water in their dreams. It is because a covenant is involved. If you have incisions on your body, you need to pray to erase them. The good news is this; the blood of

Jesus is enough to redeem you. There is no need to kill a human being, an animal or the blood of the seven children of Saul. The blood of Jesus makes atonement for all our sins and mistakes.

The Remedy

You need to give your life to Christ so that the blood of Jesus that speaks better things will speak for you. No witch doctor can deliver you from the one that holds you captive. No witch can deliver you from other witches. Only Jesus has the power to deliver to the uttermost.

Prayer Points

1. O God, arise and glorify your name in my life, the mighty name of Jesus.
2. Powers fighting my destiny from the water, land and firmament, destroy yourselves, in the name of Jesus.
3. My life will not be used for sacrifice, in the name of Jesus.
4. Anti-prosperity yoke in my life, today is your end, break, in the name of Jesus.
5. Begin to plead the blood of Jesus over your spirit and soul, in the name of Jesus.
6. Covenant of suffering, break and release me, in the name of Jesus.
7. The covenant supplying my enemy ammunition to fight

me, break, in the name of Jesus.

8. Covenant of failure at the edge of my breakthrough, break, in the name of Jesus.

9. The covenant that says my problem will not be solved, break and release me, in the name of Jesus.

10. Covenant of cruel affliction, break and release me, in the name of Jesus.

11. Covenant assigned to attract battle into my life, break, in the name of Jesus.

12. O God of mercy, arise and have mercy upon me, in the name of Jesus.

CHAPTER EIGHT

Dream Interpretation

In Jude 1:8, the Bible says, "Likewise also these filthy dreamers defile the flesh, despise dominion, and speak evil of dignities."

It is important to know that there are powers using the hours of the night to oppress the children of God. **Psalm 127:2 says, "It is vain for you to rise up early, to sit up late, to eat the bread of sorrows: for so he giveth his beloved sleep."**

Part of our heritage as children of God is to enjoy sleep; sleep that is free of satanic harassment, satanic interruptions and witchcraft disturbances. Sleep plays a very important role in the life of man. When you wake up from a good sleep, you get refreshed to face a new day with energy to pursue what you need to pursue.

Proverbs 3:24 says, "When thou liest down, thou shalt not be afraid: yea, thou shalt lie down, and thy sleep shall be

sweet."

God promises to grant you pleasurable sleep. He said you will sleep well and wake up well. Your dream life will no longer be a battlefield. God will make your dream life to be full of revelation, information and blessings, in the name of Jesus. I pray that the spirit of wickedness, the spirit of the night, the amputators and those who are firing arrows at you in the dream shall die, in the name of Jesus. Powers that are roaming around in your dream life, heaven will command destruction upon them. All the masquerades of darkness that are waiting for the hour of the night to perform their activity will die suddenly. The satanic police chasing you around in the dream, the Lord will kill them one after the other. All the nocturnal caterers that are preparing satanic dishes to feed you in the night will die, in the name of Jesus. All satanic judges that are standing in judgement against you will not wake up. All those claiming that they are married to you shall die. All their children in the dream shall die violent deaths. The strange goat, dog, and cat parading themselves in your dream shall be destroyed, in the name of Jesus.

When you have a good dream, you will know that it is a good dream because of the way you will feel about it. But when you wake up from a dream, and you are jumpy and afraid, know that it is not a good dream. Dreams that you wake up from and

99

you feel weak and pain cannot be good dreams. Good dreams bring blessings, promotion, increase, advancement and acceleration. Good dreams always bring edification and a lifting. On the other hand, satanic dreams always bring confusion, fear, demotion, poverty, humiliation, pain, frustration, disfavour, suffering and evil occurrences. But as a Christian, this is the rule: anytime you have a bad dream, don't be afraid. Take any scripture that goes with the dream and use it to nullify the bad dream. The Bible says, **"No weapon that is formed against you shall prosper and every tongue that rises up against you in judgement shall be condemned (Isaiah 54: 17).** That is the kind of scripture you can use to counter evil dreams. Once you confess the scriptures, cancel the dream and pray that it will never stand. God has given you the opportunity to see what the enemies are planning so that you can cancel it. As soon as you do that, have faith and believe that it is settled. Don't let the dream terrify you. After you have prayed about the dream, soak yourself in the power of God by speaking in tongues.

However, when you have a good dream, for example, you see somebody giving you good things, or you are being congratulated, or you are travelling out or you see yourself seated in a high position, when you wake up, look for scriptures to bring the dream to reality. You need to speak and

100

make pronouncements that you believe what you have dreamt about and that it shall manifest in a short time. One very important thing to focus on after a dream is how the dream ended. If it ended in you having upper hand, irrespective of what the enemy had done, for example, it ended with you quoting the scriptures, praying, or challenging them out of their hiding places by using the scriptures boldly, it means that you have already paralyzed the enemy. If the dream ended and you were unable to do anything, it means that you need to pray seriously.

Dreams and Interpretation, and way out
1. Being lost in the forest and trying to find your way out. It means that you would be stranded. It also means that confusion, hardship and suffering are awaiting you or are already happening to you. Cancel the dream, set the forest, desert or lonely place ablaze and command all those who were gathered there or those who organized it to be destroyed by the fire of God.
2. Missing your appointment, flight or getting late for an exam. It means abortion of good things and programmes that you want to achieve and the enemy is trying to frustrate you. The enemy is trying to bring disappointment and demotion. You need to counter

the plan of the enemy by praying very well about it.

3. Drinking dirty water. It means the enemy wants to poison your spiritual life and make you weak spiritually. Challenge your body, soul and spirit with the fire of God. Command the dirty water you drank to be flushed out by the blood of Jesus.

4. Counting coins. It is the spirit of poverty, lack and want at work.

5. Shedding tears, crying. It means the enemy is planning sorrow or tragedy for you. You need to cancel it by fire.

6. Wearing rags. It is the dream of lack. You need to pray and cancel it.

7. Being naked where people could see you. It is the spirit of shame, embarrassment and disgrace at work. You need to pray and war against the spirit violently.

8. Being chased by masquerades. It means that strange spirits have been assigned against you. The strongman, marine spirits and ancestral spirits are after your life. You need to pray deliverance prayers.

9. Rivers blocking you or you are walking in a place and you see a river ahead of you and you are unable to cross to the other side. It means hindrance, blockage and frustration in realizing your dreams. You need to dismantle the blockage with prayers.

10. Seeing cobwebs. It is a sign of poverty, delay,

abandonment, rejection or disappointment. You need to pray against it.

11. Seeing dead people. That is the spirit of death and hell and ancestral spirits coming to attack you. You need to pray against the spirit of death, ancestral and marine spirits.

12. Being tied down in prison or in a lonely place. It means delay, hardship and frustration. You need to pray and cancel them.

13. Seeing yourself swimming in the water. It means you are under the attack of marine spirits. You need to deal with marine spirits and queen of the coast through violent prayers.

14. Flood carrying away your properties. It means that you are about to lose something precious to you. You need to pray against it and recover what belongs to you.

15. Writing an exam that you have once passed. It signifies setback. You need to cancel the dream.

16. Climbing a mountain and you are unable to get to the top. It is talking about difficulty and frustration. You need to deal with it and make sure that such a dream does not plague your life.

How to conquer and receive your blessings

1. Repent of all your sins.

2.   Agree with God that prayer can solve your problems. Have genuine faith in the power and ability of God.

3.   Address foundational issues that you may have because if all the foundational problems are not dealt with, they may continue to open doors for the bad spirits invading your life.

4.   Deal with the strongman.

5.   Deal with ancestral spirits.

6.   Pray by faith and fervently. Make sure that your heart is free from evil thoughts, evil imaginations, lust, unforgiveness etc. before you start praying.

Prayer Points

1.   The finger of witches and wizards on my body, wither by fire, in the name of Jesus.

2.   O God, arise and give me victory in my dream life, in the name of Jesus.

3.   Whatever the enemy has done to make me remain useless in life, scatter, in the name of Jesus.

4.   Whatever the enemy has stolen from me in the hour of the night, right now, I command you to restore them, in the name of Jesus.

5.   Strongman delegated to steal my glorious destiny, fall down and die, in the name of Jesus.

6.   You the spirit from the grave assigned to attack me with

sudden death, die, in the name of Jesus.

7. Demonic power of delay and disappointment assigned against my life in the dream, die, in the name of Jesus.

8. You the work of my hands, I prophesy to you, prosper, in the name of Jesus.

9.   Anointing of all-round breakthrough, fall upon me, in the name of Jesus.

10. Satanic camera and satellite monitoring my dream life, catch fire, in the name of Jesus.

11. Satanic remote control working against my dream life, catch fire, in the name of Jesus.

12. Serpentine spirit of delay delegated against my life, die, in the name of Jesus.

13. Lord Jesus Christ, by your wonder working power, prosper me, in the name of Jesus.

14. Holy Ghost, burn the evil seed and satanic plantation to ashes, in the name of Jesus.

CHAPTER NINE

Deleting the Day of Sorrow from your Calendar

We shall consider this topic by looking at Ecclesiastes 3: 1-8: "To every thing there is a season, and a time to every purpose under the heaven: A time to be born, and a time to die; a time to plant, and a time to pluck up that which is planted; A time to kill, and a time to heal; a time to break down, and a time to build up; A time to weep, and a time to laugh; a time to mourn, and a time to dance; A time to cast away stones, and a time to gather stones together; a time to embrace, and a time to refrain from embracing; A time to get, and a time to lose; a time to keep, and a time to cast away; A time to rend, and a time to sew; a time to keep silence, and a time to speak; A time to love, and a time to hate; a time of war, and a time of peace."

From this Scripture, you can see that the world, where we find ourselves is spiritual as well. That is, before anything happens in the physical world, it has first occurred in the spiritual world. Before any event takes place in the physical world, that event has already happened in the spiritual world. Everything you see happening in our world don't just happen, they are made to happen. They are programmed to happen, they are orchestrated to happen, they are planned to happen, and nothing happens for nothing. Everyone has a calendar. A calendar is a programme of what happens by the second, minute, hour, day, week, month and year. So everyone has his daily, weekly, monthly and yearly calendar. That is, each person has his stake in this matter whether, the person likes it or not, and regardless of whether the person knows or not.

What the enemy does is to pick a particular date in the year and then programme evil, calamity and sorrow into it. Before a person dies, it has been programmed. It is not the day the person died that he died; he had been prgrammed to die long before then. The enemy must have first of all picked a date in the spirit realm and then do some programming, some coding, some enchantment, and spell casting to mark the particular day of sorrow. Before the enemy does anything, they will first determine where, how and who it will be. For instance before an accident happens, the enemy knows who will be involved in it, where the accident will take place and when it will take place. Before the accident happens, their blood tanks would be made ready so that as the blood is being spilled, it is being collected into their banks. Their witchcraft drum is always very close by as well as their witchcraft pipe to drain the blood into their demonic world. What I mean is that no death takes place unless the agents of darkness have already worked it out. There was a demonic man, who wanted to kill all the Jews but before he did that, he consulted the oracle. When he got to the oracle, he told the oracle to work out the day the incident would take place. A day was picked for the extermination of the Jews.

We know the story of Ahab in the Bible. Even before he died, God called a meeting in heaven and said, "Who will go and persuade Ahab for me?" The Bible said all kinds of spirits began to speak and finally one of the spirits said he would go and become a lying spirit in the mouth of all the prophets. That was how Ahab was eliminated. God already decided that Ahab must go to the battlefield and die. So, a prophet was needed to deceive him to go to the battle and eventually, the lying spirit took over him. Ahab went to the battlefield and was wasted there. In Job's life, the enemy picked a day in their calendar to waste all he had; his investment, wealth, health and children. The enemy attacked all he had and Job came back to nothing. Job was devastated, as everything happened on the same day, one after another. **Psalm 49:5 says, "Wherefore should I fear in the days of evil, when the iniquity of my heels shall compass me about?"** There is a day called the day of evil. **Psalm 50:15 says, "And call upon me in the day of trouble: I will deliver thee, and thou shalt glorify me."**

Different Kinds of Days

1. A day of feasting. A day of feasting is a day of joy, celebration, and exchange of gifts. Job 1:5 says that all the children of Job were celebrating, rejoicing, and dancing. We see the same thing in Esther 9:22, which talks about a day of feasting, drinking and enjoyment.
2. A day of recompense (Hosea 9:7).
3. A day of reward.
4. A day of distress. A day of distress is a day of calamity, tears, and weariness.
5. A day of famine.
6. A day of sorrow or mourning – Genesis 50:4.
7. A day of weeping – Deuteronomy 34:8.
8. A day of appointment. Death is an appointment. The enemy can programme an appointment with death for a

person before his time. For example, someone who dies through an accident. The Bible says in Psalm 91:6, "With long life will I satisfy him, and shew him my salvation." The meaning of this passage is that you will not die before your time. You will leave this world when you have been satisfied.

9. A day of your youth – Job 29:4.
10. A day of affliction.
11. A day of adversity – Psalm 94:13.
12. A day of siege – It is a day you wake up and it is one calamity after another; as one bad news is going, another one is coming.
13. A day of trouble.
14. A day of vengeance. The Bible says in Psalm 20:1, "The Lord hear thee in the day of trouble; the name of the God of Jacob defend thee." The day of trouble is a day you must not be silent or the Lord be silent to your prayers.

Nahum 1:7 says, "The Lord is good, a strong hold in the day of trouble; and he knoweth them that trust in him."
God is a stronghold for His children in the day of trouble. What you need to know is that the enemy programmes evil into days and weeks. We must beware of the devices of the enemy. They programme sickness, death, arrows and trouble. Everything happening in life is programmed and nothing just happens for

nothing. All the domestic accidents, plane crashes, tragedy, etc. are programmed at a particular day for a particular time. We must learn to delete evil programmes in our daily, weekly, monthly and yearly calendar. For instance, every Monday morning, you wake up early and delete evil from the calendar of the week for your life. As you do that, you will discover that no evil shall befall you. It is real that these powers project evil into the calendar of people for the day, week, month and year.

Prayer Points

1. Where is the Lord God of Elijah? Arise and make haste to help me, in the name of Jesus.
2. I receive power to rise and never fall, in the name of Jesus.
3. Satanic embargo on my head, break, in the name of Jesus.
4. Every chain of darkness on my hands, break, in the name of Jesus.
5. My life, refuse to follow the evil pattern of your father's house, in the name of Jesus.
6. The evil seed the enemy planted into my life during the hour of sleep, come out now, in the name of Jesus.
7. Every arrow of the enemy fired against the work of my hands, backfire, in the name of Jesus.
8. Powers that suck blood, my life is not your candidate, die, in the name of Jesus.
9. Witchcraft animals appearing to me in my dream, fall

down and die, in the name of Jesus.

10. Holy Ghost, connect my head to fresh oil of favour, in the mighty name of Jesus.

11. I paralyze the evil desire of the enemy against my life this year, in the name of Jesus.

12. Ancestral chain holding my destiny, break, in the name of Jesus.

13. Arrows of spiritual and physical blindness fired against me, go back to your sender, in the name of Jesus.

14. Every battle of gradual loss of good things, go back to your sender, in the name of Jesus.

15. Every investment of household wickedness in my life, scatter, in the name of Jesus.

16. I declare by the Spirit of the living God that good things shall happen to me this year, in the name of Jesus.

17. Every arrow of evil dedication working against my life, break, in the name of Jesus.

18. Poverty yokes in my life, break, in the name of Jesus.

19. Thou power of the Highest, release favour into my life, in the name of Jesus.

20. Counterfeit garment covering my head in the spirit realm, catch fire, in the name of Jesus.

21. Thou power from the grave working against my progress, catch fire, in the name of Jesus.

22. The bondage of wrong handling of placenta, break, in the

name of Jesus.

23. Environmental yoke affecting my life, break, in the name of Jesus.

24. Every band of wickedness blocking my blessing, catch fire, in the name of Jesus.

25. Every witchcraft bird flying for my sake, crash land, in the name of Jesus.

26. I shall be fruitful in the land, whether the enemy likes or not, in the name of Jesus.

27. Padlock of darkness withholding my breakthrough, break into pieces, in the name of Jesus.

28. Let prosperity appear in my life, in the name of Jesus.

29. Every evil command given to hell to carry out against me, scatter, in the name of Jesus.

30. Every instruction of barrenness, shame and reproach programmed against me, backfire, in the name of Jesus.

31. I shall not die the death of another man, in the mighty name of Jesus.

32. Any power that wants me to die suddenly shall replace me in the grave, in the name of Jesus.

33. Eaters of flesh and drinkers of blood, eat your own flesh and drink your own blood, in the name of Jesus.

34. Vulture of darkness preparing to feed on my flesh, die, in the name of Jesus.

35. Witchcraft calendar programming evil against me, catch

fire, in the name of Jesus.

36. Every evil word that is meant to attack my destiny, catch fire, in the name of Jesus.

37. The power that has vowed that I will cry this year, I silence you, in the name of Jesus.

38. Every mark of tragedy, my life is not your candidate, be removed, in the name of Jesus.

39. Appointment with sorrow, pain and tears, be cancelled, in the name of Jesus.

40. Mark of Christ, protect me from every danger, in the name of Jesus.

41. Blood of Jesus, silence the evil prayer offered against me, in the name of Jesus.

42. I shall not die but live to declare the works of God, in the name of Jesus.

43. My glory, do not accept any evil calendar, in the name of Jesus.

44. My star, do not accept to be under the control of evil calendar, in the name of Jesus.

45. Calamity and sorrow waiting to catch up with me, die, in the name of Jesus.

CHAPTER TEN

Pulling Down
Satanic Altars

Altars constitute a serious problem in our environment. Many lives have been corrupted and many more are being harassed in every area by these altars. Pray this prayer loud and clear before you read further: **"Any altar working against me, right now, catch fire, in the name of Jesus."**

Number 23:1 says, "And Balaam said unto Balak, Build me here seven altars, and prepare me here seven oxen and seven rams." Numbers 22:2-6: "And the children of Israel set forward, and pitched in the plains of Moab on this side Jordan by Jericho. And Balak the son of Zippor saw all that Israel had done to the Amorites. And Moab was sore afraid of the people, because they were many: and Moab was distressed because of the children of Israel. And Moab said unto the elders of Midian, Now shall this company lick up all that are round about us, as the ox licketh up the grass of the field. And Balak the son of Zippor was king of the Moabites at that time. He sent messengers therefore unto Balaam the son of Beor to Pethor, which is by the river of the land of the children of his people, to call him, saying, Behold, there is a people come out from Egypt: behold, they cover the face of the earth, and they abide over against me: Come now therefore, I pray thee, curse me this people; for they are too mighty for me: peradventure I shall prevail, that we may smite them, and that I may drive them out of the land: for I wot that he whom thou blessest is blessed, and he whom thou cursest is cursed."

Balak, the king of Moab was afraid of the children of Israel, who came out of Egypt and were moving towards their Promised Land. Balak became distressed because of them; he believed that the children of Israel would consume or overpower him. He called the elders of his people and concluded that they would call Balaam, a priest, to curse them in order to weaken their strength. Balak told Balaam, "I know that if you do something on your altar such as casting spell on them or chanting their names, they will become weak and then we will defeat them." When Balaam came, he instructed the king to build seven altars with the materials for sacrifice.

An altar can either be for good or for evil. God has His own altar and the devil too has his own altar, we must know that. Altars are not strange to the Bible. Those who walked with God in the Bible like Noah and Abraham were people of the altar. In Genesis 8:20, the Bible says that immediately after the flood, Noah built an altar and performed sacrifice on it, and the smell went up to God and God blessed him. The journey of Abraham can be traced with altars. As he moved from one place to another, he built altars in those places (Genesis 12:7).

Isaac built an altar (Genesis 26:24-25).

Jacob built his own altar (Genesis 35:5-7).

Gideon built an altar (Judges 6: 24).

David built an altar (1 Chronicles 21:26).

Elijah built an altar. He repaired the altar of the Lord that was broken before the fire came down (1 Kings 18:31-32).

Job built an altar. Every morning, he would gather his family and they would pray and talk to God (Job 1:1-5).

The above-mentioned people did not joke with altars. They also serve as proof that altars are very important in the life of God's children. A man is as strong, useful and relevant as his altar. People who belong to the occult and other secret societies don't joke with altars. They are very rigid and committed to their altars. They ensure that they are very consistent with their sacrifices. They abide by all the rules

117

given to them by their witch doctors.

Anytime you talk about altars, you also talk about priests because every altar must have a priest who officiates on it. A priest is the man who stands between the people and a deity. A priest is an intermediary. His work is to appease or summon the spirits or gods. A priest is the person who ministers at the altar. A priest is someone who invokes spirits. There is no satanic priest that doesn't know how to make incantations or chant words. The purpose of the chanting is to summon spirits. A priest is as powerful as his altar. A priest offers prayers on behalf of the people. For satanic priests, theirs is usually for commercial purposes.

A priest is someone who sues another person on an altar. Satanic priests are satanic intermediaries. They offer sacrifices on behalf of people. They are the ones who chant and summon the spirits. And their major purpose is to destroy, bury, attack, waste, transfer blessings and so on. There is no altar without a priest. There are mobile altars, which people carry around and there are also stationary altars. Some altars are located in particular places and whoever wants to appease them must go there. There are people, who even swallow their own altars; their altars are inside them. What we need to do as Christians is to send fire on these altars to release the people that have been tied down there and set the captives free.

118

Types of Altars

1. **Personal Altar:** A personal altar is a place where we commune with God; where we have fellowship with God. Anyone who calls himself or herself a child of God must have a regular altar with God just like we saw in the cases of Abraham, Isaac, Jacob, etc. They had their own personal altars. The question is, do you have your own personal altar, a place where you meet regularly with God? I am not talking about where you put carved images that you are bowing down to. I mean your personal relationship with God in the place of prayer and fellowship. Where you do praises, study the word of God and meditate on the word of God. It is called an altar. As little as it may seem, the altar is the strength of any man. Imagine a car without an engine, it cannot go anywhere. Likewise a Christian that doesn't have an altar. Any Christian that doesn't have an altar cannot go far. The reason many Christians are being moved up and down is that the altar which they claim to have is not a regular one. It is true that they meet with God, but only when it is convenient for them. The fire on their altar cannot cope with the barrage of battles that are coming against them.

The altar of many Christians don't have fire so when the enemy's altar is released against them, they are unable to cope. Those whose altars have no fire pray when they feel like praying and they read Bible only when they feel like. God can't do serious business with such people. As far as God is concerned, such people are not serious. So, when you talk about altars, you talk about regularity and consistency. If your capacity is thirty minutes, it must be regular and consistent. All the great people we read about in the Bible did not joke with their time of prayers. They kept a regular schedule as far as the things of God were concerned. This is very important because that is where our strength lies, where we are able to withstand the forces of darkness militating against us in these last days. The enemy is not joking in these last days and many people have been brought down because they are treading on surface water not knowing that they have to do business with deep waters to survive.

2. **Family Altar:** What we do at our family altars is fellowship: sharing the word of God, praising and worshiping God, meditating on the word and encouraging ourselves. A combination of your personal altar and family altar makes you formidable to withstand whatever comes from any direction. When these two altars are weak, the person becomes vulnerable in the battle of life.

In Genesis 18:17, God said that He trusted that Abraham would not joke with fellowship with his family, he must pray with his family. Abraham was consistent when it came to his family altar. Job too always gathered his family every morning to pray, seek the face of God and sacrifice to the Lord. In the

New Testament, in Acts 10, we read about a man called Cornelius; he was very consistent with his prayers and fasting. **Jeremiah 10:25 says, "Pour out thy fury upon the heathen that know thee not, and upon the families that call not on thy name: for they have eaten up Jacob, and devoured him, and consumed him, and have made his habitation desolate."** In the Bible also, we read about Elkanah, the husband of Hannah. He too had an altar, where he gathered his family. They went to Shiloh every year, where they had regular prayer and fellowship with God.

3.   **Church Altar:** When brethren gather in the presence of God, there is power in such fellowships; there is power in united prayers. That is why the Bible says we must not forsake the assembly of the brethren or the assembly of one another (Hebrews 10:25). When we gather together and raise our voices together in prayer and praises, we are strong, powerful and unbeatable. You cannot compare the gathering of the saints in the church with the gathering in our homes. Sadly, the people serving the devil are more serious in their service to the devil than the way some Christians serve God. They take the matter of their altars very serious. You would see a big man with his SUV car parked while he enters into a dirty bush to serve the devil in his altar. They are ready to do anything to

121

satisfy the devil. We too, must take our altars serious, particularly the altar of the church. Any calamity in a nation can be traced to the altar. If anything goes wrong in a family, check the altar. If you see the devastation caused by problem of altars in some families, you would not imagine it come near you and your family. It has caused destruction, wasted destinies, destroyed lives and wasted many good things.

What is an Altar?
1. It is a platform constructed for the purpose of worship.
2. It is a place of spiritual exchange.
3. It is a place of sacrifice.
4. It is a place of dedication.
5. It is a place of enquiry.
6. It is a place of power.
7. It is a place of decision.
8. It is a place of covenant.
9. It is a place of initiation.

Many people are being harassed today as a result of the effect of the altar that exists in their families, either visible or invisible. Altars are real and if you want to be free, make sure your own altar is strong. If you want to be strong, take time to deal with your own altar.

Altars around us

1. Traditional medicine centres.
2. Sacred trees.
3. Sacred hills.
4. Crossroads.
5. False places of worship.
6. Herbal homes.
7. Night clubs and disco halls.
8. Evil forests.
9. Ancient gates.
10. Occult altars.
11. Markets.
12. Local shrines.
13. Brothels.
14. Palaces.
15. Cemeteries.
16. Rivers.
17. Religious altars.
18. Crystal ball centres.
19. Astral altars.
20. T-junctions.
21. Mobile altars.
22. Visible altars.
23. Covens.
24. Ancestral altars.
25. Photograph altars.

26. Marine altars.
27. Clothing altars.
28. Coffin altars.
29. Territorial altars.

How to be free from evil altars

1. Make sure you are born again.
2. Have your personal altar and service your it regularly.

Prayer Points

1. Holy Ghost, touch me with the touch of fire, in the name of Jesus.
2. I tear away every veil of darkness covering my face, in the name of Jesus.
3. Every witchcraft projection into my life, scatter, in the name of Jesus.
4. O God, arise and let me experience your possibility power, in the name of Jesus.
5. I fire back every arrow of stagnation, limitation and frustration fired at me, in the name of Jesus.
6. I shall not die but live to declare the wonders of God, in the name of Jesus.
7. I prophesy, my hands shall feed me, in the name of Jesus.
8. Angels of my breakthrough, what are you waiting for? Manifest, in the name of Jesus.

124

9. I shall move from labour to favour by the power in the blood of Jesus Christ, in the name of Jesus.

10. Every altar of darkness that conspires against me, catch fire, in the name of Jesus.

11. Every demonic altar working against my life, I pull you down, in the name of Jesus.

12. Every fetish material buried to be working against me, catch fire, in the name of Jesus.

13. Witchcraft transfer of affliction into my body through inflicting injury upon any object bearing my name, catch fire, in the name of Jesus.

14. Satanic intelligent network of killer altars, catch fire, in the name of Jesus.

15. Every altar of delay and denial of my place of birth, catch fire, in the name of Jesus.

16. Battles ordained against me from a satanic altar, go back to your sender, in the name of Jesus.

17. Burial of my money, clothes and certificate working against me, catch fire, in the name of Jesus.

CHAPTER ELEVEN

The Leadership Quality of The Eagle

Psalm 71:21 says, "Thou shalt increase my greatness, and comfort me on every side."

Esther 9:4 says, "For Mordecai was great in the king's house, and his fame went out throughout all the provinces: for this man Mordecai waxed greater and greater."

The eagle is a great bird and God uses so many qualities of the eagle to teach us great lessons. The eagle is a bird that flies very high. God has called us to go high. The eagle is a very strong bird that perseveres. It doesn't eat dirty things and doesn't mix up with all kinds of birds. An eagle sticks to one partner for life.

Qualities that make you an eagle

1. Keep your promises. Learn to keep the promises you made to God, to people and to yourself. If you want to

126

excel in life, if you want to be great, if you want to wax stronger, and to reach greater heights, keep your promises to God. Are there things you told God that you would do if He did some things for you? You must keep those promises. But oftentimes when God does His own part, we don't fulfil our own part. I have seen people who said, if God blessed them, they would do this or that, but as soon as God blessed them, they forgot the vow they made to God. If you want to go far in life, don't be that kind of person. Keep the promises you make to God, men and yourself. Many people make resolutions during New Year or their birthdays but they don't keep them.

2. Walk with the right people. Many times our problems are the wrong company. I have seen many people who were very decent but not until they connected to the wrong people. It is better to move alone than to move with the wrong crowd. Anytime God wants to lift you up, He sends good people to you. Anytime satan wants to bring you down, he sends the wrong people to you. The people we meet every day are like mathematical symbols of subtraction, division, addition and multiplication. Some of them come into your life to subtract from you. Some come into your life to divide you. But some come into your life to add to you. There are others who come into your life and they multiply

you. This is the kind of people you should move with. Don't move with people that would subtract from you or divide you. Don't move with the company of unserious people. Don't move with people, who don't take the things of God serious, those who don't have value for the things of God. Avoid them.

Measures against destiny loss or wastage

1. **Mind your association:** Samson was a very great man but his association with Delilah finished him and his destiny. So, if you want to achieve greatness, be careful who you move with. Select who you associate with. You may not have the choice of where you were born, the parents who gave birth to you, or the location where you were born. You may not have those choices but the choice of friends is yours to make. So, choose wisely. **Proverbs 13:20 says, "He that walketh with wise men shall be wise; but a companion of fools shall be destroyed."**

2. **Pursue Excellence:** The eagle represents excellence. The eagle is different from all other birds. There are birds that eat carcass; there are some that eat raw and dirty things. Birds like vultures know who is going to die, and hover around them but not the eagle.

128

Ecclesiastes 9:10 says, "Whatsoever thy hand findeth to do, do it with thy might; for there is no work, nor device, nor knowledge, nor wisdom, in the grave, whither thou goest." Joseph had the gift of interpretation of dreams but he didn't stop at that. When he interpreted the king's dream, he had the wisdom for solution to the problems highlighted in the dream. If he stopped only at interpreting the dream, the king would have thanked him and maybe give him a gift, and let him be taken back to the prison. But after he interpreted the dream, he proffered solution; how they were going to preserve food. That one was not a gift. If you don't read, or do things to develop yourself, you will remain where you are. Preparation and opportunity always lead to success. **Proverbs 22:29 says, "Seest thou a man diligent in his business? He shall stand before kings; he shall not stand before mean men."**

3. Start each day with God: Ensure that you look into the word of God and meditate upon it every day. Pray, praise and worship God on a daily basis. Don't be a Christian that doesn't read the Bible or a Christian that doesn't have a prayer altar. Don't be a Christian that just floats.

129

4. Be disciplined: Be disciplined in the way you talk and the way you live your life generally. Lateness to church activities and other things is a sign of indiscipline. Unfortunately, many Christians do not consider keeping appointments with God a serious matter. Oversleeping is indiscipline. You should be able to wake up when your name is called. Overeating is indiscipline. Lawlessness is indiscipline.

5. Improve your life: Keep sharpening yourself by reading, attending seminars, workshops, conferences, and seeking more knowledge. Learn to discipline your flesh by disregarding its commands. The flesh doesn't want to pray, and it loves enjoyment. So, you must be wary of the flesh.

6. Finish what you have started: Be disciplined enough to finish what you have started.

7. Don't live your life to please everyone: The day you decide to please everyone then you have decided to fail. Jesus Christ, the Saviour of the world did not please everyone in spite of what He did for mankind. The Bible says He went about doing good but the same people that shouted, "Hosanna in the Highest" for Him were the same people that said, "Crucify Him!"

130

8. Live within your means.
9. Be consistent with your tithe.
10. Become loyal.
11. Have a mentor.
12. Pray and plan.
13. Avoid procrastination.
14. Become approachable.
15. Embrace hard work.
16. Develop hatred for failure.

The eagle is a wonderful bird. It has so many features and good characteristics. There are more references to the eagle than any other bird or animal in the Bible. The eagle is a swift bird. **Deuteronomy 32:11 says, "As an eagle stirreth up her nest, fluttereth over her young, spreadeth abroad her wings, taketh them, beareth them on her wings." Job 39:27: "Doth the eagle mount up at the command, and make her nest on high? She dwelleth and abideth on the rock, upon the crag of the rock and the strong place. From hence she seeketh the prey, and her eyes behold afar off. Her young ones also suck up blood; and where the slain are, there is she."**

The eagle is a bird of great height. It doesn't fly low that is why it is not easy for a hunter to kill an eagle. The eagle lives on the tallest mountain, the tallest hill and the tallest rock. Eagles fly high, thirty-six miles above the sea level. Do you know that

God is also calling you to fly high?

There are other birds and animals that the Bible makes reference to. For example,

1. **The Dove:** In Genesis 8, after the flood, and Noah wanted to be sure that the waters had abated on earth, he sent out a dove. Dove represents the Holy Ghost (Luke 3:21). During the baptism of our Lord Jesus Christ, a voice from heaven spoke and said, **"This is my beloved Son in whom I am well pleased." In Matthew 10:16, the Bible says, "Behold, I send you forth as a sheep in the midst of wolves: be ye therefore wise as serpents, and harmless as dove."**

2. **The Lion:** The Bible says the lion is the strongest beast. It does not run away for other animals. The lion is the king of other animals. It is known for strength, agility, power and toughness. The lion is in charge anywhere it is found. It is not the biggest animal, but certainly the strongest.

The Bible says you will be the head and not the tail. God wants you to fly high but unfortunately, many people's wings have been clipped. Many have lost their wings to fly. The eagle is a bird of vision with very sharp eyes. From a great height, the eagle can see a snake crawling on the ground and from there, it can fly straight to the snake, kill it, shake it, carry it up and go and eat it. The eagle does not eat animals that have been killed, it has to eat it fresh. What does that signify? It means that without vision, you can't go far in life; it doesn't matter how prayerful you are. God is asking, "What do you want me to bless?"

Without vision, a life will rot away. The Bible says, where there is no vision, the people perish. The bigger your future, the bigger your destiny. Vision is the picture that you want for your future, so without vision, there would be problems. Many people have no vision; if you ask them what they want to do with their lives, they don't know. The reason we celebrate Joseph, Daniel, and Esther is that they had something they were running after. The question is, what are you pursuing? What are you running after? We are to pursue vision; what is your vision? What do you want to achieve? What project do you want to give birth to? It is vision that motivates people. It is vision that helps you maximize time. It is vision that helps you to be focused. Men of vision are highly focused.

The eagle is a fighter; it doesn't give up. The scripture says, we wrestle not against flesh and blood but against principalities, powers, rulers of darkness of this world, and against spiritual wickedness in high places. Our battle is not a physical combat, it is not about your muscle; it is a spiritual warfare. God has given us the weapon of prayer to battle the forces of darkness. The Bible says, "Fight the good fight of faith and lay hold on eternal life." So, even to make heaven, you need to fight. If you

133

don't fight, nobody will hear your voice. If you don't fight, nobody will know that you are around. If you don't fight, your portion will not be given to you. If you are waiting for the day your glory will be handed over to you, you will wait for a long time. Therefore, you have to fight, pursue and recover all. You have the backing of heaven to possess your possession. The reason you are sent to this earth is to possess your possession.

Eagles always take care of their little ones. A life without a successor is a wasted life. Some people are too busy to take care of their children and as a result, their children become wayward. So, the father is decent but the children are useless. The father is godly, he loves God, but the children have no heart for God. The eagle is not like that. The eagle trains its children so that they can develop their own wings too and be able to actualize their destiny.

The eagle is not afraid of storms. When other birds disappear when there is a storm or adversity, the eagle rejoices. The eagle will face the storm, release its wings and fly high. As a Christian, you should not be afraid of oppositions, enemies, betrayal, trials etc. They are all part of life. It is only when you exit the world that you stop seeing them. Jesus said, in the world, we will face tribulation and not jubilation. That is, somebody will hate you for no reason and you will be attacked

134

for no reason. These things are part of life. However, the scripture says that they that wait upon the Lord shall renew their strength; they shall mount up with wings as eagles, they shall run and not be weary, and they shall walk and not faint.

An eagle can carry something that is four times its size and fly with it. Eagles fly alone. You need the right company in life. It is better not to move at all with people that cannot help your destiny. It is better to move alone than to be with the wrong crowd. Association is very important in life because you can't improve more than your association. You can't be better than the company you keep. Anytime God wants to bless us, He sends people to us. Likewise anytime the devil wants to harm us, he sends the wrong people to us. There are children who were brought up to be decent but by association with the wrong people, something else took over.

The dominion of the eagle
Isaiah 40:30 says, "Even the youths shall faint and be weary and the young men shall utterly fall; but they that wait upon the Lord shall renew their strength; they shall mount up with wings as eagles; they shall run and not be weary, and they shall walk and not faint."

The eagle is a special bird compared to all other birds and it is

135

quite unique. The eagle is not a chicken, a vulture or a bat. All these other birds have great limitations. The chicken is known for low ambition. The raven is a bird of destruction and war. The vulture is a bird associated with death. The bat is known for its blindness. The sparrow is only good at talking. There are birds that only sing. Farmers in the villages don't have time pieces, they can only tell the time when they hear the birds sing. When they are working in the farm and they hear the birds sing, they would know it is evening, and time to go home. There are birds that come to announce evil. Whenever such a bird begins to cry, people will know that there is trouble. That is just their assignment. But the eagle has strength, power and authority. It is a bird of flight that doesn't fly low. It flies high with strength. It is a bird of vision that has supernatural strength. It is used to symbolize good character. The eagle is disciplined; it doesn't mate with more than one eagle at a time. It stays with only one for life.

Eagles are always battle ready. They are very vigilant and they are strikers. It is not known for defense; it is always on the offensive. It takes the battle to the gate of the enemy. The eagle also signifies royalty, honour, colourful destiny, etc. The eagle is also known as a bird of speed. It is usually used to describe excellence. However, do you know that as powerful as the eagle is, it can be caged? I heard of a hunter, who in one of his hunting expeditions, saw an egg that was laid on top of a mountain. He took the egg to his house and put it under one of his hens that was incubating its eggs. Eventually, the eagle egg was hatched with the chickens. The eaglet followed the mother hen and chicks to go and pick dirt. The mother hen thought the eagle was a chicken because it lived with them. The eaglet too saw the mother hen as its mother until one day, it saw a big bird fly across. The mother hen saw the bird and ran away because it was actually coming to attack them. But the eaglet among the chicken stood back and was looking at the big bird. As it was looking at it, it saw that they were similar; they had the same features. That was how the eaglet flew away, left the chickens and joined the eagle.

But, I want you to understand that the eagle can be caged. Samson was the strongest man that ever lived; nobody could defeat him. With a jawbone in his hand, he was able to kill thousands of people. One day, they locked the gate of the city against Samson and when he got to the gate, he used his hands to pull down the gate, carried it and climbed the hill with it. But one day, the same Samson walked into the trap of the enemy, the enemy captured him and removed his eyes. An eagle can be caged and many eagles have been caged.

Many people with great potential, ability, vision, authority, royalty, and honour have been caged by the enemy. Many have been caged in ancestral cages, environmental cages, domestic witchcraft cages, cage of ignorance, cage of confusion, demonic cage, religious cages, demonic sexual partner cages and career cages. Many people need to come out from these cages so they can recover the seat that was reserved for them. There is a seat reserved for you and whoever is occupying it must be cleared away so that you can get it back. You can get back that honour, and you can get back to that seat.

There was a certain lady, who was a student of pharmacy in the university. Her parents were very rich and could afford anything for her. All her clothes were bought from overseas anytime they travelled. But she had a problem; she would leave the clothes bought for her from abroad and be going to the backyard of the university, where other girls hung their clothes to steal them. One day, she was caught where she stole one leg of shoe. The question is, what does she want to do with one leg of shoe? A girl, who lacked nothing, stealing from others. That is a serious matter.

A certain lawyer was caught like that in the supermarket. I got to know about it because I heard him giving testimony in the church. He stole a candy and put it inside his pocket without paying for it. Then he broke down and cried saying, "This problem followed me here. How much is the sweet? I have money in my pocket." As he wanted to bring money out to pay, they said to him, "You put this sweet inside your pocket because you wanted to steal it." That was an eagle that was caged; something was following him about to disgrace him.

There was also the story of a young man, who went to the office and did his work normally. He was committed to his work but the problem was anytime he collected his salary, he would go to the Newspaper stand and use all the money to buy Newspapers. What was he doing with the Newspapers? Nothing. But that is what happens when the eagle is caged.

In Mark 5, we read the story of a young man, who left his home and relocated to the cemetery. He was a fierce demoniac, who terrorized his environment. Anytime, he was on the street, nobody dared walk that way. It was that bad. The Bible said sometimes, he would cut himself with stones and would be bleeding seriously. He would be in pain and yet continue to cut himself. Even his family members could not help him. He broke every chain used to bind him. Several men came around to see whether they could bundle him out of the cemetery but they could not, he was always there. That was a caged destiny. When a destiny is caged, it is corrupted, amputated, fragmented, and aborted, instead of glory, there would be shame. Instead of honour, there would be dishonour.

Many destinies have been battered. A lot of people have become slaves where they are supposed to be kings. That is why there are so many underachievers today. Many people are tossed here and there by the oceans of life. A lot of people are fishing in fishless waters, while there are many clouds without rain and many wells without water.

Signs to know that an eagle is caged

1.   **Mental dullness:** There are some people, who have university degrees but lack the ambition to rise in life. They have no ambition to rise and make impact in life. They are dull, and have not discovered themselves. Many people do not yet realize that they have a big assignment to do for God. They don't know that they are men of substance. They don't know that heaven is waiting for them to fulfill destiny. They don't know that they are the ones sent from heaven to solve their families problems. Some of them are unknowingly complaining about the assignment that heaven has for them on earth. They complain about the problems in their families, which God has sent them to come and solve. What an irony!

2. Loss of memory.

3. Mistaken identity.

4. Embargo.

5. Destiny transfer.

6. Evil attraction.

7. Addiction.

8. Insanity.

9. Demonic attacks.

10. Evil plantations.

Prayer Points

1. I cover myself and my family with the blood of Jesus, in the name of Jesus.

2. I plug my life to the divine socket. Let the current of favour flow into my life, in the name of Jesus.

3. O Lord, give me the testimony that will advertise your name and power in my life, in the name of Jesus.

4. In the race of life, I shall not be a latecomer, in the name of Jesus.

5. O Lord, this year, my expectation shall not be cut off, in the name of Jesus.

6. Every chain of darkness binding my finances, career and health, break, in the name of Jesus.

7. Thou power of spells, charms and sorcery over my destiny, die, in the name of Jesus.

8. O Lord, bless me and increase me on every side, in the name of Jesus.

9. Father, I declare that this month shall favour me, in the name of Jesus.

10. Every evil prayer against me, your end has come, die, in the name of Jesus.

11. Any impossibility in my life, become possible, in the name of Jesus.

12. Every gang up against me on my way to the top, scatter, in the name of Jesus.

13. Powers tying me down to the wrong location where my destiny does not belong, die, in the name of Jesus.

14. Powers that have vowed that my battle will not end, die, in the name of Jesus.

15. Powers that want to scatter my harvest, die, in the name of Jesus.

16. Arrows of intimidation, limitation and frustration programmed into the work of my hand, catch fire, in the name of Jesus.

17. Every house that I have lived before that has covenanted me to failure and non-achievement, catch fire, in the name of Jesus.

18. Wherever my name is mentioned, mercy and favour of God, answer for me, in the name of Jesus.

19. My destiny is not available to be devoured, in the name of Jesus.

142

20. Whether the enemy likes it or not, I will fly high, in the name of Jesus.
21. Every pit dug to bury what should not die in my life, bury your owners, in the name of Jesus.
22. Powers assigned to take me where I should not go, you are failures, die, in the name of Jesus.
23. My glory, what are you doing in the cage of witchcraft? Come out now, in the name of Jesus.
24. Any problem in my life that has the agenda to mock God, today is your end, expire, in the name of Jesus.
25. Anything within me, anything around me and anything inside me working against my success, die, in the name of Jesus.
26. Arrow of frustration at the edge of breakthrough, die, in the name of Jesus.
27. Every ancient rope of darkness tying me down, break, in the name of Jesus.
28. Power to rise from story to glory, fall upon me, in the name of Jesus.
29. This month shall favour me, in the name of Jesus.
30. I declare that my destiny shall not be stagnated and my life will move forward, in the name of Jesus.
31. Father, wherever my eagle is tied down, release it now, in the name of Jesus.
32. O God, arise and let my glory shine, in the name of Jesus.
33. O God, arise and deliver me in every area of my life, where I am stagnated, in the name of Jesus.
34. Poverty assigned to mock me and my future, die, in the

name of Jesus.

35. Powers refusing my dominion on earth, die, in the name of Jesus.

36. Any satanic document where it is written that I must suffer, I tear you into pieces, in the name of Jesus.

37. Help of God and man for my next level, appear by fire, in the name of Jesus.

38. The good things I have been looking for, where are you? Appear, in the name of Jesus.

39. My hands begin to handle great things, in the name of Jesus.

40. My hands, you shall not gather wind, you shall gather prosperity, in the name of Jesus.

41. O God, arise and anoint my hands to recover my wasted years, in the name of Jesus.

42. O God, anoint my hands for favour and dominion, in the name of Jesus.

43. O God, arise and empower my hands for total takeover, in the name of Jesus.

44. Witchcraft chains binding my hands to wrong assignments, break, in the name of Jesus.

45. Every evil hand fighting the work of my hands, wither, in the name of Jesus.

46. Evil attachment to my hands, burn to ashes, in the name of Jesus.

47. Evil hands displacing my hands, wither, in the name of Jesus.

48. My eagle, what are you doing among chickens? Arise and fly, in the name of Jesus.

49. O God, I am not satisfied with this my level, promote me by fire, in the name of Jesus.

50. I am not a chicken. I am an eagle, therefore I will arise and shine, in the name of Jesus.

51. Powers removing my name from greatness, wherever you are, die, in the name of Jesus.

52. Powers fighting me because of my glory, your end has come, die, in the name of Jesus.

CHAPTER TWELVE

Breaking The Evil Pattern of Demonic Cycle

The Bible rightly says that there is nothing new under the sun (Ecclesiastes 1:9). Whatever you are experiencing today, whether good or bad, has happened to somebody before. The delays, attacks, demonic forces, disappointments, rejection, etc. somebody, somewhere has gone through them before. Today, there is a cycle of events that wants to repeat itself in your life. It has happened to an older generation and now, it wants to happen to you. By cycle, I mean series of events that are being repeated. The same way it happened before, it is trying to happen now to somebody else. That is what is called an evil cycle.

In Ecclesiastes 1:9-10, the Bibles says, **"The thing that hath been, it is that which shall be; and that which is done is that which shall be done: and there is no new thing under the**

146

sun. **Is there anything whereof it may be said, See, this is new? It hath been already of old time, which was before us."**
The passage in the foregoing is teaching us that life is in cycles. A young man is born as a baby. A young baby is so tender and fragile; you have to carry it very carefully because everything is tender. If you rough handle the baby, it may cause a permanent damage on it. But after sometime, going through natural biological processes, the baby would begin to sit down, crawl and after sometime begin to make attempt to stand up and walk. The baby would be falling down, but after sometime, it would become an expert by itself. That is what a cycle is all about. We have different seasons; we have the rainy season and the dry season. It is just a cycle. Every year, they come and go. It is a cycle. In the case of man, the fact that a boy is taller than his father doesn't mean that he can father a child. He can only do that when the cycle has been completed. Women have their periods or monthly cycles; it is only natural.

If a cycle or pattern is possible in nature, it is also possible spiritually. Sometimes, when you are facing some problems and you have prayed but the problem persists, you need to make some enquiries. Many people at such a point, when they made enquiries, discovered that things turned around in their favour. That is why it is often said that life is a seed we sow every day. What we do is being recorded. Our actions and the

147

things we do are being recorded for us. There is recording somewhere of the things we do even in the secret, when nobody is there. If man can devise a camera that records what happens in the traffic, how much more the God of heaven and earth, who sees in secret and in the open. I beg you, what you don't want to reap, don't sow it. What you don't want to go through and what you cannot accept, don't do it to another person. What you don't want your children to reap, please don't sow it. That is the stand of scriptures. Try not to sow what you don't want to reap. That is why when the names of the departed are mentioned, people would either say, they were good or they were bad, depending on the type of seed they sowed when they were alive. As much as possible, try not to sow what you don't want to reap.

The Bible makes us to understand that when you are facing some problems, which defy prayers and fasting, you may need to go home and ask your father and mother what they did. **Deuteronomy 32:7 says, "Remember the days of old, consider the years of many generations: ask thy father, and he will shew thee; thy elders, and they will tell thee."**

The reason you need to ask is that when you know the source of your problem, you can easily get answers or solution to it. Abraham had challenges with childbearing (Genesis 11). Isaac, his son too had the same problem. That is called a cycle.

148

When Jacob got married, the same thing happened to him. What I am saying is that some of the things happening to you now have happened before; it is only you didn't take notice.

There was a family, where the firstborn got married and had four daughters. The next one got married and had three daughters. The third one got married and had two daughters. When the fourth one got married, he said to himself, "This trend cannot be normal." Being a child of God, he started praying and was able to break the chain and evil cycle. So, he had both male and female children.

In Mark 12:21-22, we read the story of a woman, who was married to seven brothers, one after the other. It says, **"And the second took her, and died, neither left he any seed: and the third likewise. And the seven had her, and left no seed: last of all the woman died also."**

The first one married her and couldn't have any child. The second to the seventh, all had her, but all of them died without having any child. That is what happens when there is an evil chain in place. It will not allow common sense to prevail. The seven brothers married the same woman and died without having children. When two of them died, the rest could have withdrawn from the lady, but no, they went ahead and also married her and ended up with the same result as others.

David loved the Lord but was sexually loose with the opposite sex. He loved women. It was an evil inheritance from his forebear, Judah. We read about it in Genesis 38. Even when David was well stricken in age, a young woman had to be brought to warm his bed, and this helped to keep him happy and his life was prolonged. The thing came and smuggled itself into his lineage. This evil cycle was passed to David's children. When Solomon became a king, he married seven hundred wives and three hundred concubines. The son of Solomon also married many wives and had many concubines. Absalom went a little further by sleeping with his father's wives publicly, in the eyes of everyone. That is to tell you that this evil cycle perpetuates wickedness in the family. It got so bad that incest was recorded among the children of David.

What propagates the evil cycle? It is sin. When we continue in sin, the evil too continues. When we continue in drunkenness, fornication, adultery, etc. the enemy uses them to gain ground in our families and begins to perpetuate wickedness and evil. This situation needs to be tackled with prayer and deliverance before there can be freedom. In some families, marriages don't work because of this evil cycle. Those affected do everything they can for it to work because they don't want to be associated with marital failure, but no way because the root has not been dealt with.

Prayer Points

1. I break every evil cycle of rising and falling, in the name of Jesus.
2. Evil pattern of 'this is how far you will go', break, in the name of Jesus.
3. Powers that want to render my destiny useless, die, in the name of Jesus.
4. Every chain of evil cycle holding me down, break, in the name of Jesus.
5. Powers that say even if I am successful now, I will fail later, die, in the name of Jesus.
6. Evil chain holding my family down, break, in the name of Jesus.
7. Powers pursuing me with sickness unto death, you are liars, die, in the name of Jesus.
8. The gate of my breakthrough that is under lock, open by fire, in the name of Jesus.
9. My destiny shall not be meat on the dining table of darkness, in the name of Jesus.

CHAPTER THIRTEEN

Binding the Strong Man

There is a personality of darkness called, the strong man. There is a ruler of the wicked world in the demonic realm called the strong man. **Matthew 12:29 says, "Or else how can one enter into a strong man's house, and spoil his goods, except he first bind the strong man? And then he will spoil his house."**

We are told here that the strong man has a house and he has goods in that house. The goods the Bible is talking about here are the good things that belong to God's people; and if we want those things back, we need to storm the strong man's house, overpower the strongman, bind the strongman, move inside and collect our goods.

Mark 3:27 says, "No man can enter into a strong man's

house, and spoil his goods, except he will first bind the strong man; and then he will spoil his house."

The Bible introduced all kinds of spirits to us. It talks about the spirit in the air **(Ephesians 2:2)**. This spirit is not a good spirit; it works in the children of disobedience. It is roaming around in the air and its assignment is to work in the children of disobedience. The Bible calls the strong man the prince and power of the air. He is a prince and ruler over the air and he decides the affairs of men. For example, he decides how many people would not be able to fulfill their destiny, and how many would be kept in obscurity?

In **1Peter 5:8, it is written, "Be sober, be vigilant; because your adversary, the devil, as a roaring lion, walketh about, seeking whom he may devour."** This scripture is also talking about the strong man who is walking about looking for people he can afflict with problems. He does no one any good, he attacks and devours men. **Ephesians 6:12** calls them principalities, powers, rulers of the darkness of this world and spiritual wickedness in high places. The rulers of the darkness of this world are more wicked than principalities and powers, and spiritual wickedness in high places is wickedness of the highest order; what they do is terrible wickedness.

The strong man is a ruler over another group of spirits. This is

153

why the deliverance environment is very interesting. Sometimes, when deliverance ministers are praying deliverance prayers, all kinds of spirits challenge them. They would say: "We will not go, he was handed over to us," or "We are not going to let her go." At times the spirits would say, "Well if we must let her go, we would kill her." A man brought his boy to the disciples of Jesus Christ to help him cast out the spirit that was troubling the boy. The disciples of Jesus could not cast out the spirit and eventually, Jesus appeared. The father of the boy told Jesus that the spirit tormenting the boy threw him into the fire sometimes. It is amazing to see somebody neatly dressed manifesting and rolling on the floor because of the strange powers inside him or her. The person could be swimming like a fish on hard concrete floor as if he is inside water. Sometimes, you hear them talking with a strange voice, or behaving like a snake. These are strange manifestations.

Jesus entered into the temple one day, and demons challenged Him saying, "We know that you are the Son of God, why have you come to torment us? It's not yet our time, don't cast us out of here. We are here to finish them, harm them, trouble and inflict pain on them." Anywhere demons find comfortable accommodation, they stay put and don't want to leave. Rather than leave, they will go and bring all their friends

154

to come and join them to make the life of the person really terrible. When Jesus asked the demoniac, "What is your name?" He said his name is Legion, meaning that they are many. When Jesus commanded the spirits to come out, they came out and entered into the swine around and they all perished in the water.

These spirits are aggressive, you don't talk to them gently. You don't deal with them absent-mindedly. Jesus said, if you want to deal with them, you have to be strong and you have to be ready. That is why many people are not getting result. Although they are fervent and determined, they are not aggressive enough. They don't have the kind of fire that is required to chase these things out. They don't possess the kind of violent spirit that is required to challenge the spirits to come out from their hiding place. Sometimes, these spirits hide in a secured place called the stronghold in deliverance. When there is a stronghold, it makes it difficult to chase them out. That is why as soon as they get to a particular house, they quickly turn it into a stronghold. Strongholds are impenetrable, except you have the Holy Ghost fire.

The Bible tells us that the strongman is armed meaning that he has a defence. So, for your prayer to pierce through the fence, you have to be violent. Inability to penetrate the enemy's stronghold has caused many people and families to be stagnated. There are families, where anyone who tries to rise above others will be eliminated. Anyone who wants to shine will be pushed away from the place of blessing. There are evil hands that specialize in pushing people to the back anytime they take a lead. Most of these problems were initiated by their parents, grandparents or ancestors, who go to satan and his demons for help. In order to prevent witches and wizards from harming them, they go to higher witches, wizards, wicked altars and herbalists for help. This is the reason many people find themselves in the kind of battles they did not prepare for.

These spirits manifest in different forms such as skeletons, headless beings, etc. and sometimes, when they are leaving, the wave bye-bye to their victims. They make people to behave abnormally. I know of a woman who would go to the middle of the road, stay there and refuse to leave. A strange spirit usually took her over and she would not be able to leave the place until she had struggled there for ten minutes. Motorists would honk their horns and rain curses on her not knowing the battle she was dealing with. It would amaze you to know that the woman in question was a director somewhere, in a highly exalted position. But the battles of life do not recognize positions; they are no respecter of persons.

A certain man of God, whose father was a witch doctor said that as a child, he remembered people who wanted money, high position in the office, children, etc. come to his father for help. And as a young boy, he knew that witch doctors went to the bush to gather leaves and all sorts of things, spoke to altars and spirits. But one night, at home, where they lived, he woke up to ease himself outside and saw some people conversing with his father. As he moved closer, he saw his father talking to a snake and he ran back inside the house. Now that he has grown to become a man of God, life has not been easy because of where he is coming from. The things he had done in the past and the things planted in his foundation have started to trouble him.

Many people are married to strange spirits, while some were helped by the devil but now it is payback time. Sometimes, when people search for things, they don't care to know the terms and conditions. There was a woman, who anytime she was pregnant, a man would appear and sleep with her and that would be the end of the pregnancy.

A certain young man saw a beautiful lady and they started dating. The young man noticed that anytime he requested to see her parents, she told him not to worry. One day, when the pressure was much, she accepted to show him her parents. As they were going, a few poles to the house, she pointed to the house and told the young man to go ahead and she would meet him there. When he got there, they asked him whom he was looking for and he mentioned the lady's name. He told the girl's father that he came to ask for her hand in marriage. The girl's father replied that he didn't want to see both of them. Eventually, the young man learnt that the girl died many years back. The father showed him the spot in the compound, where she was buried. From that day, the young man was not the same again; he started seeing strange things.

So many people have pushed themselves into strange things and the repercussions are coming. If you go to the deliverance ground, you will hear the kind of things that spirit husbands and spirit wives are doing. Some of them, after messing up with their victims, would drop money, and they see the money physically.

The Bible describes the strong man as a wicked entity and as a spirit that does not let go of his prisoners. That is, anytime you want to go, they pull you back. They don't open the door to their prisoners except it is by force. The strongman is not weak, he is very strong and fully armed. The strongman is a thief that has stolen from everyone. The strong man has no mercy, he is wicked and destructive. He is the masquerade of darkness. There are villages where when a woman gives birth to a child, they must go to a particular place to hear the spirit give the name of the baby. Such children grow up to face a lot of challenges. There was a certain woman, who at the age of thirty-nine, she had no breasts. In the course of her deliverance, information came that her mother went somewhere when she was looking for a child.

The strongman is a destroyer and a blocker. Have you discovered that anytime you want to move forward something happens? That means you have a strongman contending with you. The strongman is a thief that steals peace, health, joy, finance, wealth and destiny. You need to go after the strongman to collect your goods from him. When the strongman is in place, you will be hearing strange voices. Some people hear whistles blowing without seeing who is blowing them. I have seen somebody who came for counselling and said, "Man of God, they are shooting." I told him I couldn't hear anything. It is the strong man making life horrible for him. Some people will tell you that invisible hands are pouring sand on their bodies. These are all the terrible strange acts of the strong man.

What to do to be free
1. You need to give your life to Jesus.
2. You need to examine the kind of life you are living. If you have the spirit of anger, it would be a door opener to other spirits such as marine spirits, spirit spouse, strong man etc.

3. Ensure that you live a clean and holy life so that you don't open the door to these wicked spirits.

Prayer Points

1. My Father, heal me and I will be healed, deliver me and I will be delivered, in Jesus' name.
2. Satanic womb that has swallowed my blessings, I command you to release them by fire, in Jesus' name.
3. Angels of my blessings, where are you, gather my blessings, in Jesus' name.
4. I bind every familiar spirit, lose your hold upon my life, in Jesus' name.
5. Every fetish power assigned against my moving forward, expire, in Jesus' name.
6. I bind the strong man and command him to release me and let me go, in the name of Jesus.
7. Strongman assigned against my destiny, die, in the name of Jesus.
8. Chains of the strongman binding me, break, in the name of Jesus.
9. The shrine of the strongman assigned against me, catch fire, in the name of Jesus.

CHAPTER FOURTEEN

Dismantling Satanic Cages

There is something known as a cage. There is a spiritual cage as well as a physical cage. The work of a cage is to hold, to keep, to limit, to restrict, to delay, to restrain, to hinder and to obstruct. Please note that a cage does not make itself. A cage is made by someone and for a particular purpose. A life that is caged is a life that is under pressure and not under pleasure. Life is supposed to be under pleasure because the Bible says, "For this purpose the Son of God was made manifest that he might destroy the works of darkness." Jesus told us the purpose of His coming. He said, "I came to give you life and to give it to you more abundantly." So the kind of life Jesus came to give to us is abundant life; that is a life of pleasure. But when a life is inside a cage, the person will be experiencing pressure instead of pleasure and instead of triumph, he would be under torture.

A life inside the cage is a life under perpetual torture. **Jeremiah 30:8 says, "For it shall come to pass in that day, saith the LORD of hosts, that I will break his yoke from off thy neck, and will burst thy bonds, and strangers shall no more serve themselves of him."**

A cage is a terrible device that is used to render a person useless in the kingdom of darkness. Therefore, we need to be determined to come out from the cage of darkness where the enemy has put us, so that we can move to where God wants us to be. It may not be easy because the enemy does not want his captives to escape. You need to fight for your freedom.

Facts about a cage

1. A cage is designed to limit: If you are experiencing limitation in any aspect of your life, it is the work of the cage. The function of a cage is to limit. If a person is in a cage, it doesn't mean that he cannot move; the only problem is that the movement is restricted and limited. What the person may be celebrating as breakthrough will be a leftover. There are so many people today that are rejoicing over crumbs, when God has designed abundance for them. What God designed for them is plenty. God designed for them to have more than enough but they have been subjected to perpetual pressure. They don't have as much as they need. Such

162

lives are constantly under pressure.

2. There are different kinds of cages: Cages are made of different sizes. There is a cage for a bird, which is not as big as a cage that is meant for monkeys. The cage for human beings is different from the cage for animals, depending on the size of the person to be kept in the cage. Some cages are made of metal while some are made of wood depending on the strength of whatever is to be guarded in the cage. The cage that would house a bird can be made of anything but the cage that would house a lion must be strong. So, there are different types and sizes of cages that are used to hold people, animals and things. It is the size of the person, animal or thing that determines the size and strength of the cage.

3. Fight for freedom: When a person is in a cage for a long time, he might try to get out after some time. He will make effort to get out of the cage but when he is unable to come out, he gives up and tries to get used to the cage. There are so many people today, who are already used to their problems. They have gotten used to their limitation. They have gotten used to a life of pressure. They are used to their bondage and captivity.

4. Brands of cages: Please note that there are several

163

brands of cages such as cage of familiar spirits, cage of marine spirits, cage of occult powers, and cage of all kinds of evil spirits. They are not all the same. Ezekiel 4:2 says, **"And lay siege against it, and build a fort against it, and cast a mount against it; set the camp also against it, and set battering rams against it round about."**

5. Movement in the cage doesn't mean freedom: Every cage still gives the captives some allowance to move around but it doesn't mean they are free. Freedom comes only when the cage is opened and they walk out. Any movement in the cage is limited, restricted and restrained. Many people are experiencing some progress now but that doesn't mean they are free from the cage. All they are doing is only a little movement here and there. Birds can move about in the cage, and sometimes, the owner of the bird can carry the cage with the bird inside from one location to another. Likewise a person in a cage can move about, and can be taken from place to place, albeit in a cage.

6. Somebody in a cage depends on those that are free for survival: The person inside a cage cannot sustain or take care of himself. He would always depend on the people outside to feed and take care of him. That is

exactly what happens to a person that is inside a cage. When you discover that you are always depending on others for survival, it means you are in a cage.

7. Somebody in a cage is kept under close watch: This is to ensure that he doesn't escape. The owner or keeper of a cage always ensures that those in the cage never escape. The devil doesn't grant freedom to his captives. Anytime they are praying to escape his prison, he fortifies it the more. That is why in the physical prison, you have prison warders and controllers that keep the prisoners to make sure that they don't escape.

8. Someone who is in a cage always sees himself tied down in the dream: He sees himself in the prison, carrying load, or as a slave running errands for other people. He would always dream of being engaged in hard work and sweating. That is a life in the cage. He always dreams of seeing himself in handcuffs standing trial, wearing rags, or being locked up and unable to escape.

Description of a life in a cage

The life of the children of Israel whilst in Egypt is a typical example of a life in a cage. They were slaves under torture in Egypt. They built towers for Pharaoh, and their labour was not

165

rewarded. In fact, the king got angry when they demanded for their release and as a result, he commanded that their bondage be increased. Before then, they were given materials for the work, but this time around, the king instructed they must source the materials by themselves. That was the extent of the suffering of the children of Israel in Egypt or in the cage, you might say.

The cage must either be destroyed or set ablaze if you want to be free. There is no other way to negotiate your freedom. You must be determined to fight your way out. Don't get used to the life of the cage because that is not the good life that heaven has designed for you. When a person is inside the cage, he would work hard but has little or nothing to show for it.

The power that enslaves

The power that keeps people in the cage is sin. Sin of immorality, drunkenness, addictions or pornography. Any form of sin in your life will ensure that you continue to be in the prison of the enemy. Repent of your sin and ask the Lord to come into your life.

Prayer Points

Make sure that you are properly born again before you take the following prayer points:

1. Witchcraft cage that does not want me to go, break into

pieces, in the mighty name of Jesus.

2. Ancestral cage holding me down, break, in the name of Jesus.

3. Every ancestral house holding me down, break, in the name of Jesus.

4. The wickedness of the wicked in my life, expire, in the name of Jesus.

5. Every satanic arrow of poor finishing assigned against me, die, in the name of Jesus.

6. Arrow of suffering in the midst of abundance, go back to your sender, in the name of Jesus.

7. Every crystal ball of darkness monitoring my life for evil, scatter, in the name of Jesus.

8. My life and destiny, receive power to overcome every battle of life, in the name of Jesus.

9. Every appointment with sorrow, be cancelled, in the name of Jesus.

10. Holy Ghost, rewrite the story of my life to carry prosperity, in the name of Jesus.

11. I break and loose myself from every invisible chain of darkness, in the name of Jesus.

12. Enemy of my open heaven, be paralyzed, in the name of Jesus.

13. Powers asking me to appear where I am not supposed to appear, you are liars, die, in the name of Jesus.

14. Satanic house legislating to stop my success, die, in the

167

name of Jesus.

15. Every bondage from my place of birth that is following me wherever I go, break, in the name of Jesus.

16. Satanic conspiracy against my full-scale laughter, scatter, in the name of Jesus.

17. The chain of glory killers around my neck, break, in the name of Jesus.

18. Every battle that is older than me and wants to disgrace me, die, in the name of Jesus.

19. The blessing of the Lord without sorrow, explode in my life, in the name of Jesus.

20. O God of performance, glorify yourself in my life, in the name of Jesus.

CHAPTER FIFTEEN

Dreams that Hinder Progress

Jude 1:8 says, "Likewise also these filthy dreamers defile the flesh, despise dominion, and speak evil of dignities."

The book of Jude identifies a group of powers known as filthy dreamers that defile the flesh. These powers use the hour of the night to defile the flesh. They plant all kinds of diseases and arrows into the body at night.

I pray that any power that is using the hour of the night to defile your body, the Lord will destroy them, in the mane of Jesus. Any power that is using the hour of the night to oppress you, the mighty hand of God will break them into pieces, in the mighty name of Jesus.

Our dreams are very important. In fact, our dreams are our spiritual monitors. Our dreams reflect what is going on in our lives. Just as God is interested in our dreams, the enemy too, is interested in our dreams. Dreams are the visions you have when you sleep. Every normal human being sleeps, and at that time of sleep, the visions you have are what we call dreams.

Dreams are thoughts or images that occur in your mind while you are asleep. Dreams are visions of the night. The enemy knows that every human being is vulnerable when asleep. Even the strongest of men is powerless when he is asleep. Whatever happens in your dreams is a reflection of your spiritual life. You cannot influence anything there. You may have physical muscles but when it comes to the world of dreams, physical muscles are useless. So the only thing that can save you in the dream is sound spiritual health.

The devil knows that many people are powerless in the dream therefore, he prefers to come during that hour to attack and plant evil seeds. He also comes at that hour to oppress, destroy, inflict sicknesses and steal from man. You should know as a child of God that the desire of heaven for you is to move forward and to make progress physically and spiritually. As a child of God, it is your covenant right to be doing well. The Bible says the path of the just is like a shining light that shines more and more unto the perfect day (Proverbs 4: 18).

170

Whatever you are doing as a child of God, be you a student, businessman or career person, you are supposed to be making progress and moving forward. But when you have a particular dream that stagnates, steals from you, arrests your progress, attacks your destiny or buries good things in your life, progress will be very difficult. The kind of dreams that you should have as a child of God should be dreams where you see yourself praying, reading the Bible, quoting Scriptures or singing good Christian songs. Such dreams show that your spiritual life is healthy. When the enemy comes to attack you in the dream, you can quote the Bible to launch a counterattack. It shows that your spirit is strong and that you are doing well.

There are dreams that you must not take lightly. Once they occur and you don't do something immediately, it can result in a very serious calamity or tragedy. That is why you should take them seriously by praying to cancel them quickly before they explode to harm you. When you have a dream where somebody shoots an arrow at you or you receive a gunshot, it must not be taken lightly. Many people who thought that such dreams were a joke ended up with some strange sicknesses and before they realized what was going on, it was already too late. Therefore any dream where you see yourself being shot, falling from a height into a ditch, being injected by a satanic nurse or something taken out of your body, is not a dream to

171

take lightly. When you have such a dream, you need to counter it when you wake up by praying those things out of your life.

Dreams where you see yourself with a satanic pharmacist prescribing drugs for you or forcing you to swallow certain things are not ordinary dreams. Don't wake up and think it is normal. Such dreams need to be destroyed. They are the dreams that hinder blessings, or stagnate people's glory. When you see somebody battling you in the dream, it is not an ordinary dream. The enemy can use such dreams to steal your glory or something very precious from you. The enemy can also use such things to plant terrible things in your life. The most terrible things that have happened to people came through dreams because they regarded such dreams as normal. They did nothing about them, only to discover strange things happening to them. The purpose of this message is to ensure that the activities of dream criminals, dream oppression and dream enemies are completely destroyed. The wicked spirits behind these evil dream operations must be battled to a standstill, if not, they will continue to operate unhindered.

Your dream is very important because it can make or mar your destiny. Your dream has the key to your promotion, success and victory in life. Your dream reveals your spiritual strength; how strong you are spiritually. Dreams always occur in the realm of the spirit. Dreams occur when we sleep and the battles of many lives can be traced to their dreams. Meaning that if they can secure victory in their dream life, they would certainly secure victory in other areas of their lives. With your understanding of this, the Lord will do a mighty work in your life and all the dreams of setback, stagnancy and failure will come to an end.

Your dreams reveal the content of your spiritual life. That is, if you want to know how much progress you are making spiritually, it is through your dream life. Your spiritual progress will reflect on your dream life. If you are the kind of person that always accepts and does anything you are instructed to do in the dream by the enemy, it means that your spiritual life is light and unhealthy. You do whatever the enemy asks you to do, they take you to places you don't want to go, you always see yourself serving others and you cannot fight back, it means you have a weak spiritual life. It is your spiritual life that determines your strength in the dream. Your physical power has no contribution at all. It is the content of your spiritual life that determines whether you would be strong in the dream and be able to fight back with the spiritual weapons made available to you.

Your dream is a reflection of how strong your spiritual life is. That is why you should be strong in the Lord and be serious with prayers. Our body is able physically to fight off sicknesses if our immune system is high. In the same vein, when our spiritual immunity is high, we are able to fight back in the dream. You can only attack the enemy in the dream or fight back when your spiritual life and immunity is very strong. That is why you need to pray seriously for your spiritual immunity to be strengthened if it is already weak.

God wants your dream life to be a place of information, a place of revelation. Several people in the Bible were given the blueprint of their lives in the dream. God gave them the direction to follow. He spoke to them and instructed them on what to do. Jacob received confirmation of the Abrahamic covenant in the dream (Genesis 28:12-14). Solomon received wisdom in the dream (1 Kings 3:5-9).

Your dream is a reflection of your prayer life. It is a reflection of how sophisticated or how strong your prayer life is. It shows your level of purity; that is if you are pure in spirit, trying your best to avoid a life of sin or trying to draw close to God through the reading of the word of God. Your dream life shows how much you try to avoid anything that can contaminate your spirit. For example, dirty films and dirty movies. Your dream also reflects the level of your brokenness or closeness to God. That is why you need to call on God Almighty to release power into your life. I believe that you want to have spiritual stability so that you can defeat any

174

enemy that comes against you.

Witchcraft Dreams

Witchcraft dreams are dreams that show that you need to pray very well. When you see red objects in your dream such as red pepper, red clothes, palm oil, etc. these are witchcraft dreams. When you see yourself in your village or the places you have left many years ago, or you see yourself wearing the school uniform of the school you have left many years ago, or you see yourself wearing rags in the dream; they are all dreams of setback, stagnancy, failure and inability to make progress.

Other types of evil dreams:

- A river blocking you and you are not able to cross to the other side.
- Seeing yourself inside a vehicle that has broken down and you are unable to repair it.
- Flood carrying away your things.
- Your Bible being snatched away from you.
- Standing trial before a judge or you are being accused.
- Summoned into a witchcraft meeting and strange questions thrown at you.
- Accused in an evil meeting of things you did not do.
- Finding yourself in a prison.

175

- Chained down somewhere.
- Wandering about in the bush and unable to find your way.
- Finding yourself naked.
- Carrying load.

These are not dreams of progress. When you begin to have these kinds of dreams, your life will be sluggish. There will be delay, poverty, rejection, limitations and frustration at the edge of breakthroughs. These things make life to become stagnated. I pray that God will give you victory over satanic dreams, in the name of Jesus.

Prayer Points

1. Powers intercepting my blessings in the dream, fall down and die, in the name of Jesus.
2. Every dream undertaker assigned against me from the bottom of the sea, fall down and die, in the name of Jesus.
3. The journey of my life will not end in disaster, in the name of Jesus.
4. Dark angels stealing, hijacking and diverting my blessings, die, in the name of Jesus.
5. Every satanic decision that has been taken against me in any witchcraft coven, scatter, in the name of Jesus.
6. Great door of abundant testimonies, open by fire, in the name of Jesus.
7. I shall be above only, I shall not be beneath, in the name of Jesus.

176

8. Anointing of multiple restoration, fall upon me, in the name of Jesus.

9. Every dream assigned to scatter my prophetic destiny, scatter, in the name of Jesus.

10. Strongman assigned against my destiny, be frustrated, fall down and die, in the name of Jesus.

11. Witchcraft barbers stealing from me whenever I am asleep, die, in the name of Jesus.

12. Every dream of perpetual servanthood, break and release me, in the name of Jesus.

13. Gunshots and arrows fired at me in the dream, backfire now, in the name of Jesus.

14. My dream life, become a place of divine revelation, in the name of Jesus.

15. Dream of defeat and failure in my life, expire, in the name of Jesus.

16. Lord Jesus, replace satanic dreams with heavenly dreams in my life, in the name of Jesus.

17. Curses and spell of darkness affecting my life, break, in the name of Jesus.

18. Masquerade of darkness troubling my dream life, die, in the name of Jesus.

19. Powers using the hour of the night to torment my life, be destroyed, in the name of Jesus.

CHAPTER SIXTEEN

Deep Calleth Unto Deep

Psalm 42:7 says, "Deep calleth unto deep at the noise of thy waterspouts: all thy waves and thy billows are gone over me."

It takes only deep people to access the Almighty God. God is a deep God, so if you are not deep, you cannot have access to Him. All the men and women that walked with God were very deep people.

ELIJAH

Elijah was a deep man of God, and he shook his generation. Everyone in Israel knew him. In fact, they nicknamed him, "He who called down fire." He called down fire upon the prophets of Baal and fire came down and consumed them. When fire came down, it consumed the sacrifice, licked up the water and dust. The fire consumed everything that was on the altar.

Eventually, those prophets of Baal were slaughtered. The fire was a fire of spell. After it came down, Elijah led all the prophets of Baal to a particular place, where they were all slaughtered without any resistance. One day, an army came to arrest him and they said to him, "Man of God, come down." Elijah said, "If I am a man of God, let fire fall." It takes a great man to talk like that. It takes a deep man to speak and heaven will hearken to his voice. To call down fire from heaven, and the fire burning the army that came to arrest him, was no mean feat. Elijah was such a powerful man of God, he was a great man of God.

ELISHA

Elisha was also a great man, who was very deep with God. He was the man of God to whom God revealed all the secret plans of the king of Syria against the nation of Israel. He would go and tell the secrets to the king of Israel, instructing him on what to do so that he would not fall into the trap of the king of Syria. The king of Syria became worried and asked his people, who amongst them was the mole reporting their secret plans to the king of Israel? Somebody said to him, "It is not any of us. There is one man called Elisha, he is the one reporting all your plans to the king of Israel. He can see your kingdom and whatever you are doing from far away." He was indeed a deep man of God.

I pray that Jehovah God will lay His hands upon you and you shall be deep, in the name of Jesus.

One day, Elisha came into town after his master Elijah had been taken up to heaven. Some children gathered together and were mocking him, calling him a bald-head. Elisha turned and commanded a bear to consume them and immediately a bear came out from nowhere and destroyed those children.

I can imagine, God seated in heaven with the angels present and then Elisha made a request. Heaven asked, "Who is that person that ordered that a bear should devour those children?" And the angel said it was Elisha. And God said, "Approved." And then the bear came from nowhere and devoured the children who were forty-two in number. That was a deep man.

One thing you must know as a Christian is the fact that all the men and women that walked with God were deep. Abraham, Moses, Joshua, Deborah, Daniel etc. were deep people. However, you must also know that even our enemies are deep too. The powers that are fighting our destinies are very deep. Men and women are going deeper into the occult and ready to pay any price that satan requires from them in order to obtain the power of satan in their generation. A lot of people are visiting strange places at night. A lot are going to the forests to meet one demonic man or woman to acquire power from them. A lot of people are sleeping in the cemetery every day in order to acquire power. Many too, will not mind to fast as long as it would enable them to obtain the power of satan. They want to have money, power, and ability to control things.

Many people visit strange places at night to offer sacrifices. They are ready to pay any amount that satan demands of them because they want power. Strange things are going on in our world and you as a believer cannot afford to be neutral. There are satanic beings and satanic activities all over the place. We cannot afford to remain asleep while the agents of satan stay awake causing havoc. Many things take place when men are sleeping. Secret meetings hold when you are sleeping. There are wicked plans against you in the coven and all kinds of places. So, you too cannot afford to be empty. This is the time to wake up from your slumber and get power from God so that you can be a voice in your generation.

MOSES

The question is, do you want to demonstrate the glory of God in your generation like Moses did in his generation? **Leviticus 9:6 says, "And Moses said, This is the thing which the LORD commanded that ye should do: and the glory of the LORD shall appear unto you."**

181

It is not easy to get the glory of God. You cannot just wake up from your bed and the glory of God comes like that. There is something you need to do, there is a price to pay. Moses paid a price for the glory of God to come upon him. After he got it, he had to use a mask to cover his face so that his people would be able to communicate with him. The glory of God overshadowed him so much that his face was glittering like fire and his people could not look at his face. Moses did an amazing work in his generation including speaking to God face to face. He spoke to the rock and water came out of it. God did many miracles through the hands of Moses because he made up his mind to get the glory of God upon his life.

The pertinent questions to consider are: Wouldn't it be wonderful for you too to experience the glory of God before you leave this world? Don't you think that you too must not depart this world unless God has used you to achieve something? Don't you think that you must be a voice for God too, and that God should use your voice to accomplish so many things in your generation? Don't you think that God can lay His hands upon you and use you mightily for His work? Do you not desire to know the secrets of the Lord? The Bible says, **"The secret of the Lord is with them that fear Him; and He will show them His covenant" (Psalm 25:14).** Don't you also desire to have a place in the heart of God in your generation?

182

Don't you want to be a man or woman who commands power? Don't you want to become mysterious to the powers of darkness? Don't you want to know the secrets of God, and have a name with God? Don't you want God to do great and mighty things through you? How about you becoming an oracle for God, becoming a voice for God? Consider these things.

DANIEL

Daniel was very deep. The king had a dream and called all his magicians to tell him the dream he had and also give him the interpretation. The perplexed magicians told the king that no human being could do that. But the king insisted they told him his dream and also the interpretation or they die. It was at this point that Daniel came forward and said, "Please king, give me some time, let me go and seek the face of the God of heaven and earth on this matter." Daniel went and prayed with the support of his friends and God revealed the dream to him and the interpretation and also gave him solution to the problem at that particular time. A deep man indeed!

Amos 3:7 says, "Surely the Lord GOD will do nothing, but he revealeth his secret unto his servants the prophets."

Are you not a servant of God? Are you not a child of God? Are you not serving the living God? Don't you go to church? Don't you pray? Why do you think that the Bible is for only a group of people? Why exclude yourself from being used by God, from carrying the grace and power of God, and from doing amazing work for God? You must know that if you are not strong, you cannot overpower the enemies. The type of enemies that we have now are very strong. No wonder the Bible says, **"Finally my brethren, be strong in the Lord and in the power of His might."**

You need to be strong to battle with the enemy because the enemy we are talking about has acquired evil powers and they are ready to kill without mercy. Their assignment is to waste and destroy. If you are not deep, you cannot fight the battles of life and these battles are increasing on a daily basis. The battles of life are becoming tougher and tougher, more aggressive and difficult. It is only deep people that can fight and win in the battles of life. Jesus said, "When the strongman armed, keeps his palace, all his goods are safe." It means the enemy is strong. It means the demons that are after your life are strong. It means that the people tying you down are strong. It means that the people chanting incantation against you are strong. You have to be stronger than them to conquer them. That is exactly what Jesus said in **Mark 3:27: "No man** can enter into a strong man's house, and spoil his goods, except he will first bind the strong man; and then he will spoil his house." You cannot defeat the strong man if you are weak. The challenge to you is to wake up your spiritual life.

God can fill you with His power. God can anoint you. You must not die in this condition. You must be used by God in your generation. If you are not strong, you can't break the yoke that is upon your life because it is the anointing that breaks the yoke according to Isaiah 10:27. And the process of getting the anointing is not cheap. If you want the anointing of God to operate in your life, you cannot be lukewarm. You must be deep in your prayer life and Bible study. You must be a man of fire. You must be consistent with your walk with God. That is what it takes. You can't wake up one day and then the power of God begins to flow. It doesn't happen that way. People pay a price to get the power of God. People pay a price to see the glory of God. People pay a price to be anointed better than they were before.

Keys to be deep with God
1. You must give your life to Jesus Christ: The beginning of a great work for God, going deeper with God, becoming a voice for God, and a person of power in your generation will all begin with having a relationship with God. This you can do by giving your

185

life to Him. It is not just about going to church, you must give your life to Jesus.

2. Enrol in the school of discipleship: After you have given your life to Jesus Christ, you must enrol in the school of discipleship. The word discipleship has it root word in discipline. Meaning that if you want to be deep with God, you must embrace a life of discipline. Anyone who will get the power of God must be disciplined. You must have a disciplined lifestyle as a Christian. You must be disciplined in your sleep, food, appetite, the way you relate with people etc. Disciplined people don't talk carelessly. They are very decent and they comport themselves properly. A disciplined person does not live carelessly. A disciplined person lives his life in compliance with the commands of our Lord Jesus Christ. You must live a life that will glorify God at the end of the day.

A disciple is not someone who has one leg in the church and the other one in the world. A disciple is not a busybody. A disciple doesn't live for his pleasure; he makes up his mind to please his master. The scripture tells us that you are a servant of whoever you obey. If you obey satan, he becomes your master and if you obey Jesus, He is your master. Whatever you submit

186

yourself to, becomes a master over you.

Some people submit themselves to alcohol, and alcohol becomes their master. I saw a man of forty years with shaky hands. He couldn't hold a cup to drink water because of his addiction to cigarette and alcohol. To serve satan, you must pay a price. That was the price he was paying for following the way of satan, his master through alcohol and cigarette.

3. You must be dead to the flesh: If you want to be a deep Christian and carry the power of God, you must be dead to the flesh. The Bible says, "**I am crucified with Christ: nevertheless I live; yet not I, but Christ liveth in me: and the life which I now live in the flesh I live by the faith of the Son of God, who loved me, and gave himself for me**" (Galatians 2:20).

The Bible says, "What shall it profit a man if he gains the whole world and loses his soul?" What is it that you will gain when you lose your soul to the devil and go to hell? Such a person has profited nothing. The truth of the matter is that the devil himself cannot give you all the money in the whole world, or all the cars, all the clothes and shoes and all the houses in the whole world. In fact, he can't give you the whole money in your

187

country let alone giving you everything in the whole world.

The flesh is our enemy within us. The flesh wants us to live a life of pleasure, eat food, sleep, roam around, go to parties, sing and dance to worldly music, etc. If you live like that, death will catch up with you fast. You must refuse to be a surface Christian. You must challenge yourself by making up your mind to pay whatever price it will take for you to get the power of God. Indeed, there is a price to pay for the power of God. You have been a member of church for five years and you can't point to one soul that you have won for Jesus, and up till now, you cannot spend more thirty minutes in prayer, you cannot become deep like that. It takes people who are ready to pay the price. Some people want to get the power of God but they overeat in the night and sleep till morning. How can you wake up to pray when you are overfed and already too weak to wake up and pray? If you want to wake up to pray in the night, you should eat light so that you won't feel too heavy to wake up and pray.

4. Receive the baptism of the Holy Ghost: Jesus commanded His disciples to tarry in Jerusalem until they were endued with the power of the Holy Ghost. If

188

the Holy Ghost was not necessary, Jesus would not have commanded His disciples to tarry in Jerusalem to receive Him. You cannot have power with God if you are not baptised in the Holy Ghost. I didn't say you will not go to heaven, what I am saying is that you will not be able to function for God as you are supposed to.

Acts 1:8 says, "But ye shall receive power, after that the Holy Ghost is come upon you: and ye shall be witnesses unto me both in Jerusalem, and in all Judaea, and in Samaria, and unto the uttermost part of the earth."

It was when the disciples waited at the upper room that the Holy Ghost came upon them. It was then they received power to witness, to do miracles and to show the power of God to their generation. I charge you now to receive the Spirit of God so that power can come upon you. This is the right time to do it.

5. You must be prayerful: The more you pray, the deeper you become. The more you pray, the more God will reveal His power to you. The more you pray, the more you carry the glory of God. The Bible says in Mark 1:35 that Jesus would wake up very early in the morning to go and pray; and that was His habit every day. If you want to be deep, your prayer life must catch fire. Your

prayer life must scare the enemy. Your prayer life must make the enemy that is travelling over the roof of your house to fall down and die. Your prayer life must disturb the coven meeting that is being held in your compound. Your prayer life must be dynamic enough to stop all the evil meetings that are being held in your street.

6. You need the word of God: If you want to be a deep Christian, you must read and know the word of God because the more of the word of God you know, the more of God you have in you. You cannot know God if you don't know His word. That is why it is important to study the word of God, read it, mediate on it and speak it out as you are reading it.

7. You must live a holy life: If you want to be deep, carnality must die in your life. All the activities of the flesh must depart from you.

Prayer Points

1. Where is the Lord God of Elijah? Arise and revive my spirit, soul and body, in the name of Jesus.
2. O God, arise and revive my life by fire, in the mighty name of Jesus.
3. Every strange power visiting my house at night, fall down and die, in the name of Jesus.

190

CHAPTER SEVENTEEN

Connecting to
True Riches

Luke 16:11 says, "If therefore ye have not been faithful in the unrighteous mammon, who will commit to your trust the true riches."
True riches here mean riches without corruption, riches without contamination, riches that are pure and riches that come from heaven. God intends to meet your needs. God wants you to exist in the world without scarcity. He wants you to have enough money to meet your needs and to be able to fulfil your assignment.

What do we mean by riches?
1. Riches are worldly possessions.
2. Riches are wealth.
3. Riches are financial resources to meet your needs and fulfil your assignment on earth. Many people believe

that once you are born again, you should not aspire to be wealthy and you should not have anything to do with worldly prosperity, wealth and riches. And the reason is simply because they believe that it is not possible for you to be spiritual and at the same time be prosperous. Their feeling is that too much money will take you away from God, make you to backslide or be distracted from serving God.

But look at this:

The purpose of Jesus Christ coming to the world to die for us is to give His life as a ransom for our lives. The principal reason is for the redemption of our souls. Christ came to die for our sins, to deliver us from the devil and from sin that entangles mankind. **Luke 1:74 says, "That he would grant unto us, that we being delivered out of the hand of our enemies might serve him without fear."** However, Christ who came to deliver us from sin, sickness and death does not intend to leave us in penury or in poverty. In fact, as you read your Bible, you will find out that His coming also makes provision for our financial wellbeing. 2 Corinthians 8:9 says, **"For you know the grace of our Lord Jesus Christ, that though He was rich, yet for your sakes He became poor, that you through His poverty might become rich."**

Psalm 35:27 says, "Let them shout for joy, and be glad, that favour my righteous cause: yea, let them say continually, Let the Lord be magnified, which hath pleasure in the prosperity of his servant."

This above-mentioned passage makes it clear that Christ did not intend to leave us in poverty. He actually made provision for our health and needs. The same death took care of everything; our wellbeing both spiritual and physical. The Bible says, **"Beloved I wish above all things that thou mayest prosper and be in health, even as your soul prospereth"** (3 John 1: 2). But I must tell you that as children of God, the kind of riches that God intends to give us is the true riches. The true riches as found in **Proverbs 10:22: "The blessing of the LORD, it maketh rich, and he addeth no sorrow with it."**

The true riches that God wants to give to us is the one that does not come with sorrow. It is not the one that will lead us to hell or lead us away from God. It is not the prosperity of the wicked. It is not ill-gotten wealth through kickbacks, stealing, bribery, corruption, cheating or all the crooked ways through which people of the world are making money. It is not the riches that cause pain or sorrow. The kind of wealth that God wants us to have is the one that will not drown our soul. God does not want us to have corrupt or polluted riches but the true riches.

193

1 Timothy 6:17-19 says, "Charge them that are rich in this world, that they be not high-minded, nor trust in uncertain riches, but in the living God, who giveth us richly all things to enjoy. That they do good, that they be rich in good works, ready to distribute, willing to communicate. Laying up in store for themselves a good foundation against the time to come, that they may lay hold on eternal life."

From this passage of the Bible, you will find that the kind of riches that God wants to give to us is not the one that will take us away from the Almighty God but the one that will give us comfort, serving God, meeting our needs and helping people around us. God intends to make us comfortable. True riches will help us to extend the good hand of fellowship to others and not the one that we will hoard. It is the kind of riches that will enable us to do good work, give scholarships, provide accommodation etc. It is the kind of money that will make us to serve God wholeheartedly without distraction. However, we must be very careful because riches have a way of occupying the place of God in our lives. We have to make sure that riches do not replace God in our lives.

We must still continue to love God and serve Him even when we have become rich. We must ensure that we continue to work to move the kingdom of God forward. We must not allow money to become the centre of attention, or begin to control us, or make us to be corrupt.

Money should not make us to look down on other people or despise them. There are many who are proud and arrogant because they are rich. They drive the poor off the road to have their way. They hold the poor in their environment in contempt. They use their money to terrorize the poor in their midst. That is not the kind of money that God wants us to have. **Psalm 68: 5 describes God as: "A father of the fatherless, and a judge of the widows, is God in his holy habitation."** God wants us to have the kind of money that Job had. **Job said in Job 29:15: "I was eyes to the blind, and feet was I to the lame."** Meaning that Job, with his money, was generous to the poor in the society; he helped the needy. That is the kind of money that God wants us to have and not the kind that will make us to close our eyes to the needs of people around us, then we become the centre of attention.

God wants us to have the kind of money that will lead us away from sin. I want you to know that money plays a major role in the kingdom of God even when our Lord Jesus Christ was on earth. **Luke 8:1-3: "And it came to pass afterward, that he went throughout every city and village, preaching and shewing the glad tidings of the kingdom of God: and the**

195

twelve were with him, And certain women, which had been healed of evil spirits and infirmities, Mary called Magdalene, out of whom went seven devils, And Joanna the wife of Chuza Herod's steward, and Susanna, and many others, which ministered unto him of their substance."

There were some people who gathered their money together and were pumping it into the ministry of our Lord Jesus Christ to help Him take care of certain things. The work of God moves on the wheel of money. You need money to do crusades, pay missionaries' salaries, buy evangelism buses, build churches etc.

During Jesus' ministry, some people requested He came to a centurion's home to heal his servant who was sick. They told Him that they had done everything to make him well but to no avail. They said to Jesus, **"This centurion is a good man; he has built a synagogue for us."** Upon hearing that, Jesus followed the man to the house to go and pray for his servant.

Some people think that money is bad, not at all. Money is a legal tender that is used to procure both goods and services. Money is also a measure of value. It is money that confirms the value of items.

Money could either be good or bad. Money would always take the character of the one that possesses it. If you are a good person, the money in your hands must be good, but if you are a bad person, the money in your hand will also be bad. It is just like having a gun. A soldier uses it to protect the citizens while the same gun becomes very dangerous in the hands of an armed robber.

Haggai 2:8 says, "The silver is mine, and the gold is mine, saith the LORD of hosts." Silver and gold are what we call money. God says they are His, meaning that money is good. Money actually helps us to live in the world. It provides food, clothing, shelter, transportation and also used to meet the needs of our loved ones.

Sources of God's true riches

1. **Favour:** As a Christian, you must not lack favour, otherwise you will be stagnated. God said in **Exodus 3:21: "And I will give this people favour in the sight of the Egyptians: and it shall come to pass, that, when ye go, ye shall not go empty."** Nobody should exist without favour because it is favour that makes people to like you. Once favour is on you, people will like you and want to assist you. They want to do things for you anyhow. Sometimes, some people don't know why they are doing you good. They cannot put their finger on why they are helping you. It is because there is something propelling them to do it. When favour is upon you, it will always bring you before great people,

197

one way or another. Your life depends on the circle of people around you. So favour makes our proposal to be acceptable in the sight of people. Once the favour of God is upon you, whatever you do will be accepted. Even if you make a mistake, the mistake will go unnoticed or will be overlooked. At the end of the day, you will scale through.

2. **Blessing:** No child of God will exist without blessing. Blessing always helps us to increase and be replenished in the land. Abraham, Isaac and Jacob stood out because they were blessed. Laban wanted to cheat Jacob while he was in his house, but it did not work because of the blessing of God upon Jacob's life. That is why you too need blessing. **Psalm 107:38 says, "He blesseth them also, so that they are multiplied greatly; and suffereth not their cattle to decrease."** Psalm 113:7: "He raiseth up the poor out of the dust, and lifteth the needy out of the dunghill."

3. **Giving:** Please do not play down on giving. The Bible says, "Give and it shall be given unto you, good measure, pressed down, shaken together and running over, shall men give to your bosom" (Luke 6: 38). That is the only way God can prosper you. If you don't give, you will not receive. Those who understand the principle of giving, don't joke with paying their offering and tithe, and sowing of seed. Learn to give and keep on

giving, and the Lord will continue to bless you.

4. **Praying against the spirit of poverty**: Many people are being harassed by the spirit of poverty. When you sleep and see yourself wearing rags, walking barefooted, carrying a basket on your head, or being blocked, it means the enemy is collecting what belongs to you. It is the spirit of the emptier. You need to pray against this demon that makes people to be stagnated and to remain in poverty.

PRAYER POINTS

1. Every evil rope tying me down to the altar of the poverty of my father's house, catch fire, in the name of Jesus.

2. Inherited limitation of my father's house in my destiny, come out and die, in the name of Jesus.

3. You the spirit of poverty in my foundation, I destroy you today, in the name of Jesus.

4. You witchcraft rat eating up my money, die, in the mighty name of Jesus.

5. The spirit of discouragement and frustration at the edge of breakthrough, die, in the name of Jesus.

6. Favour of the Almighty God, begin to operate in every department of my life as from today, in the name of Jesus.

7. Every evil power swallowing my miracles, die, in the name of Jesus.

8. Power that makes opportunity to slip out of my hands, die,

in the name of Jesus.

9. Satanic gatekeepers collecting what is due to me, fall down and die, in the name of Jesus.

10. Beginning from today, my life shall not cooperate with the spirit of poverty, in the name of Jesus.

11. Every strange fire burning in my life, be quenched now, in the name of Jesus.

12. My life, receive deliverance from the spirit of average, in the name of Jesus.

13. Powers that say my life will not be lifted up, you are liars, die, in the name of Jesus.

14. Every occult priest praying evil prayers against my success, die, in the name of Jesus.

15. Every shrine that is working against my progress, catch fire, in the mighty name of Jesus.

CHAPTER EIGHTEEN

Connecting to Great Deliverance by The Love of God

1 John 4:8 says, "He that loveth not knoweth not God; for God is love." From this passage of the Bible, we can see that God is love and anyone who does not love, does not know God. As powerful as faith is, the Bible did not say God is faith. As powerful as prayer is, the Bible did not say God is prayer. As powerful as breakthrough is, the Bible did not say that God is breakthrough. The Bible says, God is love.

The power of love can get you anything. There is no preacher that can really explain the depth of God's love for you. God loves you dearly, God loves you amazingly, and God loves you deeply. The love of God is so deep and wide that no one can go around it. It is so high that nothing can go above it. Your father may love you, your mother may love you, your wife or husband may love you, your friends, or other relations may love you, but there is no one that can really love you as much as God loves you. God loves you dearly and powerfully regardless of your colour, size or age. God loves you, whether you are educated or not, whether you are an unbeliever or a Christian. God does not love only Christians. He loves drunkards and even His enemies. The Bible says while we were yet sinners, God loved us. Meaning that before you even became a Christian, God has loved you.

Whatever you are going through, the love of God is capable of bringing healing, breaking your yoke, and removing you from the prison, where the enemy has kept you. The love of God can remove any entanglement, any mark of darkness, any battle you are facing, household wickedness, and witchcraft powers. If God can give us His only begotten Son, what else will He not give to us? Jesus loved us so much that He became poor so that we through His poverty can become rich. The Bible says, He was wounded for our transgressions, He bore all our afflictions on His body. He went through humiliation, rejection, beating and yet He endured all that because of the love He has for us.

The Bible describes the love of God as follows:
- An everlasting love (Jeremiah 31:3).
- A great love (Ephesians 2:4-6).
- An amazing love.

\- A greater love (John 10:13).

The Bible says, **"What manner of love the Father hath bestowed upon us: that we should be called the sons of God···" (1 John 3: 1).** There is no human being that can love you as much as God loves you and because of the love of God, He will not allow you to go through afflictions, bondage, suffering and pain. The important message I want to pass across to you is that the love of God is ready to do anything for you.

How do you get your deliverance through the Love of God?

1. **Compassion:** Compassion is powerful. When Jesus was in the world, He had compassion on the suffering masses, the sick, the poor, and those that were going through one affliction or another. It was compassion through His love that stirred Him to provide solution to the needs of humanity. **Matthew 14:14 says, "And Jesus went forth, and saw a great multitude, and was moved with compassion toward them, and he healed their sick."** Through the compassion of Jesus, people experienced a lot of good things: they got their healing, breakthroughs, blessing, and provision.

   The widow of Nain had only one child and that child died. As she and other people were weeping as they were going to bury the child, Jesus who was going in a different direction saw them. He met them and had compassion on the woman. Out of compassion, He raised the child and handed him back to the mother. There was another incident where they brought a boy that was afflicted by evil spirits to Jesus. The father came to Jesus and said, "Oftentimes the demon would cast him into the fire to destroy him but if you can do anything to deliver him, have compassion on us." And Jesus out of compassion, delivered the boy.

2. **Mercy:** Mercy can restore your wasted years. Mercy can bring help to you. Mercy can stop the judgement that is meant for you because of the mistake you have made. Mercy can relocate you to a new and better place. Mercy can stop the threat of the enemy against you. Mercy can work miracles in your life. Mercy can upgrade your destiny. Mercy can surprise you mysteriously. Mercy can tear the garment of shame that the enemy wants to put on you. Mercy is an amazing thing in the Bible. All the people that went to God on the platform of mercy were not turned back by Him. Mercy is an extension of the love of God. Blind Bartimaeus connected to Jesus when he appealed for the mercy of God. He said to Jesus, "Thou Son of David, have mercy on me." Jesus stopped and asked them to bring him, and when they brought him, Jesus restored

his sight.

Path to connect to the miracle power of God

How do we prove to God that we appreciate His love for us? We show appreciation when we reciprocate His love towards us. God is not a man. You could love a man or woman and give yourself to him or her, and that person does not love you in return. That is exactly what some people do to God. God loves them and gives them everything but they do not appreciate the love of God for them therefore, they give Him nothing in return. Such people hinder the hand of God upon their lives. God cannot move in their lives. If you can reciprocate the love of God, you would be amazed at the wonders He would do in your life. I counsel you to love God and serve Him by love. Do great things in the house of God by love. Be motivated by the love of God. Stop running away from sin because of the fear of the judgement of sin. Hate sin because you love God. Give to God because you love Him, make sacrifices for Him and serve Him wholeheartedly because you love Him. God is watching to see how you reciprocate His love. Let love motivate you to give without expecting back. Let the love of God motivate you to forgive those who have offended you.

Prayer Points

1. O God of mercy, arise and deliver me today, in the name of Jesus.
2. O God of mercy, bring me out of every prison of darkness,

205

in the name of Jesus.

3. O God, arise and surround me with good things, in the name of Jesus.

4. By the mercy of God, every mountain of frustration in my life, be frustrated, in the name of Jesus.

5. Rain of mercy, fall upon me, in the mighty name of Jesus.

6. By your mercy, O God, arise and intervene in my affairs, in the mighty name of Jesus.

7. O God of mercy, crown my life with your lovingkindness, in the name of Jesus.

8. Blood of Jesus, cleanse my life with your power, in the name of Jesus.

9. Blood of Jesus, dissolve any arrow of darkness in my body, in the name of Jesus.

10. Witchcraft padlock of limitation, break, in the mighty name of Jesus.

11. Satanic objects moving in my body, wither, in the name of Jesus.

12. Satanic poison in my body, be dissolved by fire, in the name of Jesus.

13. Every witchcraft basket flying against my destiny, catch fire, in the name of Jesus.

14. Holy Ghost, package me for miracles, signs and wonders, in the name of Jesus.

15. My hands, become too hot for the enemy to bewitch, in the name of Jesus.

16. The darkroom caging my wealth, release it by fire, in the name of Jesus.
17. Satanic animals appearing to me, die, in the name of Jesus.
18. Satanic investment in the works of my hands, catch fire, in the name of Jesus.
19. Every satanic seed in my prosperity, catch fire, in the name of Jesus.
20. Anti-prosperity power troubling my existence, die, in the name of Jesus.
21. Every shrine behind my problem, Holy Ghost fire, burn it up, in the name of Jesus.
22. Sicknesses and diseases that the enemy is using to tie me down, I command you to die, in the name of Jesus.
23. Glory killers, you shall not kill my glory, in the name of Jesus.
24. Every witchcraft tree harbouring my breakthrough, catch fire, in the name of Jesus.

CHAPTER NINETEEN

Breaking Stubborn Yokes and Captivity

Isaiah 10:27 says, "And it shall come to pass in that day, that his burden shall be taken away from off thy shoulder, and his yoke from off thy neck, and the yoke shall be destroyed because of the anointing." Anointing destroys yokes and captivity.

Characteristics of captivity

1. **Pain:** Captivity causes pain, inconvenience, displeasure and pressure. The reason for which Jesus died by crucifixion on the cross was to take away our pain. But a lot of people are still wondering why their pain is perpetual and their wound incurable? Can you imagine pain that is a regular occurrence? There are people going about with pain, which the enemy inflicted upon them. The Psalmist says in Psalm 55:4:

"My heart is sore pained within me: and the terrors of death are fallen upon me." When you see pain like in the above-mentioned passage, it is an indication that there is captivity in place. I decree upon your life by the power that made heaven and earth, and by the power that raised Lazarus from the dead, your captivity is expired, in the name of Jesus.

2. **Rejection:** Rejection is another characteristic of captivity. Many people are rejected and many abandoned by those who should help or accommodate them for no reason. It has become a common thing to see people being used and dumped. You see people who were accepted only for a while and they were set aside. All kinds of strange things are going on; children are abandoning their parents, husbands and wives are abandoning one another. This is the spirit of rejection multiplying in various ways. A lot people are going about with a wrong opinion of themselves; some have deep-rooted feeling of inferiority and many are wondering what is wrong with them and why their lives are like that. The reason for all these is captivity.

3. **Foul smell:** When there is captivity in place, there is what we call foul smell. Everyone has an aura around him or her; you may not be able to explain it but it is with every man or woman. There are people with bad

209

aura; when you associate with them, you have unpleasant experiences. There is an aura that drives helpers away. There is an aura of bad luck. Some people are not witches but the aura around them makes people to suspect that they are evil and could be used as instruments of attack by evil spirits. It is because they have a foul aura around them. The spirit of captivity has baptised them with an evil smell. Isaac said to Jacob, "The smell of my son is like the smell of the field that God has blessed." So there is an aura that attract good people and good things to you while there is also a bad one that drives good people and good things away.

4. **Evil covering:** Many people are going about covered with an evil spiritual veil. So, their helpers cannot see them. For some, the evil covering operates in such a way that they are projected in bad light, and they appear detestable in the eyes of men. There are many people covered and those who are supposed to see them cannot see them. Blessings that are supposed to come to them bypass them. The enemy has been using evil covering to deny so many people and their families their divine blessings. A covered person would be misunderstood and misinterpreted. The person is not seen for who he is but as the enemy wants him to be seen. The person's good future cannot be seen and his

210

potential is also hidden. His talent and even skills are also hidden. There are many talented and gifted people who are not appreciated, compensated or recognised because of the problem of evil covering. There are men and women who are endowed with special abilities but they are relegated to the back because of captivity. People need to pray these things out of their lives before they can move forward.

Prayer Points

1. My eagle, receive your wings and fly, in the name of Jesus.
2. Problems in my life that have vowed to die with me, you are liars, die, in the name of Jesus.
3. Powers that want me to remain in this condition, die, in the name of Jesus.
4. Powers that are contending for my position, you are liars, die, in the name of Jesus.
5. You the personal stronghold, blocking my way, clear away, in the name of Jesus.
6. Forces of darkness putting their legs on my breakthrough, I cut you off, in the name of Jesus.
7. Battle of thou shall not rise of my father's house, you are a liar, die, in the name of Jesus.
8. Angels of my blessing, where are you? Manifest by fire, in the name of Jesus.

9. You my enemy, leave my head alone, in the name of Jesus.

10. Anyone dancing in the palace to cut off my head, you shall dance no more, in the name of Jesus.

11. Any battle initiated to demote my destiny through my head, expire, in the name of Jesus.

12. Any power making me to forget what I should remember, I bury you today, in the name of Jesus.

13. Anointing to be the head and not the tail, fall upon me, in the name of Jesus.

14. Powers that want me to remain in this condition, you are liars, die, in the name of Jesus.

15. Powers contending for my position, you are liars, die, in the name of Jesus.

16. Personal stronghold blocking my ways, clear away, in the name of Jesus.

17. Forces of darkness putting their legs on my breakthrough, I cut them off, in the name of Jesus.

18. Battle of, "Thou shalt not rise" of my father's house, my life is not your candidate, die, in the name of Jesus.

19. Powers using my face to attack people at night, wherever you are, die, in the name of Jesus.

20. Anointing to be the head and not the tail, fall upon me, in the name of Jesus.

21. Power that wants my battle to be perpetual, die, in the

name of Jesus.

22. Any battle that wants me to labour without favour, die, in the name of Jesus.

23. Any battle that wants me to pray without testimony, die, in the name of Jesus.

24. Any battle that wants me to marry but have no peace, die, in the name of Jesus.

25. Any battle that wants me to have children, but the children will hate me, die, in the name of Jesus.

26. Any battle that wants me to be a beggar perpetually, die, in the name of Jesus.

27. Any battle that has vowed that my hands will not feed me, die, in the name of Jesus.

28. Any battle that wants me to take the back seat in destiny, die, in the name of Jesus.

29. Any battle that wants the children of my parents to convert me to servants, die, in the name of Jesus.

30. Every battle that wants me to grow old and have nothing to show for it, die, in the name of Jesus.

31. As the Lord lives, my hands shall not be empty, my hands shall feed me, in the name of Jesus.

32. Any power that wants my first to become the last, die, in the name of Jesus.

33. Problems in my life that have vowed to die with me, you are liars, die, in the name of Jesus.

34. Every veil of darkness, every chain of darkness, every chain of limitation, and every chain of rejection and disappointment at the last minute, catch fire, in the name of Jesus.

35. Anything in my hands that is pushing me backward, catch fire, in the name of Jesus.

36. As from today, my hands shall be effective, my hands shall be productive, my hands shall be efficient and my hands shall be sufficient for me, in the name of Jesus.

37. Begin to prophesy upon your life, in the name of Jesus.

CHAPTER TWENTY

Breaking The Curse of Thou Shall Not Excel

One of the greatest evils that has plagued mankind is curses. That is why every human being must pray curse-breaking prayers. Curses hinder. Curses cause a person not to be able to excel. Curses terminate or oppose progress. Curses stop success or progress. Curses frustrate people and efforts. The first person in the Bible that was placed under a curse of, "Thou shall not excel" is Reuben. Reuben was the first son of Jacob but he did something that made his father to place a curse on him. After the curse was pronounced upon him, Reuben went down. He was demoted and the sons of Joseph took his first place in the family of Jacob. The curse ravaged his life and affected his children. A close look at the Bible reveals that until the curse was lifted, the life of Reuben never amounted to anything.

In Genesis 49:2-4, Jacob was addressing his children: **"Gather yourselves together, and hear, ye sons of Jacob; and** hearken unto Israel your father. **Reuben, thou art my firstborn, my might, and the beginning of my strength, the excellency of dignity, and the excellency of power: Unstable as water, thou shalt not excel; because thou wentest up to thy father's bed; then defiledst thou it: he went up to my couch."** Reuben committed sexual immorality with one of his father's concubines. His father saw him and placed a curse on him. When he was supposed to be blessed, he received a curse from his father. The curse stuck to him until Moses prayed to destroy the curse upon Reuben. The good news is that servants of God have authority given to them to remove curses just as Moses, with the anointing of God, removed the curses upon Reuben. **Deuteronomy 33:6: "Let Reuben live, and not die; and let not his men be few."** That was how the destiny of Reuben was healed from that day.

One thing you must understand is that a curse does not just come. If you don't offend somebody, if you don't do something bad and somebody is cursing you, that curse cannot come. So, there would always be a reason for a curse to operate in a person's life, a family, community, town, city or nation.

What is a curse?

A curse is the opposite of blessing. A curse is a word of destruction spoken against a person. Curses are negative words that are meant to cause evil in the life of a person. For example, after Joshua defeated the people of Jericho, he placed a curse on Jericho. He said whoever would rebuild

Jericho would use his first and last sons to do so. As a result of that curse, Jericho remained barren until Elisha came and broke the curse.

2 Kings 2:19-21: "And the men of the city said unto Elisha, Behold, I pray thee, the situation of this city is pleasant, as my lord seeth: but the water is naught, and the ground barren. And he said, Bring me a new cruse, and put salt therein. And they brought it to him. And he went forth unto the spring of the waters, and cast the salt in there, and said, Thus saith the Lord, I have healed these waters; there shall not be from thence any more death or barren land."

A curse is an evil decree that is pronounced upon a person. In Numbers chapter 22, a king named Balak told Balaam to curse the children of Israel for him. He wanted them cursed because he believed that the curse would make them powerless. He believed that the curse would make them weak. When Balaam came, he asked Balak to build an altar for him so that he could stand on the altar and curse the children of Israel. The altar was built but each time Balaam mounted the altar to curse the children of Israel, God always reversed it and instead of cursing, he was blessing them.

Joshua too placed a curse on the tribe of Gibeon. The Gibeonites came to Joshua and deceived him into making a covenant with them. They lied to Joshua that they were from a faraway place when they were actually very close by. After Joshua had entered into an agreement with them, he discovered that they lied to him. However, the covenant had already been formed and there was nothing they could do about it. So, what Joshua did was to place a curse on them.

Joshua 9:23: "Joshua said to them, Now therefore ye are cursed, and there shall none of you be freed from being bondmen, and hewers of wood and drawers of water for the house of my God."

The word bondmen means that they would be slaves to others and nobody would serve them. They would always be doing menial jobs and would never be able to fulfil destiny. So among the tribe of the Gibeonites, you can't see anyone who is a professor. You can't see anyone excelling or anyone who will be a president or a governor. They will only do menial jobs in the society. Could it be the reason you are unable to climb high, you are always serving people and nobody is serving you? Is there a curse on the tribe, city or town from where you come?

One thing I want you to know is that a curse is not good at all. A curse will always destroy good things. A curse makes a person to labour under a closed heaven. A curse always enforces calamity. A curse always brings wastage. A curse always brings destruction. A curse always brings pain. A curse always sponsors misfortune. A curse always promotes evil.

In Genesis 3:16-19, Adam and Eve were placed under a curse because of their disobedience to God. The serpent too was also cursed by God. In Genesis 3:14, Noah cursed one of his sons for seeing his nakedness. In the New Testament, Jesus Himself placed a curse on a fig tree. He expected to see fruit on the fig tree but there was none and Jesus said, "No man shall eat from you henceforth," and within twenty-four hours, the tree dried up.

Job cursed the day he was born. The Bible says cursed is every one that does the work of the Lord deceitfully. That is why as a child of God, whatever you are doing in the house of God, do it wholeheartedly. Don't do it half-heartedly, be serious with it, be committed to the work of God. **Jeremiah 48:10 says, "Cursed be he that doeth the work of the LORD deceitfully, and cursed be he that keepeth back his sword from blood." Jeremiah 17:5 says, "Thus saith the LORD; Cursed be the man that trusteth in man, and maketh flesh his arm, and whose heart departeth from the LORD."** That is, when a man puts his trust in another man, he comes under a curse. When you totally trust in man and put your life in the hands of a man, it is condemned by God. Just trust the Lord and put your life in His hands.

Causes of curses

1. **Dishonouring your parents**: The word of God says you must honour your parents. You must not curse your parents. You must not be disobedient to your parents. Somebody who beats his or her mother and slaps his or her father automatically comes under a curse.

2. **Incest:** If you practise incest, you come under a curse.

3. **Witchcraft:** If you practise witchcraft because of what somebody did to you or for whatever reason, you come under a curse according to the Bible.

4. **Occult practice:** People who are into secret societies or into one cult or another automatically come under a curse.

5. **Oppression of the helpless:** When you oppress widows, the fatherless, orphans and the less-privileged, you come under a curse. These people are special before God. If you mistreat them, or cheat them, heaven will fight for them. And when heaven fights for them, it is always devastating.

6. **Abortions:** Mothers that are killing babies through abortion or whatever means come under a curse.

7. **Self-imposed curse:** Many people open their mouths to place curses on themselves. They curse themselves with sickness, poverty etc. The Bible says you should not curse yourself.

8. **Inherited curses:** Inherited curses are curses that are flowing in the family and have not been broken or prayed out. They may be curses from a father to the children. They may be ancestral, generational or tribal curses. One fact about curses is, as long as they are not reversed, broken, or prayed off, they will continue to operate.

9. **Stealing:** The Bible says, the curse of God will not cease in the house of a thief.

10. **Disobedience to the word of God.**

11. **Lying with an animal:** Having sex with animals puts a person under a curse. That is bestiality and God hates it.

12. **Harbouring cursed items:** If you buy or use decoration items that are possessed or accursed things that God does not want His children to keep, they can attract curses to you.

13. **Not paying your tithe:** One tenth of your income belongs to God. If you do not pay your tithe, you come under a curse and the windows of blessing will not be opened for you (Malachi 3:8-10).

14. **When you reward good with evil, it attracts curses.**

Types of curses

1. Inherited curses.

2. **Seasonal curses:** This is the curse that happens at a

221

particular time. It may be the day of a person's wedding, when tragedy will strike. It may be the day something good is supposed to come to a person that the curse will strike.

3. Personal curse.
4. Horizontal curse.
5. Mental curse.
6. Vertical curse.
7. Witchcraft curse.
8. Divine curse.

These are the reasons many people are moving from grace to grass.

Signs that a person is under a curse
1. There would be rising and falling.
2. There would be slavery.
3. There would be marital distresses.
4. There would be accident of all kinds.
5. There would be poverty.
6. There would be chain problems. Problems of childbearing, insanity, epilepsy, evil family pattern, addiction, sudden downfall, losses or huge debts, family crises, tragedy, strange infirmity, wayward children, acute frustration etc.

What do you do?
1. You must acknowledge that these things are in place

and it is time for you to remove them from your family.

2. Genuine repentance: You have to humble yourself before God and repent on behalf of your family. Confess all the sins that led to the curses. All the things the family has done wrong. For example, idol worship, maltreatment of widows, forceful collection of other people's land or properties, maltreatment of orphans etc. You need to repent and confess them to the Lord.

3. Make atonement: If it is something that can be done, go back to the people that were offended and make peace with them.

4. Prayerfully break the curses: Curses come by pronouncement. Healing and deliverance too come by making pronouncements.

5. Disconnect your family from the evil things occurring in the family. Bind the spirit in charge and cast it away. On a regularly basis, ask for restoration of everything you have lost through curses.

Prayer Points

1. Every curse of thou shall not excel, break in my life, in the name of Jesus.

2. Every curse of someone I have offended, break, in the name of Jesus.

3. Every curse of an authority figure placed upon me, break, in the name of Jesus.

223

4. Every generational curse, break, in the mighty name of Jesus.

5. Collective captivity in my bloodline, break and let me go, in the name of Jesus.

6. Curses of thou shall not excel fighting my greatness, break, in the name of Jesus.

7. Curses of repeated calamity and tragedy, break and let me to go, in the name of Jesus.

8. Curses of rejection where I am supposed to be celebrated, break, in the name of Jesus.

9. I break every curse, jinx, spell or incantation placed upon me by any unknown person, in the name of Jesus.

10. The curse of sickness and infirmity, break and let me go, in the name of Jesus.

11. Every playful curse I unconsciously placed upon myself, break and let me go, in the mighty name of Jesus.

12. I fire back every arrow of death and hell fired at me, in the name of Jesus.

13. Powers that say my glory will not shine, die, in the name of Jesus.

14. Every altar that is speaking death against my progress, catch fire, in the name of Jesus.

CHAPTER TWENTY-ONE

Breaking The Covenant of Suffering

Isaiah 28:15-18 says, "Because ye have said, We have made a covenant with death, and with hell are we at agreement; when the overflowing scourge shall pass through, it shall not come unto us: for we have made lies our refuge, and under falsehood have we hid ourselves: Therefore thus saith the Lord God, Behold, I lay in Zion for a foundation, a stone, a tried stone, a precious corner stone, a sure foundation: he that believeth shall not make haste. Judgment also will I lay to the line, and righteousness to the plummet: and the hail shall sweep away the refuge of lies, and the waters shall overflow the hiding place. And your covenant with death shall be disannulled, and your agreement with hell shall not stand; when the overflowing scourge shall pass through, then ye shall be trodden down by it."

You can see from this passage that a person can make a covenant with death and hell. These are the covenants that are troubling people's lives.

Types of covenants
1. **Good covenants:** There are good covenants. God made a covenant with Abraham and the result of that covenant is what we can see in Israel today. The result is also what we can see in the lives of Isaac, Jacob and Joseph. So, there are good covenants.

2. **Evil covenants:** There are covenants that bring suffering and hardship. These covenants make people to come under evil torment and they are responsible for slavery. There is a covenant that is responsible for oppression. There is a covenant that makes people to go from one bondage to another. These are covenants of suffering and many people are under such covenants but they are not aware. And until these evil covenants are destroyed, there will be no respite for those suffering under them. They will continue to go from bad to worse. Singing that you will not suffer or beg for bread is useless until every evil covenant that you need to destroy is completely destroyed. Until such covenants are revoked or destroyed, the affected persons will continue to experience problems. There

are also good or satanic physical and spiritual covenants.

What is a covenant?

A covenant is a binding agreement between two or more persons. For example, when there is a goal to be achieved and two more people come together and each of them agree to perform a certain task or function in order to achieve the set goals. At such a level, a covenant is enacted. A covenant has binding power. Once you enter into a covenant with somebody, you cannot wake up one day and decide to walk out, it is not possible. Covenants anywhere have binding agreement. Anyone who breaches the terms of a covenant can be sued in a court of law. However, I am talking about evil or satanic spiritual covenants. These covenants have binding power just like the physical ones and can be very destructive.

A lot of people are in one satanic covenant or another, and they are not aware. It is possible for somebody to be in a conscious evil covenant or an unconscious evil covenant. All these covenants are backed up by some powers. When a covenant is formed based on the word of God, it would be backed up by the Spirit of God. But when it is based on satanic laws, evil spirits will be in charge and then things will begin to go from bad to worse.

Ways through which people enter into a covenant:

1. **By force:** A person can be forced into a covenant. That is, he is not aware or he is forced into it against his will. There are powers that force people into evil covenants; covenants that they don't know the terms or the rules of engagement. Such covenants are very dangerous.

2. **By inheritance:** People can inherit a covenant from the family or where they come from. There are existing covenants that need to be destroyed but have not been destroyed. People or families affected by this would have problems and such problems are carried over in their lives.

3. **Through sex:** A person can enter into an unconscious covenant through sex. Any sex beyond the confines of marriage would lead to problems.

4. **Through dreams:** Many people enter into covenants in the dream. They do not know the terms of agreement, yet the covenants are binding. Eating in the dream only serves the purpose of satan. The food is not a free lunch from the enemy; it is to carry out an assignment. It is to do a particular work in the life of the person. The same way too, sex in the dream only serves the purpose of satan.

Reasons why problems remain

1. **Polluted foundation:** When the foundation of a person is polluted, the person will suffer. **Psalm 11:3 says, "If the foundations be destroyed, what can the righteous do?"** The meaning of the above-mentioned scripture is that saying you are a righteous person cannot save you. You need to do certain things. One of the reasons why many people remain in their problems for a long time is foundation. Foundation is so important that, what many people need to do to walk out of their problems is to deal with their polluted foundation; to deal with the faulty foundation that is speaking against them. Foundation is about the incident that happened before you were born, during the time you were born, and after you were born. It also has to do with the circumstances of your birth and the family you come from, including the evil powers of your father's house that have not been destroyed or defeated, the strong man in your father's house that is still active, the curses that are still running in the family which are not completely broken and the idol of your father's house that has not been completely eradicated. All these constitute your foundation. These evil powers have a way of dealing with people until they are completely destroyed.

The elders in Jericho ran to Elisha and said, "Don't be

229

carried away by the beauty of this city. The ground is barren, and all kinds of problems are happening in this city." When the man of God heard that, he put salt in water and broke the curse that was holding Jericho. The problem of Jericho started many years ago when Joshua placed a curse on it and five hundred years later, the curse remained in place until Elisha came forth and broke it. Many people come from polygamous families, and that is another cause of foundational bondage. The name you are bearing gives the enemy right to come and torment you. Strange incisions on your body could be the reason why your life is exposed to certain demons visiting you at night.

When there is an evil covenant in place, the affected person will go from one problem to another. When there is an evil covenant in place, the person will experience closed doors and short-lived open doors. He will suffer unnecessary hardship. His problem will become elongated and the journey of one day would become a journey of many years. Opportunity will slip off his hands and his life will be covered in darkness. He will be experiencing strange battles. He may be hearing voices or may be marking time and finding it difficult to move forward. When there is a hidden covenant in place, there would be unfruitfulness, lack of testimonies and oppression.

2. **Satanic conspiracy:** Satanic conspiracy is a situation where some satanic powers come together to punish somebody because they feel that individual attacks against the person will not be sufficient to handle the person's case. **Isaiah 8:9-10 says, "Associate yourselves, O ye people, and ye shall be broken in pieces; and give ear, all ye of far countries: gird yourselves, and ye shall be broken in pieces; gird yourselves, and ye shall be broken in pieces. Take counsel together, and it shall come to nought; speak the word, and it shall not stand: for God is with us."**

The Bible is making us to understand that certain powers can agree to pull forces together to attack a person because carrying out the attack individually will not make enough impact. So they combine together to deal with the person. That is what the Bible calls evil association. You recall that Balak invited Balaam because he felt that Balaam was a great prophet, and if they combined forces together, they would be able to deal with the children of Israel. He invited Balaam and they started building altars to deal

231

with the children of God but it did not work. I pray that any form of evil conspiracy against you will not work, in the name of Jesus.

In **Acts 23:12-16**, a group of men came together and bound themselves with a covenant concerning Apostle Paul. They intended to deal with Apostle Paul, whose only offence was preaching the gospel. These people agreed together and placed themselves on fasting; refusing to eat until they have terminated the life of Paul. Sometimes, witches too operate in like manner. Domestic witches combine forces with external witches to harass or to punish a person. Household witchcraft will collude with the external one to deal with a person. Sometimes, the forces from somebody's mother's house can combine with the forces of his father's house just to deal with him. Many people are suffering because they are not dealing with one power but a conglomeration of forces. The powers from the waters combine with the powers from the land. The powers that are working in the firmament combine with terrestrial powers.

A good reader of the Bible would note that Herod and Pilate were enemies and they were struggling for power in the days of Jesus. But because they wanted to deal with Jesus, they came together. They agreed

232

momentarily just because they wanted to fight Jesus. Some of these powers have information. They have monitoring gadgets to monitor people. They have what we call evil eyes, and operate in their areas of specialisation. The one that is coming to press you on the bed is different from the one that would be working against you in your place of work. They distribute their assignments to make sure that they deal with their victims from all angles. They make life difficult for their victims. They keep evil records for their sakes, and mount satanic satellite to monitor them. Sometimes, they send people as informants and the moment the informants come close to their targets, they will dig out information for the enemies in the satanic kingdom. They come and pretend that they love you and are concerned about your life. They push themselves to you and you would think they are friends not knowing they are coming to dig out information about you so that they can deal with you.

3. **Evil covenants:** The covenants that disturb people are evil covenants. Evil covenants stagnate lives. I pray that if you are already involved in such covenants, God will deliver you, in the name of Jesus.

Different kinds of covenants

1. Blood covenant

Blood covenant is very powerful and a lot of people have entered into blood covenants at one time or another. If you have ever at any time allowed incisions on your body, then you are already involved in a blood covenant without any doubt. If you have ever sacrificed animals or done anything that involved blood in any type of sacrifice, then you have formed a covenant with blood. A good reader of the Bible would know that there were good covenants too before the death and resurrection of our Lord Jesus Christ on the cross at Calvary. God told Abraham to go and sacrifice his son. In the Old Testament, you would see that the people always took animals to the temple to sacrifice to God. But the Bible says that God put an end to blood sacrifice when He offered His only begotten Son, Jesus Christ. So Jesus became a sacrifice, and the blood of Jesus replaced the blood of animals as we find in **Hebrews 9:28: "So Christ was once offered to bear the sins of many; and unto them that look for him shall he appear the second time without sin unto salvation."** The blood of Jesus replaced the shedding of the blood of goats, rams etc.

Blood is very powerful. The highest article in the spirit world is blood. There is no occult group that doesn't deal with blood. There is no sacrifice that they do without using blood because blood is very powerful. Blood can speak, blood can fight, blood can pursue a person, blood is an entity, and blood has capacity to fight. Blood can witness against a person that is why when the blood of an innocent person is shed, the person may die but the blood will continue to witness against the killer.

Many people have been involved in one covenant or another that has to do with blood. Many people entered into an agreement to marry their boyfriends or girlfriends and they sealed the agreement with blood. They cut themselves and drank the blood of one another to seal up the covenant that they would never leave one another. That is a satanic blood covenant and the devil ceases the opportunity of such a situation to torment people's lives, and to refuse to let them go. Other ways through which people enter into blood covenants are:

a. **Tattoo:** Many people do not understand that putting tattoos on their skin gives satanic powers access to their blood. They do not know that they are unconsciously donating their blood to the satanic kingdom.

235

b. Abortion: Abortion is another way through which people enter into blood covenants consciously or unconsciously.

When these categories of people start having problems, they will not understand that it is as a result of their involvement in blood covenant. People under blood covenant have suicidal tendencies. They suffer from depression and all kinds of health challenges, and some even die as a result. It is the attack of blood.

2. Dream covenant

Another kind of evil covenant that many people get involved in is dream covenant. Every human being sleeps. When you sleep, what happens? How conscious are you in the dream? The enemy of man knows that when a man is asleep, he loses consciousness. The enemy has succeeded in getting many people involved in evil covenants in the dream. Many people have said yes to many strange things that the enemy proposed to them in the dream without them knowing it, and now they are seeing the effects physically.

The Bible says, "While men slept, his enemy came and sowed tares among the wheat, and went his way" (Matthew 13: 25). It is the invasion of darkness. The enemy uses this means to corrupt a man's destiny. I have seen people who cursed themselves in their dreams thinking they were sleeping; they said some strange prayers in the dream over themselves unconsciously. Many people have been initiated into evil groups or forced into satanic marriages in the dream. If a spirit husband or spirit wife appears to you in the dream and you enter into a marriage agreement with them, they will take over your spirit and begin to control you. Spirit spouses have marriage certificates, which are legal instruments that they use to torment people. The marriage certificates give them the legal right to control and torment their victims. There are many people that are unconsciously producing children in the dream for satan. Some of them are used as sex slaves and toys in the dream. They project all kinds of strange sicknesses into their bodies in the dream and they are not aware.

3. **Covenant with idols**
    Another covenant that people enter into consciously or unconsciously is covenant with demons or idols. These are strange areas through which the enemy is invading man's destiny to pollute and to corrupt it.

Other types of covenants that people get themselves involved in are the following:

I.   Marine covenant.

ii. Familiar spirit covenant.

iii. Occult covenant.

237

iv. Sexual partner covenant.

v. Inherited family covenant.

vi. Witchcraft covenant.

vii. Witch doctor covenant. If you have visited a witch doctor for help, know that you have paid a visit to an evil altar, and automatically, a covenant has been formed. Something is connecting you to that place even though you no longer go there. You need to consciously remove yourself from it.

viii. Evil altar covenant.

ix. Cultural covenant.

x. Sacrifice covenant.

xi. Religious covenant.

xii. Twins covenant.

Signs of an evil covenant in place

1. Confusion in every area of the person's life.
2. Slippery blessings.
3. Constant bad dreams.
4. Always being chased or pursued in the dream.
5. Stagnancy.
6. Mental attacks.
7. Constant health challenges.
8. Incapacitation.
9. Inability to exercise free choice.
10. Slavery mentality.
11. Bondage to fear.

Prayer Points

1. The evil eye monitoring me, receive blindness, in the name of Jesus.

2. Covenant of poverty operating in my life, break, in the name of Jesus.

3. Satanic altar delegated against me from the coven, fall down and die, in the name of Jesus.

4. Monitoring hand of witchcraft, I cut you off, in the name of Jesus.

5. Every weapon of cultism and sorcery fashioned against me, catch fire, in mighty name of Jesus.

6. Evil tree housing my blessings, receive thunder, in the name of Jesus.

7. I overthrow and overturn every evil power working against my life, in the name of Jesus.

8. I recover all my benefits from the altar of witchcraft, in the name of Jesus.

9. Every evil voice calling me to come and die, be silenced, in the name of Jesus.

10. I disband any evil meeting being held against my destiny, in the name of Jesus.

11. Evil covenants binding me to sickness and failure, break, in the name of Jesus.

12. Witchcraft registration assigned against my destiny, expire, in the mighty name of Jesus.

13.   Every witchcraft material programmed into my body, catch fire, in the name of Jesus.

14.   Powers stealing from me, your time is up, die, in the mighty name of Jesus.

15.   Powers that want me to go from bad to worse, die, in the name of Jesus.

16.   Evil pattern of poverty, barrenness and frustration in my father's house, die, in the name of Jesus.

17.   I decree healing and success in my life right now, in the mighty name of Jesus.

18.   Enemies that have vowed that I will not prosper this year, you are liars, die, in the mighty name of Jesus.

19.   O God, arise and defend me every time of the day, in the name of Jesus.

20.   Witchcraft network assigned against my breakthrough, scatter, in the name of Jesus.

21.   I declare by the decree of fire, affliction shall not come the second time in my life, in the name of Jesus.

22.   Yoke of affliction in my life, be destroyed, in the name of Jesus.

23.   Any power that is bent on destroying me, destroy yourself, in the name of Jesus,

24.   Yoke of witchcraft power in my body, catch fire, in the name of Jesus.

25.   Arrow of delay fashioned against my breakthrough, I

destroy you, in the name of Jesus.

26. Spirit of failure and spirit of poverty operating in my life, die, in the name of Jesus.

27. Arrows of infirmity fired into my life, go back to the sender, in the name of Jesus.

28. Breakthrough amputations, I command you to leave my breakthrough and die, in the name of Jesus.

29. Every covenant of suffering under which my life is labouring, O God, arise and destroy it, in the name of Jesus.

30. Witchcraft marks on my body, vanish by fire, in the name of Jesus.

31. Ancestral evil covenants working in my life, I destroy you by the blood of Jesus, in the name of Jesus.

32. Every generational covenant working in my life, I destroy you today, in the name of Jesus.

33. Any covenant between me and any water spirit, break, in the mighty name of Jesus.

34. Every conscious and unconscious covenant that is troubling my life, be destroyed, in the name of Jesus.

35. Evil covenants in the foundation of my destiny, break, in the name of Jesus.

36. Every conscious and unconscious covenant that I have made with powers of the night, break, in the name of Jesus.

37. Every hidden and unknown covenant troubling my

destiny, break, in the name of Jesus.

38. Every satanic law enforcement agent in charge of evil covenants in my life, die, in the name of Jesus.

39. Every power backing up any evil covenant against me, die, in the name of Jesus.

40. Covenant with idols, break and release me, in the name of Jesus.

41. Covenant with the sun, moon and stars, break and release me, in the name of Jesus.

42. Evil covenants that I have been forced into in the dream, break, in the name of Jesus.

43. Every common and uncommon problem confronting me, break and release me, in the name of Jesus.

44. I bulldoze my way to breakthrough, whether the enemy likes it or not, in the name of Jesus.

45. Every evil cycle affecting my life negatively, break, in the name of Jesus.

46. I bind and cast out every spirit of failure at the edge of my breakthrough, in the name of Jesus.

47. I overthrow every altar of wickedness fashioned against me, in the name of Jesus.

48. Cage of witchcraft targeted against the works of my hands, catch fire, in the name of Jesus.

49. Every soul tie and covenant between me and my parents, break and release me, in the name of Jesus.

50. I break every covenant empowering the enemies

against me, in the name of Jesus.

51. Every covenant between me and any native doctor, break and release me, in the name of Jesus.

52. Every inherited family covenant, break and release me, in the name of Jesus.

53. Altar of losses fashioned against me, scatter, in the name of Jesus.

54. Spiritual rags fashioned against me, catch fire, in the name of Jesus.

55. Foundational pollution of my father's house, release me by fire, in the name of Jesus.

56. The curse of thou shall not excel holding me down, break, in the name of Jesus.

57. Every ancient prison of my father's house holding me down, break and release me, in the name of Jesus.

58. Covenant of failure in my foundation, be dissolved, in the name of Jesus.

59. Every evil hand troubling my life, I cut you off, in the name of Jesus.

60. Covenant of suffering under which my life is labouring, break, in the mighty name of Jesus.

61. You placental strongman, release me, in the name of Jesus.

62. Negative words spoken against my promotion, be nullified by the blood of Jesus, in the name of Jesus.

63. My glory, come out of the cage of my location, in the name of Jesus.

64. Every evil power from my place of birth pursuing my life, die, in the name of Jesus.

65. Strongman that has stolen my favour, release my favour by fire, in the name of Jesus.

66. Every evil record and evil marriage certificate that are kept against me, catch fire, in the name of Jesus.

67. Any power that has commanded the sand of the ground to work against me, I bury you today, in the mighty name of Jesus.

68. O God, arise and lift up my head, in the mighty name of Jesus.

69. Every enemy of my next level, wherever you are, expire, in the name of Jesus.

70. God of enlargement, enlarge my coast by fire, in the name of Jesus.

71. Angels of my breakthrough, where are you? Appear by fire, in the mighty name of Jesus.

72. Wind of affliction, go back to your sender, in the name of Jesus.

73. God of signs and wonders, let my life experience your signs and wonders right now, in the name of Jesus.

74. Arrows of spiritual blindness fired at me, go back to your sender, in the name of Jesus.

75. Every cage of domestic witchcraft, release my wealth by fire, in the name of Jesus.

76. Arrows of bewitchment fired into my body, go back to the sender, in the name of Jesus.

77. Every witchcraft tree that is caging my destiny, catch fire, in the name of Jesus.

78. My Father, uproot every evil seed that you have not planted in my life, in the name of Jesus.

79. This year shall favour me, whether the enemy likes it or not, in the name of Jesus.

80. I shall be at the right place at the right time, in the name of Jesus.

81. Serpents and scorpions assigned to swallow my wealth, die, in the name of Jesus.

82. Anything in my life that is cooperating with the enemy of my destiny, come out now, in the name of Jesus.

83. Any power contending for my blessing in the spirit realm, fall down and die, in the name of Jesus.

84. Eaters of flesh and drinkers of blood, your assignment over my life shall fail, in the name of Jesus.

85. Agents of darkness assigned against me, scatter, in the name of Jesus.

86. Witchcraft bank, release all my wealth in your custody, in the name of Jesus.

87. Witchcraft ladder limiting my progress, break into pieces, in the name of Jesus.

88. Every witchcraft burial that is limiting my success, catch fire, in the name of Jesus.

89. What is difficult for others shall be easy for me, in the name of Jesus.

90. Every demonic organized network to stop my breakthrough, scatter, in the mighty name of Jesus.

91. According to Psalm 7:9, every wickedness against my life shall expire, in the mighty name of Jesus.

92. All stubborn powers working against my life, your time is up, die, in the name of Jesus.

93. Evil consultation with the powers of my father's house to demote me, die, in the name of Jesus.

94. I break and release myself from every environmental strong man, in the name of Jesus.

95. Any situation in my life that wants me to beg for bread, you are a liar, die, in the name of Jesus.

96. Spirit of lack and poverty, lose your hold upon my life, in the name of Jesus.

97. Every stubborn case of evil dream and dream manipulation, die, in the name of Jesus.

98. Every linkage between me and the serpent of my father's house, scatter, in the name of Jesus.

99. You the spirit of infirmity assigned against my prosperity, die, in the name of Jesus.

100. I withdraw my name from every evil register, in the mighty name of Jesus.

101. No serpent shall swallow my glory, in the name of Jesus.

102. I violently uproot the seed of failure from my life today, in the name of Jesus.

103. You my destiny, hear the word of the Lord, move forward by fire, in the mighty name of Jesus.

104. Powers contending for my financial success, I judge you today, die, in the name of Jesus.

105. Habitation of serpentine powers in my house, become desolate, in the name of Jesus.

Be Strong in
The Lord

Ephesians 6:10 says, "Finally, my brethren, be strong in the Lord, and in the power of his might."

God is calling you to depart from a low level life. This is the time to set yourself on fire for God so that the world can come and see you burn for God. This is the time to become the kind of person that God wants you to be. God wants you to be an outstanding commander. He wants to fill you with His power and fire. So the time has come for you to collect fresh fire from God and begin to do what He has called you to do. I believe that God will lift you up spiritually, and if there is anything the enemy has killed in your life, the fire of God will revive it, in the name of Jesus.

The word of God says in **Hebrews 1:7: "And of the angels he saith, Who maketh his angels spirits, and his ministers a flame of fire."**

The only people that will be heard in these last days are the ministers with flaming fire. The Bible says we must be strong in the Lord, it didn't say we must be strong in the flesh. It didn't say we should be strong in the street by fighting. He didn't say we should have strong muscles. He said we should be strong in the Lord, which means the time has come for you and me to dig deep into our spiritual lives and to make sure that our spiritual lives are not superficial. It means that it is time to ensure that we are deeply rooted in Christ Jesus so that we cannot be easily plucked off.

In **Psalm 42:7, the Bible says, "Deep calleth unto deep at the noise of thy waterspouts: all thy waves and thy billows are gone over me."** It takes depth to have access to God. Only a deep person can have access to God because God is a deep God. All the men and women that would keep the company of God must of necessity be deep. Men and women that have ever walked with God were deep men and women. The Bible says Enoch walked with God and he was no more because God took him. All the men of God such as Moses, Joshua, Daniel etc. were deep. God cannot be accessed on the surface, you must have the fullness of Christ to achieve that. Elijah was so deep that the whole of his generation felt his impact. Elijah single-handedly brought down fire from heaven. He single-handedly brought water down. When the fire of God came down through his command, it sacrifices, licked up water, destroyed

249

wood, and consumed stones. That was not an ordinary fire. God has called us to carry the same power and fire that Elijah had.

Elisha was another extraordinary person; he was very strong and deep. Elisha was such a man who could sit in his house and be watching events happening five thousand miles away. He commanded the presence of God. He was in his room watching the activities of the king of Syria, who was plotting to deal with the king of Israel, and every attempt that the king of Syria made was revealed by Elisha to the king of Israel. When the king of Syria saw that all his attempts to get the king of Israel failed, he began to accuse some of his cabinet members thinking that they were reporting his plans against the king of Israel to him. One of his servants told him that it was Elisha, who was revealing whatever he did, even in his bed chamber to the king of Israel. One day, Elisha was walking in town filled with power and anointing, and forty-two children saw him and began to make mockery of him. He simply turned and commanded a bear to appear. The bear appeared from nowhere and devoured the children that insulted him. God approved the command of Elisha because of his close walk with God. Heaven could not ignore his command because of his sacrifice and seriousness with God.

Why must we be strong in the Lord?

1. **Our enemies are very strong:** Our enemies are not weak; Jesus told us that our battle is a battle with the strong man. And for Jesus, the Creator of heaven and earth to call him a strong man, he is certainly so. The battle against us is not a weak battle. The enemy is growing wings on a daily basis. Men and women are going deeper into the occult and witchcraft. Men and women go to different strange places to acquire power. They are giving over themselves to satan in order to get power. Many people are making a covenant with satan every day. There are people who travel far into the forest to meet herbalists and all kinds of people in order to get power. All kinds of strange things are going on in our world. There are people who are ready to do anything to acquire the power of satan.

   Sometime ago, a certain Christian lady was at the airport waiting for her plane to arrive and she sat close to a young man. At some point, she got up and went to buy some drinks and snacks to eat while she waited. Then she noticed that the young man was calm, and she said, "How are you young man? If you wouldn't mind, you can have some snacks and drinks." The young man said, "No, I am fasting." The lady became curious and said, "You must be a Christian." The young man said, "No, I belong to a group of satanists. We are fasting in order to destroy the children of pastors. We are fasting to make sure that the children of pastors are disgracing the ministry of their fathers."

There are actually people who are fasting just to ensure that you fail, or make mistakes. There are people who have sold their souls to satan. A certain young lady got admission to the university, and one day, while in the campus, some satanists came to her and said, "We want to make you powerful." The lady was reading law and they told her that they would make her a very powerful lawyer by initiating her into their group so that at the end of her studies, she would be endued with power that would enable her win her cases anytime, anywhere. They took her into the forest and got her initiated into their satanic group. The rituals included drinking blood and eating frogs. They also gave her some rings to swallow. Later, she discovered to her dismay that what they did was to make her an instrument of seduction, to make pastors to fall. After the initiation, she became very wild and was going from one church to another hunting down pastors. Any pastor that is unserious will fall prey to such powers.

That is the extent the enemy is going to ensure that he ridicules the children of God.

I heard the story of a demonic person who left the north through astral travel, and came to attack somebody in the east at night. He came neither by road nor by air but by a demonic flight to attack a child of God. The Bible says in **2 Corinthians 10:3-5: "For though we walk in the flesh, we do not war after the flesh: (For the weapons of our warfare are not carnal, but mighty through God to the pulling down of strong holds;) Casting down imaginations, and every high thing that exalteth itself against the knowledge of God, and bringing into captivity every thought to the obedience of Christ."**

Many of us have a sense of spirituality but we are not strong. Those days, many brothers and sisters we thought were strong were not but we did not know until we got to the campus and discovered to our surprise that they were not strong. One can have a false sense of spiritual stability. Sometimes, when such a person is confronted with the reality, he will be unable to stand. If you are not strong, you cannot bring down the giant confronting you. David was very strong. He built his spiritual muscle at the back of the desert, singing songs to the Lord all alone and doing all the things that would empower him and before you knew it, he became a very strong man in the Lord. One day, a bear appeared and took one of his sheep, and he killed the bear and released his sheep. Another time too, a lion came and did the same thing and he killed the lion and released his sheep. David was known as a giant slayer. On the day of the coronation of King Saul, everyone thought King Saul was strong. The whole of Israel looked up to Saul because the Bible says, he was taller than everybody; they thought he was a strong man. They didn't know that it was a false sense of strength until Goliath showed up for battle. When Goliath showed up at the battlefield, the people discovered that Saul had no strength to confront the giant; he was a weak man. But David who built himself up in secret demonstrated God's grace and power in the open. David said to the giant, "I will bring you down." Giants are very fearful; they have extraordinary appearance. If you are not strong, you cannot confront giants because giants are made for battle. They are extraordinarily big, they intimidate and harass people. If you are not strong, you cannot defeat your giant, and you cannot win the battle of your father's house or overcome the enemy.

2 Samuel 3:1 says, "Now there was a long war

between the house of Saul and the house of David: but David waxed stronger and stronger, and the house of Saul waxed weaker and weaker." David was building capacity and increasing his strength on a daily basis while his opponent was getting weaker and weaker. The Bible says it is the anointing that breaks yokes. It is not crying that breaks yokes. It is not emotional breakdown that breaks yokes. Isaac told Esau when Jacob came behind him to collect his birthright: "When you are strong, you shall be able to break the yoke off your neck." When you are strong, you can break the yoke. When you are strong, you can destroy any captivity. When you are strong, you can destroy the evil powers of your father's house. When you are strong, you can disgrace the powers that have been disgracing everybody in your family.

I heard the story of a certain man of God who was transferred to work in a particular place, which was known for witchcraft activities, voodoo and so on. He was sent there because their church there wasn't growing. So, he was sent there to help grow the church. When he got there, they welcomed him, showed him the mission house where he would stay. But because the journey was so tedious for him and he was very tired, immediately, they showed him the place, he dropped his bags, jumped on the bed and slept off. By the time he woke up the next day, he found himself outside the house near the dust bin where they threw dirt. The man who was sent to come and help the people found himself in the dust bin, surrounded by some of the villagers, who made mockery of him. The door was still locked the way it was when he went to bed. If you are not strong, you cannot break the yoke off your neck.

There was also a man of God who was sent somewhere for revival. As he arrived, he was given a place to stay. When he woke up in the morning after the first night, and opened the door, he saw a plate of sacrifice in front of his door. He quickly went inside, collected a spoon and ate the sacrifice. When he got to the church, he said to them, "I saw what you sent, it was delicious. Please can you send more of that kind of delicious food?" That man of God was the only one that could bring revival in that place.

What does it mean to be strong?

1. It means to have stability: One of the problems of Reuben was his instability. Reuben was unstable, falling here and there. He was not accountable for anything. **Genesis 49:3-4 says, "Reuben, thou art my**

firstborn, my might, and the beginning of my strength, the excellency of dignity, and the excellency of power: Unstable as water, thou shalt not excel; because thou wentest up to thy father's bed; then defiledst thou it: he went up to my couch."

Jacob said that Reuben was unstable as water. Water is not stable, it has no stable identity. If you boil it, it will evaporate. If you put it in the refrigerator, it will become iced, and if you put it in the freezer, it will become iced block. Anytime you do not take your spiritual life seriously, you become unstable. You become unreliable and cannot be trusted. Reuben was cursed by his father before God and his place was taken by another.

2. **It means to have spiritual strength:** The Bible says, they that wait upon the Lord shall renew their strength. They shall mount up with wings as eagles, they shall run and not be weary and they shall walk and not faint. God wants you to walk and not faint, He wants you to have spiritual strength. As a soldier of the Lord, you need to endure hardness; be hard on yourself, don't pamper yourself. If you are not hard on the flesh, you cannot help yourself. The flesh loves enjoyment, it likes the easy way out. It wants to be pampered, to sleep and indulge in all kinds of things. But when you are strong, you have power over your flesh and you are to put it

where it belongs. You are meant to subdue the flesh.

3. **It means to be forceful:** You need to be fearless. You need to have spiritual power. You need to be anointed. To be strong, you should be able to hear the voice of the Lord. All the men of God that did exploits for God were people who heard the voice of God. The moment you begin to hear the voice of God, you begin to make progress in every area of your life. Make effort to hear the voice of God. God can speak to you through dreams, visions, His word, the still small voice etc. You must be able to develop at least one area through which you can hear the voice of God.

The process of becoming strong in the Lord

Becoming strong in the Lord takes a process. It is not an easy task. Dieticians say we are what we eat. When you eat strong food, you become strong. For example, milk is for children while meat is for adults; that is the way it works. The spiritual food that you consume produces strength. A man who does serious manual work in the farm cannot be fed with milk and tea; that won't help him to do the necessary work that is needed. He needs strong food to enable him to do the work. Tea and milk is for those who are in the office.

1. **Prayer:** No man can be stronger than his prayer. No man can rise beyond the strength of his prayer life.

Mark 1:35 says, "And in the morning, rising up a great while before day, he went out, and departed into a solitary place, and there prayed." Jesus continuously prayed every day. If you are not praying, there is no way you can be strong.

2. **The word of God:** You must feed on the word of God on daily basis. The Bible says in **Hebrews 4:12: "For the word of God is quick, and powerful, and sharper than any two-edged sword, piercing even to the dividing asunder of soul and spirit, and of the joints and marrow, and is a discerner of the thoughts and intents of the heart."**

3. **The baptism of the Holy Spirit:** No Christian can be strong without the power of the Holy Spirit. The Holy Spirit comes to energize and empower us, to make us strong Christians, and to help us to do the work of God (Acts 1:8).

4. **You must be disciplined:** You must make a deliberate attempt to subject the flesh, your body to the Spirit of God. Let the Spirit of God rise and let the flesh come down so that you can wake up in the night to pray and do spiritual exercises. When you overfeed the flesh, by the time you land on the bed, you will sleep off. You need to create time to fast and pray because some spiritual heights cannot be attained without adding fasting to your spiritual exercises.

5. **Avoid wrong company:** Your association

determines your future. **Proverbs 13:20 says, "He that walketh with wise men shall be wise: but a companion of fools shall be destroyed."** That is whoever you walk with determines your destination. Anytime satan wants to destroy a person, he assigns a wrong person to him. The people that come to you will either subtract, minus or divide you. It is like simple arithmetic.

6. **Undergo regular deliverance:** You must always subject your life to regular deliverance. Whenever you notice that an aspect of your life is difficult for you to control, it means you need to subject yourself to serious deliverance.

Prayer Points

1. Confess every sin that is capable of hindering your prayers.
2. Covenant of blood and sacrifice keeping my problem in place, break, in the name of Jesus.
3. Powers that make good things to jump over me, die, in the name of Jesus.
4. Every satanic resistance to my progress, I break you into pieces, in the name of Jesus.
5. The spirit of almost there, operating in my life, die, in the name of Jesus.
6. Every concluded work of darkness in my life and

career, scatter, in the name of Jesus.

7.   The wind of positive change, blow towards me one more time, in the name of Jesus.

8.   I shake off from my body, sicknesses, bondage and satanic arrows, in the name of Jesus.

9.   My life and destiny shall not be covered with darkness, in the name of Jesus.

10. Dark forces sitting where I am supposed to sit in life, fall down and die, in the name of Jesus.

11. Every spell of thou shall not excel on my life, break, in the name of Jesus.

12. O God, arise and let every yoke, curse and evil covenant holding me down break, in the name of Jesus.

13. Powers and forces that will not allow me to reach my potential in life, die, in the name of Jesus.

14. Satanic embargo refusing my dominion on earth, die, in the name of Jesus.

CHAPTER TWENTY-THREE

31 Prayer Points to Kill Infirmity

Supernatural healing is healing by the power of God. Supernatural healing is healing by the blood of Jesus Christ. Supernatural healing is healing by the finished work of Christ on the cross at Calvary. Supernatural healing is when the hand of the Lord touches you and you are healed of all your infirmities.

God can heal all sicknesses and diseases. In **Acts 10:38, the Bible says, "How God anointed Jesus of Nazareth with the Holy Ghost and with power: who went about doing good, and healing all that were oppressed of the devil; for God was with him."**

Types of sickness
   -Hidden sicknesses.
   -Sicknesses at the root.
   -Spiritual sicknesses.

-Bodily sicknesses.

-Psychological sicknesses.

-Demonic sicknesses.

-Brain sicknesses, etc.

God will heal all your sicknesses, in the name of Jesus.

The power of God is still very active to heal and to remove any sickness from your body. **Malachi 3:6 says, "For I am the LORD, I change not; therefore ye sons of Jacob are not consumed."** It means that the Lord has not changed, if He healed in the past, He can heal now. Jesus gives all those who believe in Him power to heal sicknesses and diseases. That is, if you are a child of God, Jesus has given you power to heal sicknesses. Even if you are sick, you can lay your own hand on your head and pray for healing. **Matthew 10:1: "And when he had called unto him his twelve disciples, he gave them power against unclean spirits, to cast them out, and to heal all manner of sickness and all manner of disease."**

The power of healing that God gives to you is not for other people alone but also for yourself. You can lay your hands on yourself to experience your own healing.

Sickness or disease is not the will of God for His children. God wants us to be well because we can serve Him better when we are well. It is in our wellness that we can serve God. It is on our wellness that we can attend services and worship God. Someone who is sick cannot move around. Actually, God wants us to be well and in good health. Our healing has already been paid for; that is why Jesus went to the cross.

Isaiah 53:4-5 says, **"Surely he hath borne our griefs, and carried our sorrows: yet we did esteem him stricken, smitten of God, and afflicted. But he was wounded for our transgressions, he was bruised for our iniquities: the chastisement of our peace was upon him; and with his stripes we are healed."** It is the will of God that you receive total healing. **Psalm 103:2-3: "Bless the Lord, O my soul, and forget not all his benefits: Who forgiveth all thine iniquities; who healeth all thy diseases."** All thy diseases means physical sickness, spiritual sickness, emotional sickness and all kinds of sicknesses, Jesus can heal them. Some sicknesses are not visible, you cannot see them with your naked eyes. The Bible talks about a broken heart, a heart that has been wounded.

Proverbs 18:14 says, **"The spirit of a man will sustain his infirmity; but a wounded spirit who can bear?"** When the spirit of a person has been wounded, it becomes a difficult thing to bear. The Bible talks about sorrow of heart. These are sicknesses that are not visible.

Different types of sickness

1. **Anniversary sicknesses:** There are people who suffer from certain ailments at a particular month of the year. In fact, by the time it is getting to that particular month, you hear them saying, "This sickness is coming again."

2. **Programmed sicknesses:** These are sicknesses programmed by the enemy into people's lives. Any time something good is coming their way, the sickness will start. I have seen ladies, who anytime they get a marriage proposal, demonic skin rashes will cover their faces until the suitor disappears. Once the suitor goes away, the rashes will clear off.

3. **Seasonal sicknesses:** This type of sickness comes when money comes into the victim's account, and until the whole money finishes, the person will not recover.

4. **Inherited sicknesses:** These are sicknesses that parents pass to their children. This type of sicknesses travel along the bloodline. That is why when you go to the hospital and complain to the doctors that you have a particular disease, the first thing they would ask is if you have any member of your family that has suffered the same sickness so that they would know how to treat it.

5. **Sicknesses from evil arrows:** The enemy fires evil

arrows at people to make them fall sick. When the arrows are fired at a person in the night, they wake up in the morning to discover that the particular place where the arrow was fired is no longer the same. One sickness or another would arise as a result of the arrow that was fired. That is why we normally pray, "Any arrow of sickness fired at me at night, go back to your sender, in the name of Jesus." All sicknesses and diseases have their arrows. There are arrows of diabetes, arrows of stroke, arrows of infertility, and arrows of different kinds of sickness.

6. **Demonic sicknesses:** Sicknesses that you can trace to a particular attack in the night is not an ordinary sickness. Trying to take drugs or seeking physical solution to spiritual sicknesses would aggravate the problem. Demonic sicknesses can only be solved by prayers. For instance if the sickness came as a result of dream attacks, may be you were fed in the night or you woke up and saw all kinds of marks on your body and you are treating it with drugs, you are wasting your time.

7. **Sicknesses as a result of sin:** Every disobedience has its own consequences. When you disobey the word of God, you would suffer for it, unless you repent.

8. **Sicknesses caused by ancestral powers.**

266

9. **Sicknesses as a result of sexual sin:** If you commit adultery, fornication, or any immoral act, you will invite sickness. If you overeat or you do anything in excess, you attract sicknesses to yourself. If you engage in anything that God has said we should not do, for example, God said all His children should not drink alcohol and you are busy consuming alcohol, you will pay for it. The same thing goes for smokers, when it is clearly written on the pack that all smokers are liable to die before their time. But in spite of that, people are still smoking. David said, "I went astray and I was afflicted." Because David went astray, he became afflicted. So, the affliction came because he went astray. Proverbs 26:2 says, **"As the bird by wandering, as the swallow by flying, so the curse causeless shall not come."** That is, if you don't go against God's commandment, there is no way the enemy can put sickness on you.

10. **Emotional sickness:** This is the sickness of the mind. It includes all anti-social behaviours, insanity, compulsive behaviour etc.

11. **Accidental sickness:** This type of sickness is not caused by an evil arrow or evil programming. For example, if you go close to a Covid-19 patient, or somebody who has a contagious disease, you will contract it. It has nothing to do with whether you sinned or not. As far as you come close to an infected person, it will be transferred.

How does God Heal?

1. God heals when you give your life to Christ. Immediately some people give their lives to Christ, they discover that their sicknesses disappear.
2. God heals by your belief in the saving power of the blood of Jesus.
3. By confessing and exercising faith in the name of Jesus Christ.
4. By confessing the promises of the word of God.
5. By casting out the demon of sickness.
6. By applying the blood of Jesus as a weapon for healing.
7. By the use of anointing oil.
8. By living a life that is free from sin.
9. By forgiving those who have offended you.
10. By living a life of thanksgiving and praise to the Almighty God.

Prayer Points

1. Sickness with an agenda to terminate my life, lose your hold and die, in the name of Jesus.
2. Power in the blood of Jesus, uproot every wicked plantation from my body, in the name of Jesus.
3. Witchcraft arrow fired into my body at night, come out, in the name of Jesus.
4. Holy Ghost fire, burn off every satanic property from my body, in the name of Jesus.
5. Holy Ghost fire, consume all the inherited sicknesses

and diseases in my body, in the name of Jesus.

6. Serpent and scorpion of inherited disease, die, in the name of Jesus.

7. Evil voice seeking death in any organ of my body, be silenced and die, in the name of Jesus.

8. Owners of the load of suffering in my life, catch fire, in the name of Jesus.

9. Witchcraft vulture appearing in my dream, die, in the name of Jesus.

10. The seed of witchcraft growing in my body, die, in the name of Jesus.

11. Any dark power using sickness to tie me down, die, in the name of Jesus.

12. Serpent and scorpion of none achievement, die, in the name of Jesus.

13. Ancestral chain of stagnancy, break, in the name of Jesus.

14. Every dark food I have consumed, come out of my system now, in the name of Jesus.

15. My spirit, soul and body shall not be habitations for sicknesses and diseases, in the mighty name of Jesus.

16. Every satanically sponsored medical report, catch fire, in the name of Jesus.

17. The hand of the wicked laid upon my body, wither, in the name of Jesus.

18. Witchcraft poison, come out of my body, in the mighty

name of Jesus.

19. Terminal disease in my life, be terminated, in the name of Jesus.

20. Bondage of infirmities in my body, break, in the mighty name of Jesus.

21. Curses of infirmity, break, in the name of Jesus.

22. Yokes of infirmity, beak, in the name of Jesus.

23. Every sickness that has a name in my life, die, in the name of Jesus.

24. All external and internal sicknesses waiting to kill me, die, in the name of Jesus.

25. Blood of Jesus, kill every sickness in my body, in the name of Jesus.

26. My head, reject the arrow of sickness, in the name of Jesus.

33 PRAYER POINTS TO BREAK SATANIC EMBARGO

Isaiah 10:27: "And it shall come to pass in that day, that his burden shall be taken away from off thy shoulder, and his yoke from off thy neck, and the yoke shall be destroyed because of the anointing."

I want you to know that the anointing is a yoke destroyer. Anointing destroys yokes, spells, jinxes, curses, oppression, wickedness, failure and embargoes.

Joshua 6:1 says, "Now Jericho was straitly shut up because of the children of Israel: none went out, and none came in." Jericho was closed because of the children of Israel. And the outcome of the closure according to the Bible is that none went out and none came in. That is a situation that aptly describes what an embargo is. When there is an embargo in place, there would be nothing to celebrate. Nothing will go in and nothing will come out. There would be no outflow or inflow. There would be no rejoicing. The life of a person who is under a satanic embargo will be in isolation. The person will be cut off from blessing, goodness, testimony and joy. That is what an embargo does. It would appear as if there is a satanic umbrella covering the person and when the rain of blessings wants to fall, the satanic umbrella would cover the person from the blessings.

What is an embargo?
1. Lack of progress.
2. Lack of favour.
3. Lack of productivity.
4. Lack of earnings.
5. Lack of helpers.
6. Lack of open doors.
7. Lack of breakthroughs.

Signs to know that there is an embargo in the life of a person

- The person will be a permanent resident in the school of failure.
- The person's effort will yield nothing.
- Spiritual robbers will be collecting the person's benefits.
- The person will be suffering from the "Almost there" syndrome.
- The person will be experiencing failed expectations.
- There would be closed heavens.
- There would be arrested progress. Doors of opportunities would be shut.
- There would be embarrassing delay.
- The person's talents and virtues would be buried.
- The person's speed would be embarrassingly slowed down.
-

How do you deal with embargo?

1. Decide that your situation must change.
2. Ask God to show you the area you need a change in your life.
3. Refuse to hold on to the past because it is already in the past and there is nothing you can do about it.
4. You need to know that no problem has come to stay; every problem has come to pass.

5.   Break every embargo through violently prayers.

Prayer Points
1.   The voice of impossibility speaking loudly against my breakthrough, be silenced, in the name of Jesus.
2.   Serpent of paralysis assigned against my life, die, in the name of Jesus.
3.   Crippling power in my place of success, die, in the name of Jesus.
4.   Witchcraft powers tying me down, release me and die, in the name of Jesus.
5.   Powers enforcing satanic wishes and dark prophecies over my life, die, in the name of Jesus.
6.   O God, arise and deliver me from every satanic detention, in the name of Jesus.
7.   Seasonal battle of my father's house, die, in the name of Jesus.
8.   My hands, you shall not beg for bread in the land of the living, in the name of Jesus.
9.   Witchcraft marks suppressing my testimony, die, in the name of Jesus.
10. Strong man sitting on my glory, be unseated by fire, in the name of Jesus.
11. The finger of any dark personality troubling my life, wither, in the name of Jesus.

12. Every ancient prison rope tying me down, break and release me, in the name of Jesus.

13. Any evil utterance that is tying me down, expire, in the name of Jesus.

14. Power that has vowed that people will not rejoice with me, die, in the name of Jesus.

15. Serpent's venom on my progress, be removed, in the name of Jesus.

16. Evil odour chasing destiny helpers away from me, clear way, in the name of Jesus.

17. I confess every sin that is capable of hindering my prayer, in the name of Jesus.

18. I confess the sins of my parents that are giving the enemy power to oppress me, in the name of Jesus.

19. Covenant of old and new sacrifice keeping problems in place in my life, beak, in the name of Jesus.

20. Curse of perpetual slavery in my foundation, break, in the mighty name of Jesus.

21. Anti-success, anti-progress and anti-breakthrough powers working against my life, break, in the name Jesus.

22. The spell of thou shall not excel on my life, break, in the name of Jesus.

23. O God, arise and let every yoke and covenant of stagnancy in my life be destroyed, in the name of

Jesus.

24. By the power in the blood of Jesus, I shall not follow the evil pattern laid down by my ancestors, in the name of Jesus.

25. Powers that make good things to jump over me, die, in the name of Jesus.

26. On the platform of God's mercy, I pull down every stronghold of failure in my house, in the name of Jesus.

27. Witchcraft barricade in my life, clear away, in the name of Jesus.

28. Powers that will not allow me to reach my full potential in life, be destroyed, in the name of Jesus.

29. Satanic embargo that is refusing my dominion on earth, die, in the name of Jesus.

30. Thunder fire of God, blast every cage built around my life and destiny, in the name of Jesus.

31. Strongman behind continuous closed heaven in my life, fall down and die, in the name of Jesus.

32. You dragon power behind my lack of favour, die, in the name of Jesus.

33. I challenge my life with the fire of God, in the name of Jesus.

CHAPTER TWENTY-FOUR

Battle Against Manipulation

Isaiah 47:12: "Stand now with thine enchantments, and with the multitude of thy sorceries, wherein thou hast laboured from thy youth; if so be thou shalt be able to profit, if so be thou mayest prevail."

Please take this prayer: Anything standing as the work of the devil in my life and family shall be destroyed, in the name of Jesus.

There are people who live by enchantment. There are those who make progress by enchantment. There are those who kill by enchantment, and there are those who stagnate destinies by enchantment. Every enchantment working against me and my children shall scatter, in the name of Jesus.

Manipulation is so complex and it is so deep. It is like a trap that the enemy uses to catch people, to bury destinies and to cage people in wrong marriages, wrong careers, wrong locations, wrong friendship and wrong jobs. It is used by witchcraft powers to influence a person to do what he or she does not want to do. Manipulation is a weapon employed to make a person obey strange orders.

How to know a person who is under manipulation
1. He has no idea of his wrong decisions; he sees the people correcting him as those who are wrong.
2. He has no ability to reason correctly. The power may be controlling from a distance but unless the power expires, the person will be subjected to sabotage, torment, oppression, evil diversion, and untimely death. Please take this prayer: "Any weapon of manipulation working in my life and family, catch fire, in the name of Jesus."
3. He will be praising the person destroying him.
4. He will see his enemies as friends and his friends as enemies.
5. He will pick up the wrong jobs and pursue the wrong careers and he will be in the wrong location.

The ultimate aim of manipulation is to cage a person. When the person is supposed to get married and good people are coming, he or she won't see it. I pray that any form of

manipulation against you ends today, in the name of Jesus.
One day, a man was driving and suddenly the road divided into two and he did not know which one to follow. Then a voice told him to turn right, so he turned to the right and it became a disaster; he crashed. He saw the road divided into two because of manipulation.

Somebody used his legs to climb to the top of a storey building, and on his way down, he heard a voice which said, "You don't need to go through the same stair-case; just take the direct route" and he jumped down and crashed. It was due to manipulation. Take this prayer: "Any power that wants me to harm myself or to destroy my destiny shall be wasted, in the name of Jesus."

There was a girl who had burnt the midnight candle in preparation for her examination which she was determined to excel and make A1 in all subjects. In the exam hall, immediately, the invigilator asked them to start, she slept off and when he asked them to submit, she woke up. That was manipulation. We must fight against these powers.

What to do at this juncture

Accept Jesus as your Lord and personal Saviour. Say the following prayer: Lord Jesus, I come to you today, be my Lord and Saviour, I repent of my sins and I will not go back to them, in Jesus' name, I pray. Amen.

Prayer Points

1. Any problem that has been following me about for a long time, depart from me, in the name of Jesus.
2. I destroy every evil soul-tie with any dead member of my family, in the name of Jesus.
3. Anyone using sorcery, magic or satanic power at night against my life, I destroy you, in the name of Jesus.
4. Witchcraft chain binding me to the wrong people, wrong group, and wrong associates, break, in the name of Jesus.
5. Any evil material projected into my body to cause me harm or sickness, catch fire, in the name of Jesus.
6. Witchcraft agents appearing in my dreams for the control of my life, die, in the name of Jesus.
7. Witchcraft agents using my face or image to attack innocent people, die, in the name of Jesus.
8. Any person or animal programmed to appear in my dream in order to harm me, die, in the name of Jesus.
9. Enchantments, incantations, and evil pronouncements on any evil altar against my destiny, expire, in the name of Jesus.
10. Any of my image or picture on any witchcraft altar, catch fire, in the name of Jesus.
11. My blessing and breakthrough hijacked on any witchcraft altar or coven, be released, in the name of

Jesus.

12. Every witchcraft battle assigned to make me suffer from the cradle to the grave, break, in the name of Jesus.

13. Powers tracking me down from the ladder of success, die, in the name of Jesus.

14. Witchcraft powers manifesting as spirit wife or spirit husband in order to destroy me, die, in the name of Jesus.

15. Witchcraft powers using my dream life to control my destiny, wherever you are, die, in the name of Jesus.

16. Fire of God, burn to ashes every material of poverty in my body, in the name of Jesus.

17. Witchcraft powers closing the door of good things, be destroyed, in the name of Jesus.

18. Fire of God, arise and burn to ashes the clothes, pictures, photographs, images or rings representing me on any demonic altar, in the name of Jesus.

19. Witchcraft agents trading with my glory in any witchcraft market, expire, in the name of Jesus.

20. I recover my blessings, virtues and properties from the possession of domestic witchcraft, in the name of Jesus.

21. Every weapon of witchcraft deployed against me, turn against your owners, in the name of Jesus.

22. Every witchcraft handwriting of failure, defeat and frustration in my life, catch fire, in the name of Jesus.

23. Arrows fired into my spirit, soul and body to confuse me, catch fire, in the name of Jesus.

24. Witchcraft arrows of manipulation to make me believe in lies, catch fire, in the name of Jesus.

25. Witchcraft poison in my body causing weakness and spiritual slumber, catch fire, in the name of Jesus.

26. Any power on assignment to place embargo on the work of my hands, my finances, health and career, be broken, in the name of Jesus.

27. Powers that have vowed that this is how far I will go in life, expire, in the name of Jesus.

28. Any power that wants to make me a local champion, I bury you, in the name of Jesus.

29. Powers working against me in the night, you will work no more, in the name of Jesus.

30. Night caterers feeding my spirit with demonic food and drinks in order to cage my life, die, in the name of Jesus.

31. Masquerades of darkness showing me red objects, blood and pepper in order to afflict me, catch fire, in the name of Jesus.

32. Satanic nurses and doctors injecting me with poison in the dream, angels of death, visit them, in the name of Jesus.

33. Witchcraft barbers removing the glory of my star, wherever you are, die, in the name of Jesus.

CHAPTER TWENTY-FIVE

Destroying The Hands of Oppression

Acts 12:1: "Now about that time Herod the king stretched forth his hands to vex certain of the church."

There are hands capable of destroying what a person gathers. There are hands capable of drawing someone back and there are hands capable of stagnating people's lives. Herod stretched forth his hand against some people in the church, meaning that he selected some people to destroy in the church.

Many people have been sweating and struggling to make progress but there is a particular hand that is scattering their work. A lot of people are struggling in life but the enemy gets hold of their labour. A Yoruba adage says, "There are hands upon a person". It means that the person's life is gone. It means that nothing good can come out of that particular person because there are hands already on him or her. There is nothing the person would do to prosper or move forward. He is simply working in vain. Sometimes, if such a person makes any progress, he or she would be pulled back. That is why you see some people take one step forward and two steps backwards. Some people are just moving about in a circle because a particular hand has got hold of them.

In verse 3 of Acts 12, the Jews were happy that certain of them were being destroyed. Anyone that is happy about what you are going through now, the Lord will destroy them, in the name of Jesus. There is another hand that can save and deliver to the uttermost. That hand will deliver you, in the name of Jesus.

Prayer Points
1. Glory destroyers assigned against me, die, in the name of Jesus.
2. Opportunity wasters assigned against me, you are liars, die, in the name of Jesus.
3. This week, I will go out victorious and not come back empty handed. I will come back victorious, in the name of Jesus.
4. Powers beating the drum of shame for me to dance, you are liars, die, in the name of Jesus.

283

5. Powers saying, "Let us kill him," you are liars, die, in the name of Jesus.

6. Powers shifting the door of greatness from me, scatter, in the name of Jesus.

7. Every wicked hand scattering what I have gathered, wither, in the name of Jesus.

8. Wicked hands pressing down my head, you are wicked, die, in the name of Jesus.

9. Every hand of oppression upon my life, I cut you off, in the name of Jesus.

10. Every hand of the oppression upon my career, die, in the name of Jesus.

11. Begin to sing songs of praise.

CHAPTER TWENTY-SIX

The Eagle Christian

Psalm 71:21 says, "Thou shalt increase my greatness, and comfort me on every side."

The eagle is a great bird. God often uses the leadership qualities of the eagle to teach us many wonderful lessons. The eagle is the bird of sight and you need vision to succeed in life. The eagle is a bird that flies very high and God has called us to go high. The eagle is a very strong bird, which perseveres. It doesn't eat dirty things and sticks to one partner for life.

Qualities of the eagle Christian

1. **Trustworthiness:** Eagles are trustworthy. As children of God, we must keep our promises to God, other people and even ourselves. If you want to become great in life, to excel, wax stronger and attain great heights,

you have to keep your promises to God and to fellow men. God does things for us and sometimes, we ought to play our own part but we fail to fulfil it. Some would say, "God, if you do this for me, I will do this for you." But as soon as God blesses them, they forget about their promise.

2. **Good company:** Walk with the right people. Many Christians keep the wrong company and it hinders them from making progress. Many people are decent but because they are connected to the wrong partners, they don't move forward. Anytime God wants to lift you up, He sends good people to you. Likewise anytime satan wants to bring you down, he sends the wrong people to you. The Bible says the companion of fools will perish. That will not be your portion, in the name of Jesus.

3. **Excellence:** The eagle represents excellence and this is the quality that differentiates it from other birds. For example, the bat. The bat is blind, it cannot see. There are other birds which eat carcasses; they feed on dead bodies. They don't eat fresh things; they are attracted to the foul odour of death and rottenness. But the eagle is not so. It is excellent. An excellent spirit shall be your portion, in the name of Jesus. Ecclesiastes 9:10 says, **"Whatsoever thy hand findeth to do, do it with thy might; for there is no work, nor device, nor**

286

knowledge, nor wisdom, in the grave, whither thou goest."

4. **Start each day with God:** It is very important to start each day with God; read the word of God, meditate on it and pray. Don't be a Christian that doesn't read the Bible or a Christian that doesn't have a prayer altar.

5. **Be disciplined:** Be disciplined in the way you talk, and in the way you live your life generally. Some people can't even keep an appointment with God and that is an act of indiscipline. Too much sleep is an act of indiscipline. As a child of God, you should always be alert. Don't be the kind of person that slumbers all the time. Even, when the alarm rings, you put it off and continue sleeping; it is indiscipline. Gluttony too is indiscipline. Lawlessness is an act of indiscipline.

6. **Seek self-improvement:** Keep developing yourself by reading, attending seminars, conferences, etc. Seek more knowledge because that is how to become great. Learn to do what your flesh doesn't want you to do. Learn to control your flesh. The flesh doesn't want us to pray or read, the flesh loves enjoyment.

7. **Learn to always finish what you have started:** It is discipline that can help you to finish what you have started.

8. **Don't be a men pleaser:** Don't live your life trying to please people. Jesus did not live to please men but God.

The same people that cried, "Hosanna," were still the same people that cried, "Crucify Him".

9. Live within your income.
10. Ensure that you pay your tithe.
11. Be loyal.
12. Have a mentor.
13. Pray and plan.
14. Avoid procrastination.
15. Be approachable.
16. Embrace hard work.
17. Develop hatred for failure.

Prayer Points

1. I cover myself and my family with the blood of Jesus, in the name of Jesus.

2. I plug my life into the divine socket of God. Let the current of favour flow into my life, in the name of Jesus.

3. O Lord, give me the testimony that will advertise your name and power in my life, in the name of Jesus.

4. In the race of life, I shall not be a latecomer, in the name of Jesus.

5. Oh Lord, this year, my expectation shall not be cut off, in the name of Jesus.

6. Every chain of darkness binding my finances, career

and health, break, in the name of Jesus.

7. Thou power of spell, charms and sorcery over my destiny, be broken, in the name of Jesus.

8. O Lord, bless me and increase me on every side, in the name of Jesus.

9. Father, I decree and declare: I shall be favoured this month and sickness, failure, sudden death and affliction are not my portions, in the name of Jesus.

10. Power of God, operate in my life, glory of God, envelope my life, in the name of Jesus.

11. I reject failure and disappointment, and I refuse to be told sorry, in the name of Jesus.

12. The works of my hands are blessed, in the name of Jesus.

13. Every gang-up, conspiracy and evil prayer against me shall be scattered, in the name of Jesus.

14. I shall not be frustrated financially, physically and spiritually, in the name of Jesus.

15. Bewitchment is not my portion, in the name of Jesus.

16. The Almighty God will usher me into the arena of joy and the palace of celebration, in the name of Jesus.

17. My hands shall be stronger against all my enemies, in the name of Jesus.

18. Every gang-up against me on my way to the top, scatter, in the name of Jesus.

19. Powers tying me down to the wrong location, where my destiny does not belong, die, in the name of Jesus.

20. Any power that has vowed that my battle will not come to an end, you are a liar, die, in the name of Jesus.

21. Powers that say even if I gather, they will scatter it, you are liars, die, in the name of Jesus.

22. Arrows of intimidation, frustration and limitation programmed into the works of my hand, catch fire, in the name of Jesus.

23. Every house I have lived before that has covenanted me to failure and non-achievement, catch fire, in the name of Jesus.

24. Anywhere my name is being mentioned, mercy of God, answer for me, in the name of Jesus.

25. Begin to prophesy upon your life, in the name of Jesus.

CHAPTER TWENTY-SEVEN

O Lord, I need My Portion Now

Our prayers in this section are centered on the kind of people who appear as if they are very big and comfortable; people look at them and think they are okay and don't need any help but they know themselves that they are not okay. It is a deception of the enemy so that they will not attract the kind of blessings and favour that they are supposed to get from other people. People come to them to ask for financial assistance and when they say they can't help, the people asking for help think they are lying and don't want to help. It is a deception of the enemy.

In the book of Judges 6, we have the story of Gideon, who was supposed to be a judge in Israel. In those days, a judge is like the president or prime minister of the nation. By the destiny of Gideon, he was supposed to be a judge, but where was Gideon found when the angel was looking for him? Gideon was found in the bush where he was hiding to thresh corn to avoid being seen and attacked by the Midianites. We can see where Gideon was supposed to be by divine order and where he ended up. This story is found in Judge 6. Verse 11 says, **"And there came an angel of the LORD and sat under an oak which was in Ophrah that pertained unto Joash the Abiezrite: and his son Gideon threshed wheat by the winepress, to hide it from the Midianites."**

When the angel appeared to Gideon, he said, "Angel, it looks like you have come to the wrong person." The Angel announced to him that by destiny, he was a mighty man of valour. But Gideon said, "No, I know myself; our family is the poorest in the whole of Israel. How can you say that I'm supposed to be the president yet I am a beggar." You may be reading this and your destiny does not rhyme with your condition; you are big inside but the reality outside is different. You know yourself that you are bigger and greater than who and what you are now. How can you be so big inside and the reality is the opposite? The divine plan for your destiny is greatness but in reality, you are the least on the list. It so bad that even when the poor are categorized, you are still the poorest. That was the condition of Gideon and the angel said to him, "No it's not so."

There are some children who cater for both themselves and their parents, which is an upside down situation. But there are parents who have paid their dues in life and their children are taking good care of them. They don't do anything anymore but to sit where they are, and provision is coming in from the children. They move from one country to another or from one city to another, visiting the children in their different locations. That is why I decree that wherever your portion is hidden, the Almighty God shall give it to you, in the name of Jesus.

The purpose of the accompanying prayers in this section is for you to be in your right position because stars are meant to shine; they are not meant to be on the floor. Wherever your greatness is, you need to take it back; that is your portion. There are many people who are giants, they have greatness in them but they are on the wheelchair. They are great but nobody can see it, they are present but nobody is taking notice. They are well endowed but poverty is ravaging them. Poverty is not a plus but a minus. A man who is poor has no voice; he is talking but nobody is listening or hearing him. In a family meeting in some places, a poor person cannot speak because his words are not regarded. Nobody will listen to him; rather they will tell him that talk is very cheap, and he cannot match it with action, which is finance. They would rather listen to a junior person, who though is less endowed, has more money to fund whatever they are talking about. Beloved, that error shall be corrected, in the name of Jesus.

A poor man is an angry man. Why would he not be angry? I heard the story of a certain man, who was so poor that his younger siblings did not inform him when their father died. He was the first born but the younger ones went ahead and buried their father without telling him. Eventually, he heard about it and he was angry with his brothers. He asked, **"Why would you do that?"** And they told him that it wouldn't have made any difference; he would have asked them to send him money for transportation to come to the village. He would become a liability because when he would be leaving the village, he would also be asking them to raise his transport fare.

Proverbs 22:7 says, "The rich ruleth over the poor, and the borrower is servant to the lender."

The rich ruleth over the poor and a borrower is a servant to the lender; the rich rule because they are the ones that have a voice. They sit down and direct other people, and I am very sure God did not make you to be a servant. In the Bible, I did not see it written anywhere that you are a servant. The will of God for you is not to suffer nor to be a beggar or a reproach among men. If you read your Bible well, you would discover

294

that money was also used against the gospel even in the days of Jesus. The soldiers that were asked to watch over Him, when He arose were bribed to tell the world that they were sleeping, when His disciples came to take Him away. So, the enemy is working things out so that you will be poor and not be able to give to the work of God. He wants you to be useless and not be able to do anything. You cannot feed yourself or take good care of yourself. There are people who still come to church to write requests for financial assistance.

Proverbs 14: 20 says, "The poor is hated even of his own neighbor: but the rich hath many friends."
Those who live in the same environment with the poor hate him; they say he is a useless man and cannot make any meaningful contributions.

Proverbs 19: 4 says, "Wealth maketh many friends; but the poor is separated from his neighbour." Verse 7: "All the brethren of the poor do hate him: how much more do his friends go far from him? He pursueth them with words, yet they are wanting to him."

The friends of the poor offend him and his neighbours go far from him. He persuades them with his words and they still run away from him. That is why when some people see your number, they put their phones on busy. Beloved, you need to pray. Whatever is the root cause of the bad luck following you, Jehovah will destroy it, in the name of Jesus.

Prayer Points

1. Father, whatever is the root cause of poverty in my life, I curse it to the root, in the name of Jesus.
2. Multiple cobwebs attacking me at the edge of my breakthroughs, catch fire, in the name of Jesus.
3. Witchcraft agents using their evil hands to cover my blessing, catch fire, in the name of Jesus.
4. Powers sponsoring poverty in my life, die, in the name of Jesus.
5. I recover all my financial transactions physically and spiritually, in the name of Jesus.
6. Witchcraft garments assigned to imprison my finances, catch fire, in the name of Jesus.
7. Witchcraft coffin fashioned to bury my prosperity, catch fire, in the name of Jesus.
8. Whirlwind of the Lord, blow poverty away from my life, in the name of Jesus.
9. Every curse of feeding from hand to mouth, break, in the name of Jesus.
10. Every secret I need to know to move forward, be revealed, in the name of Jesus.
11. Anything I have eaten that is affecting my life, die to

the root, in the name of Jesus.

12. Powers programmed to make me suffer, die, in the name of Jesus.

13. Powers swallowing the greatness of my father's house, I command you to die, in the name of Jesus.

14. Marine powers behind my suffering, die to the root, in the name of Jesus.

15. Inherited mark of shame and reproach in my life, catch fire, in the name of Jesus.

16. Spirit of bad luck and poverty, I bind and cast you out of my life, in the name of Jesus.

17. Anointing of excellence, fall upon me, in the name of Jesus.

18. O Lord, teach my hands to fight and my hands to win in the battle of life, in the name of Jesus.

19. Spirit of rejection and abandonment, get out of my life, in the name of Jesus.

20. Spirit of failure, my life is not your candidate, get out of my life, in the name of Jesus.

21. O God, arise and connect me to the source of prosperity, in the name of Jesus.

22. I speak woe to every weapon that the enemy is using against me, in the name of Jesus.

23. Every anti-prosperity arrow fired at me, go back to your sender, in the name of Jesus.

24. Holy Ghost fire, burn every strange garment on my life,

in the name of Jesus.

25.   Arrows of manipulation against the work of my hands, catch fire, in the name of Jesus.

26.   I bind the spirit of lack of faith; lose your hold upon my life, in the name of Jesus.

27.   Every door closed against me that is meant to be open, hear the word of the Lord, open by fire, in the name of Jesus.

28.   My blessings shall not be given to another. What is due to me shall not be diverted and what is my mine shall not be stolen, in the name of Jesus.

29.   I refuse to be a giant on the wheelchair, in the name of Jesus.

30.   My greatness shall not be swallowed or strangulated, in the name of Jesus.

31.   O God, arise and show me favour in high places, in the name of Jesus.

CHAPTER TWENTY-EIGHT

Judgement Against Witchcraft

Ephesians 6:12 says, "For we wrestle not against flesh and blood, but against principalities, against powers, against the rulers of the darkness of this world, against spiritual wickedness in high places."

Witchcraft is referred to as realistic science or scientific realism, which is the view that the universe is real regardless of how it may be interpreted. It is the belief that things exist, whether they can be observed or not. The Bible says, our battle is not against flesh and blood. Witchcraft powers are real and there is no witch that is good, whether it is a green witch, a white witch or a black witch. In the world of witchcraft, every witch or wizard is evil.

2 Kings 9:22 says, "And it came to pass, when Joram saw

Jehu, that he said, Is it peace, Jehu? And he answered, What peace, so long as the whoredoms of thy mother Jezebel and her witchcrafts are so many?

In the above-mentioned Bible passage, we can see that wherever witchcraft is present, the peace of that place will be suspended. When witchcraft powers enter a community, the peace there will be suspended. The same thing happens when it enters a family, the peace of that family will be suspended. When a witch is in a city, she will turn the place upside down. In Acts 8:6, Philip the man of God entered Samaria and preached Christ to them and the people gave heed to those things which Philip spake, hearing and seeing the miracles which he did for unclean spirits came out of the people that were possessed with them and those that were sick of them were healed. Verse 8 says there was so much joy in that city. One man stepped into a city and peace came into the city so much that those that were oppressed were set free, those that couldn't sleep started sleeping, those that couldn't get jobs got jobs, those that couldn't get married got married, etc.

In that same chapter, the Bible introduced another man called, Simon the sorcerer, who used his evil power, his witchcraft power to bewitch everybody. You can see two men with different assignments. One man caged the people, caged their marriages, health, careers etc. but the other man came with the power of God and set the people free. Wherever you see witchcraft, whether red, white or black, marine witchcraft, corporate witchcraft, forest witchcraft, family witchcraft, junction witchcraft, terrestial witchcraft, flying witchcraft, ground witchcraft, fetish witchcraft, private witchcraft, familiar witchcraft, or whatever name they may be called; they are all evil. Please take this prayer before you read further: "Any power pressing down my head, blocking my way, attacking my family, and my health, perish, in the name of Jesus.

The Bible says in Exodus 22: 18, "Thou shalt not suffer a witch to live." The man of God, Jehu, said to Joram, "As long as the whoredoms of your mother Jezebel and her witchcrafts are so many, there would be no peace."

Prayer Points
1. Wickedness of the wicked assigned to trouble my life, die, in the name of Jesus.
2. Stubborn unrepentant witchcraft that will not let me go, die, in the name of Jesus.
3. Witchcraft powers subjecting me to harassment, die, in the name of Jesus.
4. I break and release myself from the dominion of

ancestral witchcraft, in the name of Jesus.

5.   Every coven ministering against me, catch fire, in the name of Jesus.

6.   Arrow of witchcraft hiding in my body, go back to your sender, in the name of Jesus.

7.   Battles assigned to pursue me at night and in the day, wither, in the name of Jesus.

8.   My breakthrough in the custody of domestic witchcraft, be released by fire, in the name of Jesus.

9.   Every witchcraft power troubling my health, peace, home, marriage and finances, be destroyed, in the name of Jesus.

10.   Every witchcraft activity in my place of work, expire, in the name of Jesus.

11.   Habitation of domestic witchcraft in my house, receive fire, in the name of Jesus.

12.   Witchcraft power sponsoring rejection in my life, expire, in the name of Jesus.

13.   My destiny, you shall not be food on the dining table of witchcraft, in the name of Jesus.

14.   Witchcraft worms assigned to cause sickness in my body, dry up, in the name of Jesus.

15.   Hand of witchcraft resting on my career, wither, in the name of Jesus.

16.   Owners of evil load in my life, carry your load by fire, in the name of Jesus.

17.   Any problem in my life that is making the enemy to mock God, die, in the name of Jesus.

18.   Expectation of witches and wizards over my life and family, fail woefully, in the name of Jesus.

19.   The witchcraft power that has vowed that I must suffer, you are not my God, die, in the name of Jesus.

20.   Witchcraft powers pursuing me with poverty, sickness and infirmity, die, in the name of Jesus.

21.   The presence of domestic witchcraft chasing good things away from me, be arrested by fire, in the name of Jesus.

22.   Every evil word of witches and wizards over my life, expire, in the name of Jesus.

23.   Marks of miserable existence on my life, clear away, in the name of Jesus.

24.   Masquerade of death appearing in my dream, die, in the name of Jesus.

25.   O God, arise and decorate me with favour, in the name of Jesus.

26.   Any witchcraft power blocking the flow of blessing and favour in my life, let the Angel of the Lord slap them to death, in the name of Jesus.

27.   I decree the judgement of fire upon every domestic witchcraft, in the name of Jesus.

28.   Any witchcraft power that has vowed that what I am praying for will not reach me, Angel of the Lord, slap them to death, in the name of Jesus.

29.   As from today, anyone that will fly or attend any evil

meeting at night for my sake shall only go but never return; they shall crash, in the name of Jesus.

30. Any evil mark that is making me invisible, catch fire, in the name of Jesus.

31. Whether the enemy likes it or not, I recover my portion violently, in the name of Jesus.

32. The rage of domestic witchcraft that has been released against me, wither, in the name of Jesus.

33. Every veil of darkness assigned against me, I tear them off, in the name of Jesus.

34. Every coven of darkness assigned to limit me, I am not available, catch fire, in the name of Jesus.

35. Beginning from now, I shall be visible to my helpers, in the name of Jesus.

36. Any satanic power promoting failure, defeat and delay in my life, catch fire, in the name of Jesus.

37. I refuse to become an abandoned project, in the name of Jesus.

38. Anything that has been erected or put in place to stop me, I stop them before they stop me, in the name of Jesus.

39. Every accusation from hell fire that I shall not amount to anything in life, I silence the evil voices, in the name of Jesus.

40. Every insult that I have ever received, Jehovah convert it to result, in the name of Jesus.

41. Every story in my life, O God, arise and convert it to glory, in the name of Jesus.
42. Every shame in my life shall become favour, in the name of Jesus.
43. I become unstoppable. My voice shall be heard and my helpers shall locate me, in the name of Jesus.
44. Anyone that God has been ordained to help me but the enemy is stopping them because they don't want them to locate me, by the mercies of God, be released, in the name of Jesus.

CHAPTER TWENTY-NINE

I Must Take
My Portion Now

Dear reader, I want you to know that God has already paid for your healing. God has already taken your diseases away; you only need to take hold of your healing, which the Lord Jesus has perfected over 2000 years ago. Let it manifest in your body. Let the infirmity, sickness or disease in any part of your body be healed now, in the name of Jesus.

Luke 15: 11-12 says, "And he said, A certain man had two sons. And the younger of them said to his father, Father give me the portion of goods that falleth to me and he divided unto them his living."

The young man in the above-mentioned passage said to his father, "Daddy, I am your son and by the virtue of the fact that you are my father, I don't need to beg, give me my portion. I have a portion that belongs to me. It's my own right, it's my inheritance." The Bible said the inheritance was divided which means that the other one that did not ask also got his own and kept it somewhere. I pray that your own portion in life will enter into your hands, in the name of Jesus.

Everyone has a portion, which is not another person's portion. Your portion is not my portion. All of us have our portions but the book of **Nehemiah 13: 10 says, "And I perceived that the portions of the Levites had not been given them: for the Levites and the singers that did the work, were fled everyone to his field."**

The Levites who were not only the children of God but also priests were denied their portion. I pray that your portion shall no longer be denied you, in the name of Jesus.

There are people who have collected their portion in life while there are others who are not aware that they have any portion. There are people, who even after they have collected their own portion still went ahead and collected other people's portion.

You have your earthly portion that God has given to you to trade with. If you don't have it, it would appear as if you came to the world but did not show up. If the portion that heaven

307

gave to you when you were coming to the earth is missing, it would appear as if you were not present. You are present but nobody is noticing because you are unable to get your portion.

There are earthly portions and there are heavenly portions. Everlasting life of peace, joy and happiness is for all those who serve the Lord Jesus when they exit the world. But for those who do not serve Jesus, the Bible says there would be tears, weeping and gnashing of teeth for them. That is the portion of the wicked. So it is important that you know what portion awaits you. For those who are living godly lives, the word of God says they are seated in heavenly places with Christ Jesus. All these things are already in place. God is no longer creating anything. All that we need have already been created; everything is available. So, if you are lacking anything, it is not God's fault but yours because you are not aware that these things are available. It is not even by gender that is why you see some women doing well even in a male dominated world because it is not by gender or in turns. It is not also according to age; that is why you also see many people being fed and catered for by their younger ones. In the Bible, David was not the oldest, in fact, he was the last and yet he was the one crowned king. Joseph too, was not the oldest, he was number 11, yet he was the one used to preserve the lives of his other brothers. I pray that your portion with which you are to rule your world and dominate will enter into your hand. Take your portion, in the name of Jesus.

It was the younger one of the two brothers, who asked for his inheritance and not the older one but unfortunately, he wasted it. It means that you can still collect your portion and waste it. But there is a big lesson for us to learn here. He wasted his portion, which was given to him when he asked but his brother did not open his mouth to ask; he was still managing and even when the man came back, the one that was kept for his brother was still used to celebrate his homecoming. Although he got angry and complained that his father didn't do anything for him in spite of his commitment, the father said, "Well it's not my fault. You've always been with me and you didn't ask for anything that's why you were not given." The Bible says it is he who asks that receives. I believe that now, you will ask and receive, in the name of Jesus.

Someone who has been abandoned and rejected, and it has been concluded that nothing good will ever come out of him, but all of a sudden the Son of Righteousness rules on his behalf, and the person collects his portion, he will shine forth. When a person who is barren and has nothing to celebrate, but all of a sudden he is visited by God and he collects his portion; there will be rejoicing. The bachelor who was roaming around the street and couldn't marry and settle down; he couldn't do anything good for himself but all of a sudden the Lord blessed him and he took a lady to the altar and got married, it means he has collected his portion. Beloved, at this juncture, I want to make this declaration: "I will have my portion, in the name of Jesus."

In case you are asking what is your portion? Long life is your portion; it means you must not die before your time. The Bible says both Abraham and Isaac died in good old age. Your portion is divine protection from danger; it may be happening to others but the scripture says, with your eyes, you will see the reward of the wicked. What is your portion? Prosperity is your portion. Life without money is very stressful; most of the stress that people are going through is due to lack of money, therefore you must take your portion today.

The Bible says, **"Beloved, I wish above all things that thou mayest prosper and be in good health even as your soul prospereth" (3John 1: 2).** So, a prosperous marriage is also your portion. In case you don't know that you are not supposed to be alone, **Genesis 5: 2 says, "Male and female created He them; and blessed them, and called their name Adam, in the day when they were created."** So if you are alone, it means that you have not taken your portion; you need to take it now. Fruitfulness is your portion. Increase is your portion and good life is also your portion and it is time for you

310

to take them. Say again, "I will take my portion now, in the name of Jesus."

What do you do?
You need to cry out. You need to ask or place a demand. Also, you have to make up your mind that nobody will take your portion because in the world, there are people, even after they have collected their own portion, they still want to collect other people's portions. Many have lost their portions to all kinds of people. The portion of some have also been transferred. You must declare that your portion will not be transferred, taken away, diverted, stolen or sat upon by any wicked power.

If you are serious about taking back your portion, and you have not given your life to Christ, it cannot work. You cannot take your portion because that is the Person who will give it to you; you must be at peace with Him. To take your portion, you must have a relationship with Jesus. When you give your life to Christ, what you have done is to establish a relationship between you and Christ; you become His son or daughter, and He becomes your father. He will be talking to you, guiding, directing and leading you.

If you want to become born again, make the following confessions: Lord Jesus, I come to you today. I acknowledge that I am a sinner. Forgive my sins and wash me clean with your precious blood. I surrender my life to you; be my Lord and Saviour and write my name in the Book of Life. From this day henceforth, I am now your son/daughter. I begin a relationship with you today and I will follow you all the days of my life. Thank you Lord, in Jesus' name.

Prayer Points

1. Strong man sitting on my portion, I push you away, in the name of Jesus.
2. Ancestral strongman, remove your legs from my portion, in the name of Jesus.
3. My portion in all the four corners of the earth, appear by fire, in the name of Jesus.
4. Serpents and scorpions that have swallowed my portion, right now, vomit them and die, in the name of Jesus.
5. Every witchcraft cage holding my money, catch fire, in the name of Jesus.
6. My virtues stolen when I was a baby; I recover them by fire, in the name of Jesus.
7. Power to possess my possession, fall upon me now, in the name of Jesus.
8. Rain of favour, fall upon me now, in the name of Jesus.
9. Every door of opportunity that the enemy has closed against me, right now, open by fire, in the name of Jesus.

10.   Angels of my breakthrough, I send you forth into the land of the living to gather all my portions, in the name of Jesus.

11.   My portion shall not be given to another and my portion shall not be transferred, in the name of Jesus.

12.   My portion, appear by fire, in the name of Jesus.

13.   The root of failure in my life, I curse you; die, in the name of Jesus.

14.   Backwardness in my life, I curse your root, die, in the name of Jesus.

15.   Every witchcraft pot assigned against my destiny, catch fire, in the name of Jesus.

16.   The voice of the wicked that said, this is how far I will go, I silence you by fire, in the name of Jesus.

17.   I break out from every prison of limitation fashioned against my life, in the name of Jesus.

18.   The impossibility in my life, become testimony by fire, in the name of Jesus.

CHAPTER THIRTY

When The Eagle is Caged

Isaiah 40:30-31 says, "Even the youths shall faint and be weary, and the young men shall utterly fall: But they that wait upon the LORD shall renew their strength; they shall mount up with wings as eagles; they shall run, and not be weary; and they shall walk, and not faint."

The eagle is a special and unique bird compared to all other birds. It is not like the chicken, bat or vulture, which have their limitations. The chicken is known for low ambition. The raven is a bird known for destruction. The vulture is known for death, the bat is known for blindness while the sparrow is known for talking.

The eagle is a bird of the top, it flies very high. It is a bird of supernatural strength. It is a bird of good character and discipline. It doesn't mix up sexually, it sticks with only one partner at a time. The eagle is always battle ready and vigilant. It is a good striker, known for its defensive and offensive abilities. The eagle signifies royalty, honour, colourful destiny and also speed. The eagle is also known for excellence.

However, the eagle can be caged in spite of all these good qualities, and many eagles have been caged. Many people that were born with great potential, ability, vision, authority, royalty and honour have been caged by the enemy. Many are in ancestral cage, environmental cage, domestic witchcraft cage, cage of ignorance, cage of confusion, religious cage, sexual cage, demonic cage etc. There was a certain lady who was studying pharmacy in the university. Her parents were very rich, and could afford whatever she wanted. They bought her clothes abroad whenever they travelled but this girl would leave the clothes bought for her and would go to the backyard of the university, where other girls dried their clothes and steal them. One day, she was caught stealing one of a pair of shoes, not a complete pair and people were surprised and wondered what she would do with that.

A lawyer shared his testimony in the church. He was caught in the supermarket, where he stole sweets. He broke down and started crying and saying, "This problem has followed me to this place." He said, "How much is the sweet that I cannot pay." He brought out money from his pocket but it was too late. The people shouted, "You took it and you did not want to pay!" His eagle had been caged. Something was following him about to disgrace him.

I heard the story of a certain man who worked in an office. He was committed to his work but his problem was that whenever he collected his salary, he would go to a newspaper vendor, ask for the amount of all the newspapers on his stand and buy everything. What does he want to do with all the newspaper? Nothing. That can only happen when the eagle is caged. Please pray this prayer at this juncture: "Wherever I have been caged, I come out of the cage, in the name of Jesus."

We have the story of a young man in the Bible, who lived among the tombs. He left his house and relocated to the cemetery. The Bible says that he would pick up a stone and use it to cut himself and blood would be gushing out. He would be in pain and yet he would still continue to cut himself. Nobody could stop or help him. He was possessed with so much demonic power that he could break chains. His eagle was caged. His destiny was caged. When a destiny is caged, the destiny will be corrupted, amputated or fragmented. Instead

316

of glory, there would be aborted glory, instead of honour, there would be aborted honour.

Signs to know that an Eagle is caged
1. Mental dullness.
2. Loss of memory.
3. Mistaken identity.
4. Embargo.
5. Destiny transfer.
6. Evil attraction.
7. Addiction.
8. Insanity.
9. Demonic attack.
10. Evil plantation.

Take this prayer: Anything the enemy has planted in my life to control the affairs of my life, I set it ablaze, in the name of Jesus.

Prayer Points
1. Father, I know I am an eagle, make me to fly high, in the name of Jesus.
2. Father, wherever my eagle is tied down, release it now by fire, in the name of Jesus.
3. I receive the invitation that will transform my life, in the name of Jesus.

4. O God, arise and let my glory shine, in the name of Jesus.

5. O God, arise and deliver me in every area of my life where I am stagnated, in the name of Jesus.

6. Powers assigned to mock me and mock my future, die, in the name of Jesus.

7. Powers refusing my dominion on earth, what are you waiting for? Die, in the name of Jesus.

8. Any satanic document, where it is written that I must suffer, catch fire, in the name of Jesus.

9. Help of God and help of man for my next level, appear, in the name of Jesus.

10. The good thing that I have been looking for, where are you? Appear, in the name of Jesus.

CHAPTER THIRTY-ONE

Yoke of Famine

Famine signifies lack, starvation, shortage and insufficiency. It is the opposite of abundance and plenty. The will of God for us is to have plenty of good things but famine is a time of agitation, crisis, distress, deprivation and hardship. Famine means hunger, lack of basic and essential things of life; it is a time when people manage things due to scarcity.

Types of Famine

1. Famine of food: When there is shortage of food, it is called the famine of food. It happened in the Bible days when people were buying dung of animals because there was no food. Make this declaration: "I will not experience it, in the name of Jesus."

2. Famine of water: Water is one of the basic necessities of life. Our body needs water, we use water to wash, drink and for other domestic uses. Make this declaration:

"The famine of water shall not be my lot, in the name of Jesus."

3. Famine of vision: Many people wake up in the morning without any plans for the day; they have nothing to do and nowhere to go. What a waste of destiny. If they must eat, someone has to give them food. If they must spend money, they have to borrow. It is due to the famine of vision. The Bible says when there is no vision, the people perish. Make this declaration: "I will not experience it, in the name of Jesus."

4. Spiritual Famine: This happens when people are spiritually ignorant or lazy, and when people do not have a personal relationship with the Lord.

5. Business Famine: This happens when people have nothing to do. It does not mean that they are lazy or don't want to do anything but there is nothing to do. Perhaps the capital for their businesses or trade has been eaten up because of the harsh economic situation.

6. Famine of the word of God: This happens when the word of God does not dwell richly in a person.

7. Health Famine: When someone's health is completely broken down, he or she would experience health famine. It is lack of good health. When a person who was formally enjoying good health becomes sick, all kinds of troubles coming in, and the emotions are no longer stable, it is caused by health famine.

320

8. Political famine.
9. Marital famine.
10. Social famine.
11. Moral famine.
12. Academic famine.

The power of God was demonstrated in the period of famine in the Bible. There are instances, where the people experienced creative miracles through the supernatural power God. God lifted Abraham and Isaac in the period of famine. When there was famine in the land, where Isaac lived and he was contemplating on leaving, when others were leaving, God told him not to leave that He would bless him there. And against all the evil predictions and expectations, God blessed Isaac. Make this declaration: "In this period of economic meltdown, God will prove Himself and surprise me, in the name of Jesus." **Job 5:20 says, "In famine he shall redeem thee from death: and in war from the power of the sword."**

Causes of famine
1. Idolatry.
2. Disobedience.
3. Lawlessness.
4. Wastefulness.
5. Curses.
6. Laziness.
7. Prayerlessness.

8. Stinginess; particularly stinginess towards God.
9. Lack of self-development.
10. Procrastination.
11. Lack of purpose.
12. Destructive habits.
13. Demonic attack.
14. Lack of information.
15. Giving up too soon.

Prayer Points

1. This month, everyone will know and testify that I am serving a living God, in the name of Jesus.
2. Whether the enemy likes it or not, I shall enjoy favour, in the name of Jesus.
3. Lord Jesus, by your wonder-working power, make a way for me, in the name of Jesus.
4. Sickness and diseases of any kind shall not be my portion, in the name of Jesus.
5. Wherever my breakthroughs are tied down, O God, arise and release them by fire, in the name of Jesus.
6. Holy Ghost, overshadow my life for miracles, signs and wonders, in the name of Jesus.
7. Angels of my blessing, where are you? Appear by fire, in the name of Jesus.
8. Battles of no one will help me in life, I am not your

candidate, die, in the name of Jesus.

9.   Power to be connected to the high places of the earth, fall upon me, in the name of Jesus.

10. Problems that are mocking God in my life, I bury you today, in the name of Jesus.

11. Witchcraft powers assigned to trouble my life this month, before I open my eyes, die, in the name of Jesus.

12. I take authority over this month, in the name of Jesus.

13. Sudden death is not my portion, in the name of Jesus.

14. My body shall not collect evil arrows, in the name of Jesus.

15. Every witchcraft pot fashioned against me this month, I break it to pieces, in the name of Jesus.

16. I decree; everything will work together for good for me this month, in the name of Jesus.

17. I render null and void every enchantment and pronouncement of darkness, in the name of Jesus.

18. I shall possess the gates of my enemy, in the name of Jesus.

19. I command situations to change for me this month, in the name of Jesus.

20. My breakthrough, favour and promotion, I order you to appear one after the other, in the name of Jesus.

21. This month, I will celebrate and my celebration shall not be postponed, in the name of Jesus.

22. Father, bless me and make a way for me, in the name of Jesus.

23. O God, arise and deliver me from every problem I am passing through now, in the name of Jesus.

24. I receive power to convert my famine to surplus and abundance, in the name of Jesus.

25. O God, who promoted Isaac in the time of famine, arise and promote me, in the name of Jesus.

26. I receive deliverance from every embarrassing situation, in the name of Jesus.

27. Before a need arises in my life, God's provision is already available, in the name of Jesus.

28. Jesus, the great provider will satisfy me this season, in the name of Jesus.

29. Spiritual rats devouring my harvest and prosperity, I kill you today, in the name of Jesus.

30. Begin to prophesy upon your life, in the name of Jesus.

CHAPTER THIRTY-TWO

Breaking the Circle of Negative Repetition

Prayers against wicked powers

1. Stubborn and unrepentant pursuers, O God, arise and smite them, in the name of Jesus.
2. Arrows that are looking for landing space, my life is not your candidate, backfire, in the name of Jesus.
3. Darkness and wickedness shall not cover my life, in the name of Jesus.
4. Battles subjecting my life to constant attack, die, in the name of Jesus.
5. Powers assigned to detain me in captivity, wither by fire, in the name of Jesus.
6. Arrows assigned to pursue me at night, backfire, in the name of Jesus.
7. Arrows of oppression hiding in my blood and bones, dry up, in the name of Jesus.

8. Arrows fired to make my helpers turn their backs against me, go back to your senders, in the name of Jesus.

9. Powers assigned to convert my greatness to smallness, wither, in the name of Jesus.

Powers of the night shall not trouble me

10. Wickedness programmed in the hour of the night to trouble me, wither, in the name of Jesus.

11. Let there be civil war in the camp of Herod, Ahab and Pharaoh assigned against me, in the name of Jesus.

12. Agenda of terror at night against me, perish, in the name of Jesus.

13. Agenda of death, pass through the land of my enemies, frustrate, intimidate and terrify them, in the name of Jesus.

14. O God, arise and wipe out every enchantment programmed against me during the hour of the night, in the name of Jesus.

15. Every contrary declaration of the enemy against my life, scatter by fire, in the name of Jesus.

16. The voices of retrogression and stagnation speaking against me at night, you shall speak no more, in the name of Jesus.

17. I recover all my benefits, favour and blessing from the powers of the night, in the name of Jesus.

18. Troubles and tragedy set in motion at night to frustrate me during the day, scatter, in the name of Jesus.
19. Garment of shame designed by the enemy for my sake, catch fire, in the name of Jesus.
20. Powers of the night in my habitation assigned to harass me, die, in the name of Jesus.
21. Every organized wickedness in my habitation, you shall gather no more, in the name of Jesus.

I connect to fruitfulness, increase, breakthroughs and favour

22. Angels of my breakthrough, appear and assist me this month, in the name of Jesus.
23. Every dark pot tying down my breakthrough, catch fire, in the name of Jesus.
24. Evil door opened by the enemy against me, close by fire, in the name of Jesus.
25. Any good thing that is dead in my life, hear the voice of resurrection, come alive, in the name of Jesus.
26. Environmental witchcraft tormenting my glory, expire, in the name of Jesus.
27. I shall arise above my root by the power in the blood of Jesus, in the name of Jesus.
28. Every ancestral register containing my name, vomit my name by fire, in the name of Jesus.

29. Every chain of strange gods tying me down, break, in the name of Jesus.

30. Seed of wickedness in my foundation, catch fire, in the name of Jesus.

31. The voice of Jezebel that is pursuing my star, wither, in the name of Jesus.

32. Any power using my star to shine, before seven days, heavens shall silence them, in the name of Jesus.

33. Any power that is using evil words to steal from me, before seven days, the ground will open up and swallow you, in the name of Jesus.

No more famine

34. Sing songs of praise unto the Lord.

35. Evil spirits guarding the door of my breakthrough, by this prayer, I destroy you, in the name of Jesus.

36. Secret blockages working against my success, scatter, in the name of Jesus.

37. Battles that want me to die without an achievement, you are failures, die, in the name of Jesus.

38. Glory killers searching for my glory, run mad and die, in the name of Jesus.

39. My season of advertisement and announcement, hear the word of the Lord, appear by fire, in the name of Jesus.

40. Chain of delay and stagnation holding me down, break, in the name of Jesus.

41. Cobweb of death, lose your hold upon my life, in the name of Jesus.

42. All my imprisoned benefits, hear the word of the Lord, be released by fire, in the name of Jesus.

43. Any power that is boasting over my testimonies, O Heavens, silence them, in the name of Jesus.

Prayers to open closed wombs

1. O God of Isaac, arise and give me laughter, in Jesus' name.

2. My womb shall be fruitful by the power in the blood of Jesus, in Jesus' name.

3. I break the yoke of delay militating against me, in Jesus' name.

4. I release myself from the control of the powers of the night, in Jesus' name.

5. My spirit, soul and body, become too hot for the enemy to handle, in Jesus' name.

6. Any area of my life under the control of ancestral powers, be released, in Jesus' name.

7. I reject the cycle of failure, in Jesus' name.

8. I withdraw my womb from the control of marine powers, in Jesus' name.

9. Lord, it is my turn to be celebrated, in Jesus' name.

10. I shall be fruitful physically and in marriage, in Jesus' name.

11. I fire back every arrow of barrenness fired against me, in Jesus' name.

12. Every identification mark of delay, be removed, in Jesus' name.

13. Woe to every vessel that the enemy is using to attack my womb, in Jesus' name.

14. I break the hold of financial confusion, in Jesus' name.

15. Powers wasting the sperm of my husband, I bind you, die, in Jesus' name.

16. My womb, reject any form of bewitchment, in Jesus' name.

17. Holy Ghost, explode in my life with miracles, signs and wonders, in Jesus' name.

18. Dark rivers in my place of birth, release my womb, in Jesus' name.

19. Every demonic manipulation of my menstrual cycle, be nullified, in Jesus' name.

20. Every counsel of evil priests against me, scatter, in Jesus' name.

21. Satanic priests making enchantment against me, die, in Jesus' name.

22. Goodness and mercy shall follow me all the days of my life, in Jesus' name.

23. This year, men and women shall congratulate me, in Jesus' name.

24. Witchcraft cloud over my womb, clear away by fire, in Jesus' name.

25. Evil hand holding tight to my womb, wither by fire, in Jesus' name.

26. Powers waging war against my fruitfulness, die, in Jesus' name.

27. Strange powers living with me in my house, die, in Jesus' name.

28. Serpents and scorpions of infirmity, die, in Jesus' name.

29. Evil pot of frustration, I break you to pieces, in Jesus' name.

30. Witchcraft padlock holding my womb down, break to piece, in Jesus' name.

31. Powers contesting for my blessing, I bind you, in Jesus' name.

32. O God, arise and pass through me with your fire, in Jesus' name.

33. Wherever my womb is caged, be released, in Jesus' name.

34. Powers using the hours of the night to harass me, die, in Jesus' name.

35. Angel of breakthroughs, pass through me, in Jesus'

name.

36. Evil seeds growing in my life, I cut you down, in Jesus' name.

37. O God, arise and plant the seed of joy in my life by fire, in Jesus' name.

38. The ground of my life, become fruitful, in Jesus' name.

39. Blood of Jesus, perfect everything that concerns me, in Jesus' name.

40. I am who God says I am and I am what God says I am, in Jesus' name.

Prayers to set your destiny eagle free

1. Powers holding down my eagle and preventing it from rising, die, in Jesus' name.

2. I break the yoke of limitation, frustration and affliction, in Jesus' name.

3. Every tree which God has not planted in my life, I cut you down, in Jesus' name.

4. Powers locking up the glory of my destiny, I destroy you, in Jesus' name.

5. My door of success under lock, open, in Jesus' name.

6. I recover every good thing that I have lost by the power in the blood of Jesus, in Jesus' name.

7. I break every cycle of stagnation, in Jesus' name.

8. My destiny, refuse to cooperate with failure, in Jesus'

name.

9. The handwriting of darkness, be rubbed off, in Jesus' name.

10. Arrows of delay fired against the work of my hands, backfire, in Jesus' name.

11. The anointing that breaks every yoke, fall upon me, in Jesus' name.

12. Every dark projection of my star for failure, scatter, in Jesus' name.

13. Satanic priests ministering against me, expire, in Jesus' name.

14. Let God be God in every area of my life, in Jesus' name.

15. Every garment of poverty assigned against me, catch fire, in Jesus' name.

16. I withdraw my wealth from satanic altars, in Jesus' name.

17. O Lord, strengthen me physically and spiritually, in Jesus' name.

18. Powers holding on to my blessing, release it and die, in Jesus' name.

19. Powers praying evil prayers against me, you have failed, in Jesus' name.

20. I shall not labour in vain, I shall not labour for trouble, in Jesus' name.

21. I shall not build for another to inhabit, my blessings

shall not be transferred, in Jesus' name.

22.   Every yoke of poverty working against me, break, in Jesus' name.

23.   Powers drinking the blood of my success, die, in Jesus' name.

24.   Powers contesting for my breakthroughs, you have failed, die, in Jesus' name.

25.   Plantation of darkness limiting my glory, catch fire, in Jesus' name.

26.   I reject financial embarrassment, in Jesus' name.

27.   Thou spirit of dryness and emptiness, lose your hold upon me, in Jesus' name.

28.   I shall be like a tree planted by the rivers of water; I shall not experience dryness anymore, in Jesus' name.

29.   The eagle of my life, it is your turn to arise and shine, in Jesus' name.

30.   The eagle of my life, what are you doing in the cage? Arise and manifest, in Jesus' name.

31.   Every curse of, 'This is how far you can go and no more', break, in Jesus' name.

32.   Organized battles against my progress, scatter, in Jesus' name.

33.   O God, arise and enlarge my coast this year, in Jesus' name.

34.   I receive total deliverance from the spirit of limitation, in Jesus' name.

35. Witchcraft embargo working against my promotion, break, in Jesus' name.

36. You the spirit behind sluggishness and drowsiness, lose your hold upon me, in Jesus' name.

37. Every pot of enchantment assigned against my health, break, in Jesus' name.

38. My enemies shall not meet me where they left me, I move forward by fire, in Jesus' name.

39. Sickness that swallows prosperity, die, in Jesus' name.

40. Evil eyes spying on me for evil, receive blindness, in Jesus' name.

Prayers to stop evil gang up in your place of work

1. Agenda of killer agents assigned against me, fail, in Jesus' name.

2. The Lord will perfect everything that concerns me, in Jesus' name.

3. The Red Sea standing on my way of excellence, dry up, in Jesus' name.

4. Holy Ghost, kill every infirmity in my body, in Jesus' name.

5. Anointing to possess the gates of my enemy, fall upon me, in Jesus' name.

6. My star, you shall not be caged; arise and shine, in Jesus' name.

7. Every evil gang up against me in my place of work,

scatter, in Jesus' name.

8. I bind the spirit of hostility and aggression directed at me, in Jesus' name.

9. Wasters and emptiers, lose your hold upon my life, in Jesus' name.

10. Yoke of financial stagnation, break, in Jesus' name.

11. Yoke of career limitation, break, in Jesus' name.

12. This year, my expectations shall not fail, in Jesus' name.

13. Angels of my breakthroughs, appear by fire, in Jesus' name.

14. Battles older than me that want to waste me, expire, in Jesus' name.

15. My name, jump out of the register of failure, in Jesus' name.

16. My heaven of prosperity, open by fire, in Jesus' name.

17. Angels of my goodness, where are you? Manifest, in Jesus' name.

18. My virtues caged inside the waters, be released, in Jesus' name.

19. My name shall not be removed from the Book of life, in Jesus' name.

20. O God, rearrange my life to carry favour, in Jesus' name.

21. I shall be the head and not the tail, in Jesus' name.

22. Every closed door before me, open by fire, in Jesus' name.

23. Holy Spirit, lead me to my place of blessings, in Jesus' name.

24. Curses of failure at the edge of success, break, in Jesus' name.

25. Witchcraft padlock, lose your hold on my life, in Jesus' name.

26. Holy Spirit, show me what I do not know that I need to know, in Jesus' name.

27. My hands, gather your wealth, in Jesus' name.

28. Strange voices speaking against me, I silence you, in Jesus' name.

29. Arrow of sudden death, my life is not your candidate, backfire, in Jesus' name.

30. Powers hiding the key of my success, release it and die, in Jesus' name.

31. I shall not be ashamed and I shall not be disgraced, in Jesus' name.

32. It is well with me by the power in the blood of Jesus, in Jesus' name.

33. All my delayed blessings, be released now, in Jesus' name.

34. Evil seeds growing against me, die, in Jesus' name.

35. Evil hands stretched forth against me, wither, in Jesus' name.

36. Prosperity swallowers, vomit my prosperity now, in

Jesus' name.

37. Charms working against me, expire, in Jesus' name.

38. Anything in my foundation working against my progress, be destroyed, in Jesus' name.

39. Evil covering, be removed from me, in Jesus' name.

40. O God, arise and put me at the centre of your will for my life, in Jesus' name.

CHAPTER THIRTY-THREE

Deliverance Prayers And Breakthroughs

Night Oppression Must Cease

Casting out the spirit of slumber on the altar of prayers

1. Arrows of spiritual slumber and arrows of rising and falling in the things of God, come out and die, in Jesus' name.

2. Powers poisoning my spirit, soul and body, wither, in Jesus' name.

3. Activities of destiny polluters at the hours of the night, die, in Jesus' name.

4. Marine powers of the night hour, release me and let me go, in Jesus' name.

5. I command the weapons of my enemies to turn against them, in Jesus' name.

6. I render the aggressive altar of familiar spirits impotent, in Jesus' name.

7. Hammer of the Almighty, dismantle the altar of familiar spirits in my body, in Jesus' name.

339

8. Wind of the Holy Ghost, blow away the poison of familiar spirits from my body, in Jesus' name.

9. Powers using my dreams to control the affairs of my destiny, wither, in Jesus' name.

10. I withdraw my prosperity from the hands of familiar spirits, in Jesus' name.

11. I destroy any image representing me on the altar of familiar spirits, in Jesus' name.

12. I am created to solve problems, I am not the problem, therefore, any problem planted in my life by familiar spirits, die, in Jesus' name.

13. Glory abortionists of the night, be suffocated unto death, in Jesus' name.

14. Every battle limiting my progress and success, scatter and die, in Jesus' name.

15. The internal coffins planted by familiar spirits, catch fire, in Jesus' name.

16. Strangers living with me in my house, the fire of God is against you, die, in Jesus' name.

17. Every inherited evil plantation in my life, catch fire, in Jesus' name.

18. Stubborn obstacles of familiar spirits preventing me from being great, burn to ashes, in Jesus' name.

19. Stubborn obstacles of career failure, catch fire, in Jesus' name.

20. Every agent of familiar spirits blocking my way to the top, die, in Jesus' name.

21. Every yoke of familiar spirits that has refused to break, right now, break, in Jesus' name.

22. Breakthrough swallowers at the hours of the night, run mad, in Jesus' name.

23. Every veil of familiar spirits shielding me away from my miracles, burn to ashes, in Jesus' name.

24. I receive deliverance from long term bondage of familiar spirits, in Jesus' name.

25. Anti-harvest and anti-breakthrough marks of familiar spirits, clear away, in Jesus' name.

26. Witchcraft powers afflicting my marriage, career and destiny, be buried, in Jesus' name.

27. The cage of familiar spirits, release me now, in Jesus' name.

28. O God, arise and let the evil plan and programme of familiar spirits for my life scatter, in Jesus' name.

29. Familiar spirits assigned to destroy my faith in God and make God a liar in my life, die, in Jesus' name.

30. Witchcraft nurses and doctors injecting me with satanic substances, be buried, in Jesus' name.

31. Apostolic power of the Holy Ghost, break my yokes, in Jesus' name.

32. Whatever must die for my breakthroughs to manifest, die now, in Jesus' name.

33. Satanic reports, decisions and accusations of coven powers against me, die, in Jesus' name.

34. Resurrection power of the Holy Ghost, fall upon me now, in Jesus' name.

35. Satanic object representing me in the dark places of the earth, catch fire, in Jesus' name.

Prayers for open Heavens

36. Principalities blocking my heavens, clear away, in Jesus' name.

37. Powers of environmental wickedness that manipulate destiny helpers, be wasted, in Jesus' name.

38. Thou fire of God, dissolve obstacles and barriers to answers to my prayers, in Jesus' name.

39. O God, by your mercy, let my heavens open, in Jesus' name.

40. Every traffic warden of darkness blocking my heavens, be arrested, in Jesus' name.

41. Rain of multiple favour, fall upon me, in Jesus' name.

42. Wandering spirits at night, lose your hold upon my life, in Jesus' name.

43. Satanic angels that hinder breakthroughs, clear away from me, in Jesus' name.

44. Contenders with the angels of my blessings, wither, in Jesus' name.

45. Every personalized stronghold limiting my breakthroughs, I pull you down, in Jesus' name.

46. Occult practices that hinder answer to prayers, wither, in Jesus' name.

47. Battle of pockets with holes, scatter, in Jesus' name.

48. Delegated strongman assigned to make my heaven brass, die, in Jesus' name.

49. Demonic reinforcements of witchcraft powers at night against me, be broken, in Jesus' name.

50. Bullets of death fired at me, return to your senders, in Jesus' name.

51. Breakthrough amputations assigned against my blessing, wither, in Jesus' name.

52. The Lord, the Creator of heaven and earth, establish me in your favour, in Jesus' name.

53. Confusion and mistakes shall not be my portion, in Jesus' name.

54. My heaven shall not be brass and my earth shall not be iron, in Jesus' name.

55. Powers speaking to the sun and moon against my star, expire and die, in Jesus' name.

56. Network of domestic witchcraft flying against me, scatter, in Jesus' name.

57. Projections of environmental witchcraft at night

blocking good things from locating me, wither, in Jesus' name.

58. Communication gadgets of the enemy, I block you, in Jesus' name.

59. Let the weapon of the enemy turn against the enemy, in Jesus' name.

60. Battles assigned to frustrate my efforts this year, be destroyed, in Jesus' name.

61. The word of the enchanters fighting my destiny, die, in Jesus' name.

62. Satanically empowered words caging my eagle, wither, in Jesus' name.

63. The wickedness of the wicked over my present and future, expire, die, in Jesus' name.

64. Every evil name the enemy is calling me, which is not ordained by God, be nullified, in Jesus' name.

65. The enemy that has vowed not to let me go, woe to you, die, in Jesus' name.

66. Evil association gathered to destroy me, scatter and die, in Jesus' name.

67. I release myself from the bondage of evil altars, in Jesus' name.

68. I vomit every satanic poison that I have swallowed, in Jesus' name.

69. I cancel every demonic dedication, in Jesus' name.

70. Axe of fire, cut down every tree of non-achievement in my life, in Jesus' name.

Freedom from satanic limitation by the fire of the Holy Ghost

71. Powers making my complete deliverance difficult, I set you ablaze, in Jesus' name.

72. Every sin that is giving the enemy power over me, O Lord, give me victory over them, in Jesus' name.

73. There is nothing too hard for God to do, therefore, possibility power of God, manifest in my life, in Jesus' name.

74. Every damage done to my life by forces of darkness, be repaired by the power of the Holy Ghost, in Jesus' name.

75. Spiritual sexual partners at night, die, in Jesus' name.

76. Plantation of darkness hindering my greatness, be buried, in Jesus' name.

77. Powers interfering with the flow of my favour, die, in Jesus' name.

78. Powers hijacking my favour, die, in Jesus' name.

79. Anti-greatness curses operating in my life, break and release me, in Jesus' name.

80. Strongman positioned to collect what is due to me, I overthrow you violently, in Jesus' name.

81. Witchcraft padlock holding me down at an evil bus stop, break asunder, in Jesus' name.

82. Anti-progress and anti-success powers, break and let me go, in Jesus' name.

83. Satanic embargo working against me, break, in Jesus' name.

84. Progress terminators, be terminated by fire, in Jesus' name.

85. My destiny, I prophesy upon you, you shall be great, in Jesus' name.

86. All my destiny helpers, I command you to appear, in Jesus' name.

87. Spoilers and robbers of my glorious destiny, run mad, in Jesus' name.

88. All my enemies gathered against me, before I open my eyes, scatter, in Jesus' name.

89. Satanic chapter opened against me, close by fire, in Jesus' name.

90. Woe unto every vessel that the enemy is using against me, in Jesus' name.

91. Arrow of darkness fired at me, go back to sender, in Jesus' name.

92. Satanic elders sitting on what belongs to me, I push you down from my blessing, in Jesus' name.

93. The words of enchanters fighting my destiny, die, in Jesus' name.

94. Satanically empowered word that is caging my eagle, wither, in Jesus' name.

95. I release myself from the bondage of evil altars, in Jesus' name.

96.   I vomit every satanic poison that I have swallowed, in Jesus' name.

97.   I break every evil authority over my life, in Jesus' name.

98.   Authority of any demonic strongman over my life, be broken, in Jesus' name.

99.   Authority of family shrine or idol over my destiny, break, in Jesus' name.

100.   Authority of witchcraft and familiar spirits over my life, be broken, in Jesus' name.

Bewitchment must come to an end

101.   Serpentine powers of bewitchment, wither, in Jesus' name.

102.   O heavens, mobilize adequate support for me to succeed, in Jesus' name.

103.   O Lord, anoint me with superior wisdom to beat all my competitors, in Jesus' name.

104.   Satanic resistance to my emergence as a candidate of double honour, perish, in Jesus' name.

105.   Every evil meeting being held against me, be buried, in Jesus' name.

106.   All physical and spiritual saboteurs militating against my success, expire, in Jesus' name.

107.   Anointing to be first among others, fall upon me, in

Jesus' name.

108. Marks of not living life to the full, be wiped off my life, in Jesus' name.

109. Anti-favour marks denying me my expected place in life, clear away, in Jesus' name.

110. O Lord, give me your permanent image to scare away all satanic agents from me, in Jesus' name.

111. Witchcraft marks tormenting my destiny, clear away, in Jesus' name.

112. Enemies making dark consultations to waste my life, be buried, in Jesus' name.

113. Powers using demonic marks to control my life negatively, be paralyzed, run mad, in Jesus' name.

114. Strange marks assigned to make me sorrow this year, be wiped off, in Jesus' name.

115. Satanic marks assigned to make me restless this year, clear away, in Jesus' name.

116. Mark of the enemy that wants poverty to be my identity, clear away, in Jesus' name.

117. Witchcraft marks that terminate joy and laughter, my life is not your candidate, clear away, in Jesus' name.

118. Evil marks that make one to labour and sweat without favour, clear away, in Jesus' name.

119. Demonic marks promoting emptiness and trading off my virtues, clear away, in Jesus' name.

120. Mark of 'no one shall come to your help now and in

the future,' be destroyed, in Jesus' name.

121. Powers diverting my favour to the wrong place or the wrong person, die, in Jesus' name.

122. Mark of perpetual slavery in my life and around my life, clear away, in Jesus' name.

123. Mark of darkness slowing down my speed, clear away, in Jesus' name.

124. Witchcraft baskets collecting my blessing for keeps, catch fire, in Jesus' name.

125. Witchcraft marks assigned to return me to zero, clear away, in Jesus' name.

126. All my problems shall expire today, in Jesus' name.

127. Evil marks programmed to make me fall into grievous error, clear away, in Jesus' name.

128. Mark of oppression causing confusion and delay in my life, be terminated, in Jesus' name.

129. The marks of witches and wizards denying me good things, be wiped off now, in Jesus' name.

130. Evil marks making me to work and another reap my harvest, die, in Jesus' name.

131. Marks of sorrow programmed into my calendar this year, clear away by fire, in Jesus' name.

132. Angels of war, arise, pursue my wasters and waste them, in Jesus' name.

133. Powers energizing my enemy to pursue me, die, in

Jesus' name.

134. Sword of fire, cut off the head of the serpent roaming around in the garden of my life, in Jesus' name.

Prayers to erase the marks of the enemy

135. The mark of the enemy that cannot be seen physically hiding in my body, clear away, by the Blood of Jesus.

136. Every mark of aimless existence, be robbed off, in Jesus' name.

137. Mark of slavery of the enemy, be removed, in Jesus' name.

138. Let no demon trouble me because I have in my body, the mark of Jesus Christ, in Jesus' name.

139. Mark of the antichrist, depart from me, in Jesus' name.

140. Every mark of darkness that gives the enemy access to my body, be removed now, in Jesus' name.

141. Holy Ghost, delete the mark of failure at the edge of breakthrough from me, in Jesus' name.

142. Mark of oppression, depression and obsession, clear away by fire, in Jesus' name.

143. Witchcraft trademark of ownership by satan, I am not your candidate, die, in Jesus' name.

144. Satanic identification mark, be rubbed off by the Blood of Jesus, in Jesus' name.

145. Mark of Jesus Christ, appear in my life. Mark of the antichrist disappear from my life, in Jesus' name.

146. Mark of unprofitable delay, clear away by fire, in Jesus' name.

147. Mark of finding simple things difficult, clear away by fire, in Jesus' name.

148. Mark of rejection, where I ought to be accepted, depart from me, in Jesus' name.

149. Mark of self-destruction, expire, in Jesus' name.

150. Mark of sudden death, my life rejects you, in Jesus' name.

151. Any wicked spirit spouse claiming I am married to him or her, it is a lie, die, in Jesus' name.

152. Mark of marital failure, leave me alone, in Jesus' name.

153. Mark of family idol claiming ownership of my life and destiny, die, in Jesus' name.

154. Any mark that is linking me to any body of water, clear away from me, in Jesus' name.

155. Mark of seasonal attacks, die, in Jesus' name.

156. Mark of gradual loss of property, die, in Jesus' name.

157. Mark of profitless hard work, be wiped off from me, in Jesus' name.

158. Familiar spirit marks, clear away from me, in Jesus' name.

351

159. Mark of suffering at old age, clear away, in Jesus' name.

160. Mark of strange sicknesses and diseases, die, in Jesus' name.

161. Witchcraft marks, symbol and label behind my affliction, catch fire, in Jesus' name.

162. Evil smell, depart from me now, in Jesus' name.

163. Evil marks chasing good things away from me, be erased, in Jesus' name.

164. Inherited evil marks, be cancelled, in Jesus' name.

165. O God, arise and let my potential tied down, be loosed, in Jesus' name.

166. Mark of rejection in the place of blessing, clear away, in Jesus' name.

167. All coven judgements passed on me, be nullified, in Jesus' name.

168. Money shall be not be scarce with me this year, in Jesus' name.

169. This year, I shall enjoy multiple sources of income, in Jesus' name.

170. Mark of diversion of expectations, be cancelled, in Jesus' name.

171. Mark of lack of helper, be erased, in Jesus' name.

172. Satanic pronouncement backed up by enchantment, die, in Jesus' name.

173. Mark of disfavour, die, in Jesus' name.

174. My angels of blessing, receive reinforcement, in Jesus' name.

175. Wicked horns lifted up against me, catch fire, in Jesus' name.

176. Mark of suffering for what I know nothing about, die, in Jesus' name.

177. Mark of 666 secretly encoded and affecting me negatively, catch fire, in Jesus' name.

178. Every mark of darkness on any of my items, be wiped off, in Jesus' name.

179. Visible or invisible marks of the enemy, be removed, in Jesus' name.

180. Every good thing the enemy has stolen from me, I take it back, in Jesus' name.

181. Powers attacking me from the bottom of the river, die, in Jesus' name.

182. Mark of spiritual defilement in the dream, be removed, in Jesus' name.

183. Every fetish power behind the problems I am going through, die, in Jesus' name.

184. Satanic materials projected into my body, disappear now, in Jesus' name.

185. Lord Jesus, arise and decorate me with the perfume of favour, in Jesus' name.

186. Power behind spiritual nakedness, die, in Jesus' name.

187. All my detained blessings, be released, in Jesus' name.

188. Every secretly inscribed evil mark, clear away, in Jesus' name.

189. My life shall not be overshadowed by evil marks, in Jesus' name.

190. Mark of poverty, die, in Jesus' name.

191. Every breakthrough forcefully snatched from me in the dream, I take it back, in Jesus' name.

192. Evil marks waging war against my progress, die, in Jesus' name.

193. Wind of affliction, I command you to return to where you are coming from, in Jesus' name.

194. Every coven decision taken to harm me, be nullified, in Jesus' name.

195. I shall not miss my season of divine visitation, in Jesus' name.

196. Every soul tie that connects me to any dead relative, be cancelled, in Jesus' name.

197. Any wicked sleep undertaken to harm me, the evil agent shall not wake up, in Jesus' name.

198. Every witchcraft vulture feeding on my breakthrough, die, in Jesus' name.

199. Marine altar behind the problems I am going through, die, in Jesus' name.

200. Mark of collective evil family pattern, be wiped off, in

354

Jesus' name.

201. Angelic carpenters, arise and break the horn of the Gentiles, in Jesus' name.

202. The broom of the enemy assigned to sweep away my blessings, catch fire, in Jesus' name.

203. O God, arise and anoint me for beauty and glory, in Jesus' name.

204. Since no hand can cover the glory of the sun, no evil mark shall cover my glory, in Jesus' name.

205. Sing praises to God who answers prayers

O Lord, I need a miracle (Mark 10:27)

206. O God of miracles, I need my own miracle now, in Jesus' name.

207. O God, arise and let the world know that I am serving a living God, in Jesus' name.

208. My harvest of ten years, gather together, and locate me, in Jesus' name.

209. Powers and forces blocking answers to my prayers, fall down and die, in Jesus' name.

210. Witchcraft conspiracy to delay my breakthrough, scatter, in Jesus' name.

211. By faith, I receive my long awaited breakthrough, in Jesus' name.

212. Evil birds crying against the manifestation of my

blessing, die, in Jesus' name.

213. Wind of positive change, blow in my favour quickly and speedily, in Jesus' name.

214. I shall not die before my glory shines, in Jesus' name.

215. Because of Jesus, I shall not fail, in Jesus' name.

216. I connect to mysterious breakthroughs by fire, in Jesus' name.

217. All my stolen blessings, I recover them now, in Jesus' name.

218. The spirit of get and lose, depart from me right now, in Jesus' name.

219. My life, I prophesy to you, move forward right now, in Jesus' name.

220. From now, I shall be in the right place at the right time, in Jesus' name.

221. O God, arise and raise a voice for me in unlikely places this year, in Jesus' name.

222. Every dark market, where what belongs to me is being sold, scatter, in Jesus' name.

223. Evil hands collecting what is due to me in the spirit realm, wither, in Jesus' name.

224. Evil umbrella preventing the flow of my blessing, catch fire, in Jesus' name.

225. My life, you shall not obey evil commands this year, in Jesus' name.

226. My expectations shall not be cut off, in Jesus' name.

227. Jesus said, 'It is finished', therefore, all my sorrows are over, in Jesus' name.

228. In Jesus' name, I shall not miss my season of breakthrough.

229. The eagle of my life, arise and fly high this year, in Jesus' name.

230. The enemy shall not be able to uproot me from my place of breakthrough, in Jesus' name.

231. My life must advertise the power of God this year, in Jesus' name.

232. Thou power of evil cover over my head, lose your hold over my life, in Jesus' name.

233. The God, who does great and wonderful things, remember me, in Jesus' name.

234. Jesus, the story changer, arise and change my story, in Jesus' name.

235. My problems shall bow before me, in Jesus' name.

Oppression must die

236. Every evil cabinet member legislating against my progress, scatter by fire, in Jesus' name.

237. Witchcraft pot cooking my health in any satanic coven, break to pieces, in Jesus' name.

238. The wicked hands employed against my wellbeing,

wither, in Jesus' name.

239. No one born of a woman shall use my destiny to gain promotion in any witchcraft coven, in Jesus' name.

240. Every witchcraft projection into my dream life, die, in Jesus' name.

241. O God that disgraced Haman before Mordecai, let all my stubborn pursuers experience public disgrace, in Jesus' name.

242. Anything standing on my way to the top, before I open my eyes, scatter, in Jesus' name.

243. Satanic instruction asking me to come down, I will not go down, be silenced and die, in Jesus' name.

244. Witchcraft command asking me to appear in any witchcraft meeting, I refuse to appear, die, in Jesus' name.

245. Witchcraft arrows fired against me, I command the arrows to go back to the sender, in Jesus' name.

246. I shall not die another man's death, in Jesus' name.

247. Anyone uttering incantations to Mother Earth against me, die with your incantations, in Jesus' name.

248. My head, reject evil loads, in Jesus' name.

249. Any witchcraft animal programmed into my body, wither and die, in Jesus' name.

250. Every spiritual dog barking against my breakthrough, I command the ground to open and swallow you now, in Jesus' name.

251. Thou power of affliction, frustration and limitations, die, in Jesus' name.

252. Thou power of multiple padlocks employed against me, break asunder, in Jesus' name.

253. Thou power of spiritual dowry behind my marital delay, die, in Jesus' name.

254. I break the curse of, "This is how you will go", in Jesus' name.

255. I break and loose myself from inherited family curses, in Jesus' name.

256. Spiritual chains tying me down, break and let me go, in Jesus' name.

257. O God, who answers by fire, my time has come, answer me by fire, in Jesus' name.

258. Powers attacking my source of income, the Lord is against you, die, in Jesus' name.

259. Every delegated strongman diverting my breakthrough, fall down and die, in Jesus' name.

260. Blood of Jesus, kill every disease hiding in my blood now, in Jesus' name.

261. O God, arise and let my glory manifest by fire, in Jesus' name.

262. Every altar or shrine that is killing good things in my life, die, in Jesus' name.

263. Blood of Jesus, write the obituary of all my stubborn

enemies, in Jesus' name.

264. Anything planted in me to destroy me, come out and die, in Jesus' name.

265. Every witchcraft pot cooking the affairs of my destiny, break and scatter, in Jesus' name.

266. Anointing to move forward, fall upon me, in Jesus' name.

267. Angel of my blessing, do not pass me by, in Jesus' name.

Praying off satanic arrows from your destiny (Psalm 11:2, Psalm 91:5)

268. Arrow of sudden death fired into my destiny, come out and return to where you came from, in Jesus' name.

269. Arrow fashioned to frustrate me in my place of destiny, backfire, in Jesus' name.

270. The poison of serpents from my foundation, dry up now, in Jesus' name.

271. Programmed battle intended to make me inefficient and ineffective in the pursuit of my God ordained destiny, come out and die, in Jesus' name.

272. Evil hand pressing me down, wither by fire, in Jesus' name.

273. Every arrow projected into my dream life to cause me pain, expire, in Jesus' name.

274. Tormenting arrows assigned to make me fail, come out of my life now, in Jesus' name.

275. Just as Hamman died in the place of Mordecai, my enemy must die in my place, in Jesus' name.

276. Any man who has decided to turn to other creatures in order to attack me, die suddenly, in Jesus' name.

277. All anti-progress arrows fired into my destiny from childhood, come out and never return forever, in Jesus' name.

278. Holy Ghost fire, with your purging fire, pass through my life now, in Jesus' name.

279. Every arrow of working and not seeing result in my foundation, die, in Jesus' name.

280. Every arrow designed to embarrass me, wither now, in Jesus' name.

281. Every chain anchoring my destiny to pain and suffering, die, in Jesus' name.

282. The garden of my life, yield abundance beyond the expectation of the enemies, in Jesus' name.

283. Evil rope tying me down unconsciously, break by fire, in Jesus' name.

284. Arrow of internal shame and external disgrace, backfire, in Jesus' name.

285. I withdraw my portion from the hands of domestic witchcraft, in Jesus' name.

361

286. Evil plantation of the dark world in my body, come out at once, in Jesus' name.

287. I release myself from dream contamination and pollution, in Jesus' name.

288. I withdraw my health from the control of ancient strongman, in Jesus' name.

289. Strangers programmed into my body through dreams, be suffocated to death, in Jesus' name.

290. Lord of host, by the greatness of your power, set me free now, in Jesus' name.

291. Rain of affliction behind seasonal affliction, stop right now, in Jesus' name.

292. The cord of the enemy that is dragging me to places I don't want to go in the dream, I cut you in pieces, in Jesus' name.

293. I destroy the finger of any native doctor assigned to divine evil against me, in Jesus' name.

294. Anywhere my spirit man has been arrested and caged, Holy Ghost fire, set my spirit free, in Jesus' name.

295. I put my hands on the neck of every unrepentant witch assigned against me and I break it to pieces, in Jesus' name.

296. Any arrow programmed to work against me at night, backfire, in Jesus' name.

297. The rod of the wicked, rise against the wicked, in Jesus' name.

298. Arrow of continuous affliction, die, in Jesus' name.

Killing sickness and infirmity
DAY ONE

299. O God, arise and consume any sickness in my body with your consuming fire, in Jesus' name.

300. Arrows of darkness fired into my body, come out, in Jesus' name.

301. My body, reject any terminal sickness by fire, in Jesus' name.

302. Every bloodline infirmity of my father's house, be uprooted from my body now, in Jesus' name.

303. Blood of Jesus, kill every sickness in my body now, in Jesus' name.

304. Every sickness or infirmity sponsored by demons in my body, I cast you out of my body, in Jesus' name.

305. Any arrow of sickness hiding in any part of my body, waiting to manifest as terminal sickness, die to the root, in Jesus' name.

306. Goliath of infirmity assigned against my health, die, in Jesus' name.

307. Lord Jesus, you are the healer, heal me and I shall be healed, in Jesus' name.

308. Owner of evil load in my life, appear and carry your load, in Jesus' name.

309. Eaters of flesh and drinkers of blood, I paralyze your power over my health, in Jesus' name.

310. I challenge my entire body with the fire of God, in Jesus' name.

311. All serpents programmed against my health, die, in Jesus' name.

312. Holy Ghost, redeem my body from the power of infirmity, in Jesus' name.

313. Everything in my body that is not planted by God, hear the word the Lord, come out by fire, in Jesus' name.

314. Every problem carried over from the dream world, die, in Jesus' name.

315. Blood of Jesus, become divine immunity in my body, in Jesus' name.

316. Thou power of inherited sicknesses in my life, die, in Jesus' name.

317. O God, arise and prosper the works of my hands, in Jesus' name.

318. Sicknesses and diseases, expire, in Jesus' name.

319. Every inherited infirmity and sickness in my body, die, in Jesus' name.

320. My head, reject every arrow of affliction, in Jesus' name.

321. Every money-consuming sickness and disease, die, in Jesus' name.

322. Terminal sickness and disease, be terminated, in

Jesus' name.

323. Holy Ghost fire, burn off evil arrows, in Jesus' name.

324. Programmed sickness and disease, wither, in Jesus' name.

325. Give thanks to God for answers to your prayers, in Jesus' name.

DAY TWO

326. Killer sickness and disease, my life is not your candidate, die, in Jesus' name.

327. I transfuse the blood of Jesus into my body, in Jesus' name.

328. My body, reject every garment of sorrow, in Jesus' name.

329. Every sickness in my body, dry up now, in Jesus' name.

330. Poison in my body through night feeding, die, in Jesus' name.

331. The hand of a witch assigned to introduce sickness into my body, die, in Jesus' name.

332. Evil plantation, come out of my life, in Jesus' name.

333. Witchcraft pot cooking my health, catch fire, in Jesus' name.

334. Marine materials programmed into my body, catch fire, in Jesus' name.

335. My body shall not be a dumping ground for

sicknesses and diseases, in Jesus' name.

336. Every organ of my body that is dead, come alive, in Jesus' name.

337. Witchcraft arrow fired into my blood, come out and die, in Jesus' name.

338. The smell of mortuary, depart from me, in Jesus' name.

339. Any power that wants to put me on a wheelchair, die, in Jesus' name.

340. I am for blessing, I am not for curses, in Jesus' name.

341. Spirit of insomnia, depart from me, in Jesus' name.

342. Every projection of witchcraft into my dream life, catch fire, in Jesus' name.

343. Evil hands manipulating my health, wither, in Jesus' name.

344. O Lord, Jehovah Rapha, heal me and I shall be healed, in Jesus' name.

345. Any sickness or disease waiting to eat up my body, die, in Jesus' name.

346. I shall not die but live to declare the goodness of the Lord, in Jesus' name.

347. Blood sucking demon, die, in Jesus' name.

348. Goliath of sickness, die, in Jesus' name.

349. Sickness due to inherited yokes, die, in Jesus' name.

350. O God, arise and consume any sickness in my body

with your consuming fire, in Jesus' name.

351. Arrow of darkness fired into my body, come out, in Jesus' name.

352. My body, reject terminal sickness by fire, in Jesus' name.

353. Give thanks to God for answers to your prayers.

DAY THREE

354. Every bloodline infirmity of my father's house, be uprooted from my body now, in Jesus' name.

355. Blood of Jesus, kill every sickness in my body now, in Jesus' name.

356. Every sickness or infirmity sponsored by demons in my body, I cast you out of my body, in Jesus' name.

357. Any arrow of sickness hiding in any part of my body, waiting to manifest as terminal sickness, die to the root, in Jesus' name.

358. Goliath of infirmity assigned against my health, die, in Jesus' name.

359. Lord Jesus, you are the healer, heal me and I shall be healed, in Jesus' name.

360. Owner of evil load in my life, appear and carry your load, in Jesus' name.

361. Eaters of flesh and drinkers of blood, I paralyze your power over my health, in Jesus' name.

362. I challenge my entire body with the fire of God, in Jesus' name.

363. All serpents programmed against my health, die, in Jesus' name.

364. Holy Ghost, redeem my body from the power of infirmity, in Jesus' name.

365. Give thanks and praises to the Lord for your healing and deliverance, in Jesus' name.

366. The law of sickness and disease working against me, be cancelled, in Jesus' name.

367. My body shall not be an incubator of sickness and disease, in Jesus' name.

368. Rope of darkness tying me down for sickness and infirmity, catch fire, in Jesus' name.

369. Thou spell of thou shall not prosper assigned against me, be nullified, in Jesus' name.

370. Every embargo refusing my dominion, break, in Jesus' name.

371. Seasonal sickness programmed into my body, wither, in Jesus' name.

372. Venom of serpents and scorpions, come out of my body, in Jesus' name.

373. Finger of any dark personality troubling my health, wither, in Jesus' name.

374. Give thanks to God for answers to your prayers.

Breaking Evil Soul Tie

375. I break the yoke of ancestral soul tie holding me down, in Jesus' name.

376. The curse of perpetual slavery working against me, break, in Jesus' name.

377. Covenant of blood and sacrifice keeping problems in place in my life, be dissolved, in Jesus' name.

378. Powers that have vowed that they would rather die than see me prosper, die, in Jesus' name.

379. Every soul tie with any man living or dead, break, in Jesus' name.

380. The covenant of the blood of Jesus, deliver me from evil family pattern, in Jesus' name.

381. Powers that make good things to jump over me, come out of me, in Jesus' name.

382. Witchcraft embargo of 'thou shall not excel' placed on my life, break, in Jesus' name.

383. Every blood tie with familiar or ancestral spirits, break, in Jesus' name.

384. Every ancient prison house, let me go, in Jesus' name.

385. Evil words spoken by the wicked, troubling my life, wither, in Jesus' name.

386. Seasonal battles assigned to stop my breakthroughs, die, in Jesus' name.

387. Witchcraft marks suppressing my personal

testimony, clear away, in Jesus' name.

388. O God, make haste and bring me out of satanic detention, in Jesus' name.

389. Powers enforcing satanic wishes on my life, die, in Jesus' name.

390. The voice of impossibility speaking loudly against my star, wither, in Jesus' name.

391. Serpent that wastes effort and labour, die, in Jesus' name.

392. Thunder fire of God, break the satanic cage built around my life, in Jesus' name.

393. Crippling power in my foundation, die, in Jesus' name.

394. Evil covering assigned against my head, I set you ablaze, in Jesus' name.

395. Evil arrow that paralyzes glorious destinies, go back to your sender, in Jesus' name.

396. Padlock of darkness tying down my glory, die, break to pieces, in Jesus' name.

397. Evil wind directed at me, backfire, in Jesus' name.

398. Spell and hexes of frustration, break and release me, in Jesus' name.

399. Evil commands issued against me, my life and destiny reject you, in Jesus' name.

400. Satanic burial done against my marriage, wither, in Jesus' name.

401. Evil prayers made against me on any altar, be cancelled, in Jesus' name.

402. Dark broom sweeping away good things from me, catch fire, in Jesus' name.

403. Give thanks to God for answers to prayers.

PRAYER TO DESTROY THE SATANIC REMOTE CONTROLLING POWER WORKING AGAINST YOUR LIFE

404. The foundational strongman assigned to cripple my elevation, fall down and die, in Jesus' name.

405. O God, arise and let the wicked be swallowed by the evil they have imagined against me, in Jesus' name.

406. Every door of progress shut against me, open, in Jesus' name.

407. Every resistance to my divine acceleration and promotion, be dashed to pieces, in Jesus' name.

408. Thou power of emptiers and wasters assigned against me, be destroyed, in Jesus' name.

409. Internal and external devices of domestic witchcraft blocking the rising of my star, burn to ashes, in Jesus' name.

410. Serpents and scorpions of failure at the edge of success, die, in Jesus' name.

411. No wickedness shall prevail against me, in Jesus' name.

412. My star and glory, reject bewitchment, in Jesus' name.

413. Haman diverting my breakthroughs, die, in Jesus' name.

414. Witchcraft padlock that holds destinies down in the place of frustration, die, in Jesus' name.

415. Association of wicked elders on assignment against my life, scatter, in Jesus' name.

416. Evil speaking against my success, wither, in Jesus' name.

417. O God by your power, bring me out of every valley of working without results, die, in Jesus' name.

418. Invisible chains of environmental witchcraft in my hands, break, in Jesus' name.

419. Satanic legislation working against me, be nullified, in Jesus' name.

420. The concluded work of darkness against my prosperity, scatter, in Jesus' name.

421. The key of my promotion in the hands of spiritual robbers, be released to me now, in Jesus' name.

422. Ancestral witchcraft embargo, break, in Jesus' name.

423. Wind of positive change, blow in my favour, in Jesus' name.

424. The wickedness of the wicked, expire today, in Jesus' name.

425. Every satanic set up to frustrate me, be dismantled, in

Jesus' name.

426. Thou spirit of almost there but never there assigned against me, die, in Jesus' name.

427. In Jesus' name, I shall not die before the manifestation of my glory.

428. O ye gate of hell fashioned against my progress, scatter, in Jesus' name.

429. The rod of the wicked shall not rest upon the lot of my life, in Jesus' name.

430. Enchantment from the sun, moon and stars, fail woefully, in Jesus' name.

431. Give thanks to God for answers to prayers.

DESTROY SATANIC COVENANT THAT HINDER PROGRESS

432. I break every covenant of limitation, in Jesus' name.

433. What is meant to kill me shall die in my place, in Jesus' name.

434. No organ of my body shall be donated to the dark kingdom, in Jesus' name.

435. Evil gathering of the wicked against my future, scatter, in Jesus' name.

436. The dominion of my glorious destiny shall not be crippled, in Jesus' name.

437. The strongman that does not want my glory to rise and shine, be destroyed, in Jesus' name.

438. I receive anointing to break forth and break through,

in Jesus' name.

439. The wall of Jericho standing between me and my breakthrough, fall, Jesus' name.

440. Failure and defeat shall not be my portion, in Jesus' name.

441. Witchcraft burial conducted to bury the good things of my life, die, in Jesus' name.

442. Witchcraft cage fashioned against me, break, in Jesus' name.

443. Witchcraft warehouse, release my wealth that you are holding, in Jesus' name.

444. Witchcraft garment of demotion, I set you ablaze, in Jesus' name.

445. Evil line which the enemy says I cannot cross, I cross over by fire, in Jesus' name.

446. Owner of the load of infirmity, carry your load, in Jesus' name.

447. Every closed chapter of my divine manifestation and intervention, open, in Jesus' name.

448. Thou power of collective captivity, break, in Jesus' name.

449. Holy Ghost, consume the evil seed growing in my life, in Jesus' name.

450. Every problem that has a name in my life, wither, in Jesus' name.

451. Blood of Jesus, dissolve every satanic arrow by your burning power, in Jesus' name.

452. By the power that raised Lazarus from the dead, let my stubborn problem receive solution now, in Jesus' name.

453. I shake off sickness and disease from my body, in Jesus' name.

454. I shake off evil arrows from my destiny, in Jesus' name.

455. I curse the root of slavery in my life to die, in Jesus' name.

456. Bondage expanders and yoke promoters, die, in Jesus' name.

457. Poison that leads to sudden death, come out of me, in Jesus' name.

458. Thank God for answers to your prayers.

EJECTING THE POISON OF DARKNESS FROM YOUR BODY

459. Poison of sudden death, come out of my body, in Jesus' name.

460. Dark plantation, come out of me, in Jesus' name.

461. My life and destiny, receive empowerment to succeed, in Jesus' name.

462. Witchcraft poison as a result of eating polluted food, come out of me, in Jesus' name.

463. Satanic programmed object in my body, come out ,in Jesus' name.

464. Dark table of domestic witchcraft, catch fire, in Jesus' name.

465. Dark room caging my wealth, release my wealth, in Jesus' name.

466. I declare war against poverty, sickness and failure, in Jesus' name.

467. Every sickness that has a name in my life, die, in Jesus' name.

468. Every witchcraft basket flying for my sake, catch fire, in Jesus' name.

469. Evil arrow programmed to any dark hour of the night against me, backfire, in Jesus' name.

470. My life and destiny shall not be covered by darkness, in Jesus' name.

471. My spirit, soul and body, reject evil plantation, in Jesus' name.

472. Holy Ghost, make my life conducive for your presence, in Jesus' name.

473. Demons shall not use my body as their evil habitation, in Jesus' name.

474. Death and destruction shall not feed on my body, in Jesus' name.

475. Every blood speaking against my blood line, shut up and die, in Jesus' name.

476. Every unconscious witchcraft altar ministering against me, catch fire, in Jesus' name.

477. Arrow of affliction fired against me, lose your hold, in Jesus' name.

478. Where is the Lord God of Elijah? Manifest your power and let the altar of magicians hired against me crumble, in Jesus' name.

479. Satanic dedication that speaks against my glory, be silenced, in Jesus' name.

480. Every good thing the houses I have lived in the past have stolen from me, I take it back, in Jesus' name.

481. I vomit every dark food, which I have eaten from the table of the enemy, in Jesus' name.

482. Let every stubborn pursuer of my life turn back from me, in Jesus' name.

483. My life, you shall not cooperate with evil designers, in Jesus' name.

484. Chain of oppression limiting me, break, in Jesus' name.

485. Holy Ghost, package me for miracles, signs and wonders, in Jesus' name.

486. O Lord, according to the greatness of your power, manifest yourself in my life, in Jesus' name.

487. My body shall not be a habitation of devils, in Jesus' name.

488. Any dark object representing me in the dark kingdom, catch fire, in Jesus' name.
489. Give thanks to God for answers to your prayers.

DELIVERANCE FROM THE SHADOW OF DEATH

490. Spirit of death and hell, lose your hold upon my life, in Jesus' name.
491. Any strongman sitting on what belongs to me, I push you out by fire, in Jesus' name.
492. Every mark of slavery placed upon my life, clear away, in Jesus' name.
493. Anointing of double recovery, fall upon my life, in Jesus' name.
494. O God, arise and single me out for your miracles, in Jesus' name.
495. O God, arise and make haste to bless me, in Jesus' name.
496. The enemy shall not succeed in removing me from my place of blessing, in Jesus' name.
497. My destiny helpers, where are you? Appear, in Jesus' name.
498. O God, rend the heavens for my sake and bless me, in Jesus' name.
499. The spell of wrong association, break and release me, in Jesus' name.
500. Powers that have stolen from me, give me back what

you have stolen from me, in Jesus' name.

501. Every organized warfare of witchcraft network, scatter, in Jesus' name.

502. Powers praying satanic prayers against me, fall down and die, in Jesus' name.

503. Every witchcraft mirror monitoring my life, catch fire, in Jesus' name.

504. Wicked powers swallowing the result of my prayers, fall down and die, in Jesus' name.

505. Satanic umbrella preventing heavenly blessings from reaching me, die, in Jesus' name.

506. Arrow of confusion fired at my brain, catch fire, in Jesus' name.

507. Satanic garment of demotion, Holy Ghost fire, consume it, in Jesus' name.

508. Anything done against me under satanic anointing, expire, in Jesus' name.

509. Owner of evil load, appear and carry your load, in Jesus' name.

510. Strange powers contending and protesting against my breakthroughs, catch fire, in Jesus' name.

511. The poison of darkness in my root, come out now, in Jesus' name.

512. Evil dedication that has stolen from me, I recover what you stole from me, in Jesus' name.

513. Witchcraft padlock caging me, break to pieces, in

Jesus' name.

514. Witchcraft pot of bewitchment, break to pieces, in Jesus' name.

515. Every instrument of manipulation of my star, wither, in Jesus' name.

516. Every door opened to the enemy to attack me, close, in Jesus' name.

517. Blood of Jesus, purge my foundation from all satanic pollution, in Jesus' name.

518. Poison of serpents and scorpions, come out of my body, in Jesus' name.

519. The blood of Jesus, purge my system from all satanic contamination, in Jesus' name.

520. Thank God for answers to your prayers.

PULLING DOWN SATANIC STRONGHOLDS MILITATING AGAINST YOU

521. Every dark stronghold waging war against me, I pull you down, in Jesus' name.

522. Finger of God, unseat the strongman assigned against my life, in Jesus' name.

523. Angel of God, invade every dark coven assigned against me, in Jesus' name.

524. I cut off my body, soul and spirit from every ancestral hold, in Jesus' name.

525. Anointing of all round recovery, fall upon me, in Jesus'

name.

526. Every demonic court in session against me, scatter, in Jesus' name.

527. Every evil decision taken against me in the dark, scatter, in Jesus' name.

528. O God, let all my oppressors oppress themselves to death, in Jesus' name.

529. I reject every demonic limitation of my life and destiny, in Jesus' name.

530. The strongman from both sides of my families, destroy yourselves, in Jesus' name.

531. Every spirit of Herod that wants to use me as sacrifice, die, in Jesus' name.

532. I bind the spirit of poverty; lose your hold upon my life, in Jesus' name.

533. O God, arise and subdue my enemy under me, in Jesus' name.

534. Let the blood of Jesus speak woe to every weapon the enemy is using against me, in Jesus' name.

535. Blood of Jesus, kill every spirit of infirmity in my body, in Jesus' name.

536. I curse the root of the work of darkness in my life, in Jesus' name.

537. Evil bird flying for my sake, I shoot you down, in Jesus' name.

538. O God, by your possibility power, give me the neck of my enemy, in Jesus' name.

539. The negative effect of idol worship of my father, be nullified, in Jesus' name.

540. Satanic dreams that trigger oppression, die, in Jesus' name.

541. Deposit of spiritual spouse, dry up, in Jesus' name.

542. Plantation of demons in the dream, be evacuated, in Jesus' name.

543. Holy Ghost, visit my life with your burning fire, in Jesus' name.

544. Dream criminals visiting me at night, what are you looking for? Die, in Jesus' name.

545. Every evil family pattern of marital distress, die, in Jesus' name.

546. No more frustration and satanic embargo, in Jesus' name.

547. Powers making life difficult for me, die, in Jesus' name.

548. O God, arise and let everything you have made promote me, in Jesus' name.

549. Every good thing I lay my hands upon shall prosper, in Jesus' name.

550. Thou power of stagnancy, break and release me, in Jesus' name.

382

551. Thank God for answers to your prayers.

A CRY OF SOLUTION TO DIFFICULT SITUATIONS

552. O God, arise and favour me on every side, in Jesus' name.

553. Ancient robbers stealing from me, give me back what you stole from me, in Jesus' name.

554. O God, arise and anchor my destiny to profitable success, in Jesus' name.

555. O God, arise and soak my life in the anointing of success, in Jesus' name.

556. O God, arise and increase my speed, in Jesus' name.

557. Dark powers in my foundation frustrating my efforts, die, in Jesus' name.

558. Devourers, you shall not devour me, in Jesus' name.

559. Evil chains of stagnancy, break and let me go, in Jesus' name.

560. Astral projection of darkness into my dream life, expire, in Jesus' name.

561. Dark plantation assigned to cage my health, die, in Jesus' name.

562. I shall prevail over all my enemies, in Jesus' name.

563. O God, arise and make a way for me where there is no way, in Jesus' name.

564. I withdraw my destiny from the control of domestic

witchcraft, in Jesus' name.

565. Contrary voice speaking against me, be silenced, in Jesus' name.

566. Satanic bank keeping my money, release it now, in Jesus' name.

567. The wicked spirit that promotes satanic dreams, die, in Jesus' name.

568. Anyone sacrificing animals to cage me, expire, in Jesus' name.

569. Anyone hiring evil prophets against me, expire, in Jesus' name.

570. I pursue, I overtake and I recover all, in Jesus' name.

571. Rain of abundant blessings, soak my life, in Jesus' name.

572. Anointing to succeed where others have failed, fall upon me, in Jesus' name.

573. I fire back every arrow of failure fired against me, in Jesus' name.

574. Anyone cursing my destiny in the dark, be silenced, in Jesus' name.

575. The plan of the wicked to make me labour in vain, fail, in Jesus' name.

576. The battle of life shall not consume me, in Jesus' name.

577. Dark charms buried for my sake, expire, in Jesus' name.

578. Anti-promotion dreams, die, in Jesus' name.

579. My destiny shall not be covered in shame and reproach, in Jesus' name.

580. The spirit of 'almost there' working against me, die, in Jesus' name.

581. I prophesy success, peace and progress on my life, in Jesus' name.

582. Give thanks to God for answers to your prayers.

DELIVERANCE FROM STUBBORN FOUNDATIONAL BONDAGE

583. I bind the strongman over my life and destiny, in Jesus' name.

584. Demonic instruction given to Mother Earth to harm me, expire, in Jesus' name.

585. The horn of darkness assigned against me, wither, in Jesus' name.

586. The padlock of household wickedness, break to pieces, in Jesus' name.

587. Witchcraft aggression against my star, scatter, in Jesus' name.

588. Garment of shame, catch fire, in Jesus' name.

589. O God, arise and rend the heavens for my sake, in Jesus' name.

590. Spell of darkness limiting me, break to pieces, in Jesus' name.

591. I arrest, paralyse and destroy every serpent of delay assigned against me, in Jesus' name.
592. Marine cage, break and release me, in Jesus' name.
593. The chain of glory killers, break, in Jesus' name.
594. The enemy of my open heavens, expire, in Jesus' name.
595. Powers asking me to appear where I am not supposed to appear, die, in Jesus' name.
596. Blessings of the Lord without sorrow, explode in my life, in Jesus' name.
597. O God, arise and glorify yourself in my life, in Jesus' name.
598. I break the authority of demons over my life, in Jesus' name.
599. Every crystal ball of darkness, catch fire, in Jesus' name.
600. Every witchcraft basket caging my wealth, catch fire, in Jesus' name.
601. Evil pilot of the satanic aircraft against me, crash land, in Jesus' name.
602. My talent, be connected to favour permanently, in Jesus' name.
603. Witchcraft cauldron working against me, catch fire, in Jesus' name.
604. Every bewitchment on my certificate, be removed, in

Jesus' name.

605. Evil pot cooking my flesh, catch fire, in Jesus' name.

606. Satanic trade by barter against my life, expire, in Jesus' name.

607. Witchcraft handwriting of failure and defeat in my life, clear away, in Jesus' name.

608. Spirit of divination assigned against my future, expire, in Jesus' name.

609. My life shall not harbour any seed of darkness, in Jesus' name.

610. My foundation, you shall not stop my rising, in Jesus' name.

611. O God, arise and advance my life by fire, in Jesus' name.

BREAKING THE BACKBONE OF DOMESTIC WITCHCRAFT

612. I break the backbone of stubborn domestic witchcraft powers assigned against me, in Jesus' name.

613. Witchcraft radar and mirror of darkness assigned against me, catch fire, in Jesus' name.

614. Powers that suck blood, my life is not your candidate, in Jesus' name.

615. Witchcraft animals programmed against me, die, in Jesus' name.

616. Holy Ghost, break the cord of darkness dragging me

to the wrong location, in Jesus' name.

617. Arrow of spiritual and physical paralysis fired at me, backfire, in Jesus' name.

618. Ancestral cage holding my destiny, break, in Jesus' name.

619. Battles that sponsor gradual loss of good things, die, in Jesus' name.

620. The investment of household witchcraft on my life and destiny, catch fire, in Jesus' name.

621. Thou power of sweating without results, die, in Jesus' name.

622. Evil dedication working against me, break, in Jesus' name.

623. Counterfeit garment of stagnancy, catch fire, in Jesus' name.

624. Eaters of flesh and drinkers of blood, my life is not your candidate, die, in Jesus' name.

625. Poverty yokes, break from my neck, in Jesus' name.

626. Padlock of darkness holding my breakthrough, catch fire, in Jesus' name.

627. Every band of sickness holding my favour, break, in Jesus' name.

628. Poison of marine, come out of my body, in Jesus' name.

629. Witchcraft instrument of manipulation assigned

against me, catch fire, in Jesus' name.

630. The spell of thou shall not excel on my life, break, in Jesus' name.

631. Thunder fire of God, destroy every satanic cage around me, in Jesus' name.

632. Witchcraft mirror monitoring my life, break to pieces, in Jesus' name.

633. O God, arise and break the yoke of poverty in my life, die, in Jesus' name.

634. My life shall not harbour the anointing of defeat, in Jesus' name.

635. Divine opportunity beyond explanation, manifest in my life by fire, in Jesus' name.

636. Father Lord, let your angels of blessing locate me today, in Jesus' name.

637. My glory shall not be exchanged, in Jesus' name.

638. Family strongman sponsoring poverty and failure in my life, die, in Jesus' name.

639. Rain of divine favour, fall upon me, in Jesus' name.

640. O God, arise and turn my sorrow to joy, in Jesus' name.

641. Give thanks to God for answers to your prayers.

SPEAKING DESTRUCTION TO INFIRMITY

642. Anything covering my destiny for evil, be removed, in Jesus' name.

643. The seed of witchcraft in my foundation, be uprooted,

in Jesus' name.

644. Anointing that breaks yokes, break every yoke of backwardness in my life, in Jesus' name.

645. Evil chains binding my legs and feet, break, in Jesus' name.

646. Evil growth hiding in any area of my body, be dissolved, in Jesus' name.

647. I command my problem to enter into problem, in Jesus' name.

648. The seed of poverty and hardship in my life, die, in Jesus' name.

649. Veil of darkness covering my face, clear away, in Jesus' name.

650. By the power in the blood of Jesus, my bondage enter into bondage, in Jesus' name.

651. I am ordained for success, whether the enemy likes it or not, in Jesus' name.

652. Umbrella of failure, release me and let me go, in Jesus' name.

653. I shall become everything God has ordained me to be, in Jesus' name.

654. Mark of failure upon my hands, clear away, in Jesus' name.

655. Because Jesus never fails, I shall not fail, in Jesus' name.

656. Arrow of demotion from grace to grass in my life, die, in Jesus' name.

657. O Lord, I need a change in my life today, in Jesus' name.

658. Powers keeping me on the same spot, I break your yokes in my life, in Jesus' name.

659. I release myself from the night of embarrassment, in Jesus' name.

660. Darkness hiding in my father's house, be exposed, in Jesus' name.

661. Enemy of my peace and joy, fall down and die, in Jesus' name.

662. Arrow of slow death fired against me, die, in Jesus' name.

663. Thou power of inherited bondage, break and release me, in Jesus' name.

664. Every activity of spiritual spouses behind what I am going through, die, in Jesus' name.

665. Masquerade of darkness pursuing me in the dream, die, in Jesus' name.

666. The rod of the wicked rising up against me in the dream, burn to ashes, in Jesus' name.

667. Arrow of pain and discomfort, go back to your senders, in Jesus' name.

668. O Lord, connect me to my miracles in this season, in

Jesus' name.

669. I bind the spirit of infirmity, lose your hold upon my life, in Jesus' name.

670. Every tongue contrary to my peace, dry up, in Jesus' name.

671. Every soul tie to any covenant of affliction, break, in Jesus' name.

673. Powers stealing from me, I cut you off, in Jesus' name.

673. Give thanks to God for answers to your prayers.

DESTROYING THE SPIRIT OF EMPTIERS OVER YOUR LIFE

674. I break the teeth of spiritual masquerades swallowing my blessings, in Jesus' name.

675. I release myself from every conscious and unconscious witchcraft initiation, in Jesus' name.

676. My life shall not be a habitation of devils, in Jesus' name.

677. Every good thing that witchcraft power has emptied out of my life, come back, in Jesus' name.

678. I dethrone every queen and king of darkness ruling in my life, in Jesus' name.

679. The organs of my body shall not be devoured by eaters of flesh and drinkers of blood, in Jesus' name.

680. I challenge my internal organs with burning coals of fire, in Jesus' name.

681 Poison of darkness that renders destinies useless, come out of my body and die, in Jesus' name.

682. The activities of witchcraft in my family, be terminated, in Jesus' name.

683. Evil plantations of witchcraft in my body, come out and die, in Jesus' name.

684. The blood of ritual and sacrific speaking against my moving forward, be silenced, in Jesus' name.

685. Owners of evil load, carry your load now, in Jesus' name.

686. Every inherited mark of failure, be cut off from me, in Jesus' name.

687. Dirty and filthy hands of witchcraft troubling my life, wither, in Jesus' name.

688. Every dark presence magnetizing problems into my life, be destroyed, in Jesus' name.

689. Every organized warfare to strip me naked physically and spiritually, die, in Jesus' name.

690. Whoever used my pictures to programme poverty into my life shall fail, in Jesus' name.

691. Thou power of the emptier, die, in Jesus' name.

692. Witchcraft umbrella blocking favour from flowing to me, catch fire, in Jesus' name.

693. Witchcraft animals swallowing my wealth, die, in Jesus' name.

694. Let the arrows of witchcraft organized for my sake

393

backfire, in Jesus' name.

695. I shall not be forgotten, where I am supposed to be remembered, in Jesus' name.

696. The serpent of the magician swallowing my breakthroughs, I kill you with the sword of fire, in Jesus' name.

697. The evil veil covering my eyes from seeing what I am supposed to see, catch fire, in Jesus' name.

698. Every pot of enchantment against me, break to pieces, in Jesus' name.

699. My blessing, come out of the cage of witchcraft, in Jesus' name.

700. Satanic priests operating any dark altar against me, fall down and die, in Jesus' name.

701. Every power of witchcraft cooking my flesh, break to pieces, in Jesus' name.

702. Agenda of envious witchcraft targeted against me, die, in Jesus' name.

703. The crying blood against my success and progress, be silenced, in Jesus' name.

704. Every household witchcraft employing fetish power against me, wither, in Jesus' name.

705. My spirit, soul and body shall not be bewitched, in

Jesus' name.

706. Every witchcraft food I have eaten that is bringing problems into my life, come out and die, in Jesus' name.

707. My life, possess your possessions by fire, in Jesus' name.

708. Give thanks to God for answers to your prayers.

PRAYERS AGAINST THE ATTACK OF BAD BODY ODOUR OR BAD BREATH

709. Every evil odour sprayed on me at night, be roasted by fire, in Jesus' name.

710. Every pollution in the dream that scares helpers away during the day, burn to ashes, in Jesus' name.

711. Blood of Jesus, pass through my entire system and flush out evil smell, in Jesus' name.

712. Holy Ghost, let your burning fire burn off inherited evil smell, in Jesus' name.

713. Every witchcraft injection to poison my spirit man, clear away by the blood of Jesus, in Jesus' name.

714. I break and release myself from every smell of death, in Jesus' name.

715. Thou witchcraft perfume of gradual decay, die, in

Jesus' name.

716. Every witchcraft perfume of rejection, blood of Jesus, clear it away from me, in Jesus' name.

717. Witchcraft arrow drying the oil of favour from my head, come out and die, in Jesus' name.

718. Strange personality following me anywhere I go, receive the arrow of death, in Jesus' name.

719. I release myself from the pollution emanating from the waters, in Jesus' name.

720. Witchcraft urination on my project of prosperity, dry up by fire, in Jesus' name.

721. Evil seed terminating progress and joy in my life, be uprooted by fire, in Jesus' name.

722. Witchcraft ointment on my forehead, dry up, in Jesus' name.

723. Every dream promoting setbacks in my life, be nullified by the blood of Jesus, in Jesus' name.

724. Evil visitors visiting my house at night, fall down and die, in Jesus' name.

725. O God, arise and cancel any evil prayer against me, in Jesus' name.

726. Holy Ghost, anoint me with the special ointment of favour, in Jesus' name.

727. Thou chains of dark oppression, break off from me, in Jesus' name.

728. Every witchcraft remote controlling device working against me, burn to ashes, in Jesus' name.

729. My picture on any evil altar being used against my health, burn to ashes, in Jesus' name.

730. I shake out of my life every satanic deposit of marine witchcraft, in Jesus' name.

731. Evil transfer through satanic handshake, catch fire, in Jesus' name.

732. Evil seed of demotion, come out of my life, in Jesus' name.

733. Thou power of incantations assigned to cage my spirit man, be destroyed, in Jesus' name.

734. Every conscious or unconscious soul tie with any witch, break, in Jesus' name.

735. Soul tie with any family idol, break and let me go, in Jesus' name.

736. Domestic witchcraft bent on disgracing my star, die, in Jesus' name.

737. Holy Ghost, make me too hot for any witchcraft manipulation, in Jesus' name.

738. Evil words from the tongue of Jezebel sent to make me confused, backfire, in Jesus' name.

739. Give thanks to God for answers to your prayers.

PRAYER OF DIVINE POSSIBILITY FOR UNCOMMON OPPORTUNITY (EPHESIANS 3:20)

740. My heaven of possibility, open, in Jesus' name.

741. I shall not be a deficit to heaven and a liability on earth, in Jesus' name.

742. Power of God to scale new heights this year, fall upon me, in Jesus' name.

743. The season of my celebration shall not be postponed, in Jesus' name.

744. The achievement that no one in my family has achieved, by divine power, I shall achieve it this year, in Jesus' name.

745. O God, arise and strengthen my hands to war and my fingers to battle, in Jesus' name.

746. What God did not plant in my life, which is a plantation of the enemy, be uprooted by fire, in Jesus' name.

747. I shall not be a struggler in Zion, in Jesus' name.

748. Every satanic embargo placed on my life, be lifted by fire, in Jesus' name.

749. Evil embargo placed on my family, be broken by the power in the blood of Jesus, in Jesus' name.

750. Evil barrier placed on my progress, I blot you out with the blood of Jesus, in Jesus' name.

751. I exempt myself from every foundational covenant by

fire, in Jesus' name.

752. I free myself from every evil ancestral yoke by fire, in Jesus' name.

753. You evil blockade in my life; be demolished by fire, in Jesus' name.

754. Every power that has sworn that I will not be set free as long as they are alive, die by fire, in Jesus' name.

755. You altar of my father's house, speaking against me, I silence you by the blood of Jesus, in Jesus' name.

756. I refuse to be chained to any evil altar, in Jesus' name.

757. Creative power of the Lord Jesus Christ, perfect everything that concerns me today, in Jesus' name.

758. I bind and cast the spirit of failure and defeat out of my life, in Jesus' name.

759. I withdraw my wealth from the ancient altars of my father's house, in Jesus' name.

760. The seed of my greatness, receive divine fertilizer, in Jesus' name.

BREAKING ANTI-MARRIAGE CURSES AND COVENANTS (ISAIAH 10:27)

761. The family curse that is strengthening marital delay against me, break by fire, in Jesus' name.

762. My divine ordained partner, wherever you are, appear by fire, in Jesus' name.

763. Every curse of frustration in marriage, break and let

me marry and enjoy my marriage, in Jesus' name.

764. By the power of the Lord Jesus, I shall not marry my enemy, in Jesus' name.

765. Holy Ghost, give me divine prescription that will solve my marital problems, in Jesus' name.

766. Any dream where someone claimed that I am married to him or her, let it be clear now, I am not married to you, in Jesus' name.

767. I release myself from any covenant that says I must suffer before I get married, in Jesus' name.

768. Holy Ghost, let your fire consume anything that you have not planted in my life, in Jesus' name.

769. Special announcement, I disband the marks of rejection from my life by fire, in Jesus' name.

770. Yoke of marital embarrassment, depart from me now, in Jesus' name.

771. Thou power of marital failure, leave me alone, in Jesus' name.

772. I render the spirit of marital delay powerless over my life, in Jesus' name.

773. O Lord, make my life and destiny wonders to behold, in Jesus' name.

774. I release myself from the curse of marital confusion, in Jesus' name.

775. My marriage, hear the word of the Lord, succeed by fire, in Jesus' name.

776. Programmed spirit wife/husband, leave me alone and die, in Jesus' name.

777. I stand against the covenant of marital distress, in Jesus' name.

778. The Lord will perfect everything that concerns me and make me laugh last, in Jesus' name.

779. I renounce every satanic claim of ownership concerning my marriage and destiny, in Jesus' name.

780. O Lord, begin a new thing in my life and marriage today, in Jesus' name.

781. I place my life and marriage under the cover of the blood of Jesus, in Jesus' name.

782. I refuse to make mistakes that will ruin my life and destiny in marriage, in Jesus' name.

783. My life and destiny, reject any form of witchcraft manipulation, in Jesus' name.

784. Holy Spirit, reveal to me, deep secrets concerning my marriage, in Jesus' name.

785. Let the serpent of marital failure be rendered powerless, in Jesus' name.

786. Holy Ghost, guide me to marry your perfect will for me, in Jesus' name.

PRAYERS TO REVERSE THE IRREVERSIBLE (ISAIAH 8:9-10)

787. The joy of the enemy over my life, be turned to sorrow,

in Jesus' name.

788. Everything in my life that does not give glory to God, be reversed, in Jesus' name.

789. The camp of the enemy, receive total darkness and confusion, in Jesus' name.

790. Holy Ghost, reverse every curse of ancient elders affecting me negatively, in Jesus' name.

791. The garment of filthiness and oppression will not fit me, in Jesus' name.

792. O Lord, work your miracle in my life in a way that people will know that I am serving a great God, in Jesus' name.

793. O Lord, remove anything that will drag your name in the mud in my life now, in Jesus' name.

794. The wind of God, blow blessings into my life and drive affliction away from me, in Jesus' name.

795. Lord Jesus, break the teeth of the ungodly for my sake this year, in Jesus' name.

796. The wickedness of the wicked in my life, expire right now, in Jesus' name.

797. O Lord, ordain your arrow of death against the strongman assigned against me, in Jesus' name.

798. I loose myself from the bondage I inherited from my root unconsciously, in Jesus' name.

799. The spell of this is 'how far I will go this year', break to pieces, in Jesus' name.

800. The hand of the Lord, heal me and I shall be healed, in Jesus' name.

801. Let the angel of God trouble the evil waters assigned to trouble me, in Jesus' name.

802. Any part of my body that has been shared out, I command a restoration now, in Jesus' name.

803. I reject the spirit of physical and spiritual embarrassment, in Jesus' name.

804. The enemy that rose up against me in one way, flee in seven ways, in Jesus' name.

805. I pull down the forces of limitation erected against me, in Jesus' name.

806. Every secret I need to know to move forward, be revealed to me by fire, in Jesus' name.

807. I prophesy to you my hands; gather your wealth, in Jesus' name.

808. I prophesy to you my legs, carry me to my place of blessing, in Jesus' name.

809. Where is the Lord God of Elijah? Arise and let my affliction die, in Jesus' name.

810. The association of evil prophets assigned against me, run mad, in Jesus' name.

811. Every occult material programmed to project affliction into my life, catch fire, in Jesus' name.

CONNECTING TO THE GOD OF 24 HOURS
(GENESIS 41:14)

812. The God of sudden miracle, appear in my situation, in Jesus' name.

813. The miracle of 'who did this for you', the hour has come, manifest in my life, in Jesus' name.

814. No matter how my enemies try over my destiny, they shall end in failure, in Jesus' name.

815. Anointing to succeed where others have failed, fall upon me, in Jesus' name.

816. Holy Ghost, empower me to prosper in everything I lay my hands upon, in Jesus' name.

817. Wind of the Holy Ghost, blow away all afflictions from me, in Jesus' name.

818. In Jesus' name, I shall succeed this year.

819. Altar of suffering, I set you ablaze, in Jesus' name.

820. Siege of darkness projected into my dream life, expire now, in Jesus' name.

821. Every door I knock on shall open by fire, in Jesus' name.

822. Strangers visiting my dwelling place at night, I am not your candidate, die, in Jesus' name.

823. Every serpent swallowing what is due to me, I kill you with the sword of fire, in Jesus' name.

824. I reject the rule and lordship of demonic powers

claiming ownership over my life, in Jesus' name.

825. O God, arise and open my eyes to see my divine opportunities, in Jesus' name.

826. I terminate the operation of the spirit of infirmity, in Jesus' name.

827. Holy Ghost, immunize me against any form of satanic attack, in Jesus' name.

828. Every physical and spiritual reproach, leave me alone, die, in Jesus' name.

829. The spirit of fruitfulness is upon me, therefore I shall be fruitful, in Jesus' name.

830. O God, arise and envelope me with the fire of the Holy Ghost, in Jesus' name.

831. I tear off from my body, the garment of sorrow, in Jesus' name.

832. Any power drawing evil energy against me from the sun, moon and star, run mad, in Jesus' name.

833. Satanic animals coming to me in my dream, be electrocuted by fire, in Jesus' name.

834. Any object or image representing me in the world of darkness, I set you ablaze, in Jesus' name.

835. Every source of information that is available for my enemy to use against me, be withdrawn, in Jesus' name.

836. I withdraw my blessing from the custody of the

strongman, in Jesus' name.

837. My eyes, open and see what God has provided for my comfort, in Jesus' name.

838. Domestic witchcraft, leave my destiny alone, die, in Jesus' name.

839. My angel of recovery, gather all my stolen blessings back to me, in Jesus' name.

840. The problem that came into my life through dreams, die, in Jesus' name

841. Maturity date of any inherited bondage, expire, in Jesus' name.

PRAYERS TO ABORT THE WICKED PLAN OF THE ENEMY (PSALM 7:9)

842. The battle that is older than me and the battle that is stronger than me, die, in Jesus' name.

843. The programme and effort of the enemy over my life, end in failure, in Jesus' name.

844. Thou enchantment power assigned against me, expire, in Jesus' name.

845. Angel of war, arise and terrorise every strongman assigned against me, in Jesus' name.

846. Powers making my problems to become difficult, die, in Jesus' name.

847. Every evil bird flying for my sake, crash land, in Jesus' name.

848. Domestic witchcraft, you shall not prevail over me, die, in Jesus' name.

849. The register of the wicked containing my name, I set you ablaze, in Jesus' name.

850. My season of positive change, manifest by fire, in Jesus' name.

851. I speak to my hands, gather your wealth by fire, in Jesus' name.

852. Evil altar killing stars in my father's house, die, in Jesus' name.

853. O Lord, satisfy me early in every area of my life, in Jesus' name.

854. Witchcraft projection into my dream life, die, in Jesus' name.

855. Satanic judgement and litigation against me, be revoked, in Jesus' name.

856. Spirits behind dream manipulation, die, in Jesus' name.

857. I decree mass burial in the camp of my enemy, in Jesus' name.

858. Anywhere an evil meeting is being held against me, scatter, in Jesus' name.

859. Evil voices asking me to come down, I shall not come down, die, in Jesus' name.

860. Spiritual rope tying me down, break, in Jesus' name.

861. Blood of Jesus, erase all contrary marks from me, in

Jesus' name.

862. I call forth my breakthrough to appear now, in Jesus' name.

863. Umbilical cord connecting me to the problem of my father's house, break, in Jesus' name.

864. Evil mandate of collective family captivity, break, in Jesus' name.

865. In Jesus' name, I shall be above only and not below.

866. Strongman sitting on anything that belongs to me, die, in Jesus' name.

867. I close every door to lack and poverty, in Jesus' name.

868. O earth, open and swallow all my problems, in Jesus' name.

869. Holy Ghost, turn my curses to blessings, in Jesus' name.

870. Everything that God has created, begin to work for me this year, in Jesus' name.

871. Obstacles and barriers assigned against me this year, clear away by fire, in Jesus' name.

STRATEGIC PRAYERS TO OPEN YOUR MIRACLE DOORS (I CORINTHIANS 16:9)

872. Deserved and underserved favour, envelope me by fire, in Jesus' name.

873. Every good door that is closed and also under lock,

hear the word of the Lord, open, in Jesus' name.

874. Door of abundant supply of every good thing of life, open, in Jesus' name.

875. O God, arise and connect me to miracles, signs and wonders, in Jesus' name.

876. Every irreversible condition in my life, be reversed, in Jesus' name.

877. Evil decree of delay to my breakthrough, scatter, in Jesus' name.

878. Witchcraft embargo of darkness, break, in Jesus' name.

879. Powers calling my name before any oracle, scatter, in Jesus' name.

880. Sudden shame shall not be my portion, in Jesus' name.

881. Door of mercy, hear the word of the Lord, open, in Jesus' name.

882. Door of possibility to enjoy opportunity, open, in Jesus' name.

883. Anointing of uncommon favour after the order of Joseph and Esther, fall upon me, in Jesus' name.

884. O mighty hand of God, perfect everything that concerns me, in Jesus' name.

885. O God, uproot every evil seed from my life and destiny, in Jesus' name.

886. Door of affliction that is opened against my health, be

closed, in Jesus' name.

887. Power to be remembered for uncommon promotion, fall upon me, in Jesus' name.

888. Anointing of multiple celebrations, fall upon me, in Jesus' name.

889. Invisible hand stealing from me, wither, in Jesus' name.

890. Witchcraft broom, sweeping away my blessing, catch fire, in Jesus' name.

891. The manifestation of my glory and star is now, in Jesus' name.

892. O God, arise and anoint me for beauty and glory, in Jesus' name.

893. All my buried blessings, come out of the earth where you are buried, in Jesus' name.

894. I command every good door that is closed against me to open, in Jesus' name.

895. Every environmental coven troubling me, wither, in Jesus' name.

896. Jehovah Jireh, answer your name in my life, in Jesus' name.

897. The creative wonder of God, arise and surprise me right now, in Jesus' name.

898. O Lord, make the garden of my life and destiny fruitful, in Jesus' name.

899. The mouth of the enemy shall be permanently shut when the enemy hears about my next breakthroughs, in Jesus' name.

900. My expectation shall not fail, in Jesus' name.

901. Miracles that cannot be explained, manifest in my life, in Jesus' name.

WITCHCRAFT POISON COME OUT OF MY SYSTEM (PALMS 18:44-45)

902. Evil seed that is growing in my system, come out by fire, in Jesus' name.

903. Satanic arrow fired into my head, come out and die, in Jesus' name.

904. Poison of serpents and scorpions, come out of my body now, in Jesus' name.

905. Arrow of failure at the edge of breakthrough, come out of my life, in Jesus' name.

906. Organs of my body, you must not cooperate with sickness, in Jesus' name.

907. Holy Ghost, burn to ashes strange materials programmed through evil food, in Jesus' name.

908. My days of afflictions, expire, in Jesus' name.

909. Darkness and wickedness shall not swallow my destiny, in Jesus' name.

910. Mark of rejection, clear away from me, in Jesus' name.

911. All eaters of flesh and drinkers of blood, drink your blood and eat your flesh, in Jesus' name.
912. Anti-progress forces, die, in Jesus' name.
913. O Lord, arise and make me a leading light in my family, in Jesus' name.
914. My blood, receive cleansing by the blood of Jesus, in Jesus' name.
915. I shall not be a prisoner of environmental coven, in Jesus' name.
916. Every blood sacrifice released against me, catch fire, in Jesus' name.
917. I declare war against evil arrows, wither and die, in Jesus' name.
918. I use the sword of fire to cut off the head of spirit wife/husband assigned against me, in Jesus' name.
919. I collect the key of my breakthrough from the hands of the enemy, in Jesus' name.
920. The wickedness of the wicked against me, expire, in Jesus' name.
921. Strange hands working against my success, wither, in Jesus' name.
922. Dark perfume, clear away from me, in Jesus' name.
923. Holy Ghost, immunize me against darkness, in Jesus' name.
924. Altar of affliction, catch fire, in Jesus' name.

925. East wind, I send you to scatter every evil gathering against me, in Jesus' name.

926. Powers energizing my problems, wither, in Jesus' name.

927. Mark of rejection, lose your hold upon my life, in Jesus' name.

928. Good things that have died in my life, come alive, in Jesus' name.

929. Strange voices countering my blessing, die, in Jesus' name.

930. My blessing shall not be exchanged, in Jesus' name.

931. My legs, carry me to my place of breakthrough, in Jesus' name.

SICKNESSES AND DISEASES EXPIRE (EXODUS 23:25)

932. Every inherited infirmity and sickness in my body, die, in Jesus' name.

933. My head, reject the arrow of affliction, in Jesus' name.

934. Every money-consuming sickness and disease, wither, in Jesus' name.

935. Terminal sickness and disease, be terminated, in Jesus' name.

936. Holy Ghost fire, burn off evil arrows and let them dry up, in Jesus' name.

937. Programmed sickness and disease, wither, in Jesus'

name.

938. Killer sickness and disease, my life is not your candidate, in Jesus' name.

939. I transfuse the blood of Jesus into my body, in Jesus' name.

940. My body, reject every garment of sorrow, in Jesus' name.

941. Every sickness in my body, dry up now, in Jesus' name.

942. Poison in my body through night feeding, die, in Jesus' name.

943. The hand of a witch assigned to introduce sickness into my body, die, in Jesus' name.

944. Evil plantation, come out of my body, in Jesus' name.

945. Witchcraft pot cooking my health, catch fire, in Jesus' name.

946. Marine materials programmed into my body, catch fire, in Jesus' name.

947. My body shall not be a dumping ground for sickness and disease, in Jesus' name.

948. Every organ of my body that is dead, come alive, in Jesus' name.

949. Witchcraft arrows fired at my blood, come out and die, in Jesus' name.

950. Any power that wants to put me on a wheelchair, die,

in Jesus' name.

951.   I am for blessing, I am not for curses, in Jesus' name.

952.   Spirit of insomnia, depart from me, in Jesus' name.

953.   Every projection of witchcraft into my dream life, catch fire, in Jesus' name.

954.   Evil hand manipulating my health, wither, in Jesus' name.

955.   O Lord, Jehovah Rapha, heal me and I shall be healed, in Jesus' name.

956.   Any sickness or disease waiting to eat up my body, die, in Jesus' name.

957.   I shall not die but live to declare the goodness of the Lord, in Jesus' name.

958.   Blood sucking demon, die, in Jesus' name.

959.   Goliath of sickness, die, in Jesus' name.

960.   Sickness due to inherited yokes, die, in Jesus' name.

CUTTING OF THE FINGER OF WITCHCRAFT ON YOUR DESTINY

961.   I break the powers of domestic witchcraft operating against me, in Jesus' name.

962.   Every mouth paid to curse me, be filled with gravel, in Jesus' name.

963.   Evil hands holding a witchcraft gun to shoot at me, wither, in Jesus' name.

964.   Hands of the Lord, arise and wipe away my shame, in

415

Jesus' name.

965. Every blood covenant working against me, break, in Jesus' name.

966. O Lord, mobilize divine and human support for me to succeed, in Jesus' name.

967. O God, arise and send the spirit of confusion to envelop the camp of my competitors, in Jesus' name.

968. Holy Ghost, anoint me with wisdom to beat my competitors with a wide margin, in Jesus' name.

969. Every evil nocturnal meeting holding for my sake, scatter, in Jesus' name.

970. Satanic resistance to the emergence of my candidacy, wither and scatter, in Jesus' name.

971. All external and internal saboteurs, be exposed and disgraced, in Jesus' name.

972. Fresh fire to outshine others, fall upon me, in Jesus' name.

973. Holy Ghost, journey with me, guide and instruct me in the path of righteousness for your sake, in Jesus' name.

974. Every spirit of quarrelling and misunderstanding in my camp, I bind you, in Jesus' name.

975. Every evil fraternity and collective effort to destroy me, fail, in Jesus' name.

976. All forms of sacrifice and rituals to cage my

workforce, scatter, in Jesus' name.

977. Divine warriors of heaven, unseat anyone sitting where I am supposed to sit, in Jesus' name.

978. By the power of the Holy Ghost, I shall succeed, I shall not fail, in Jesus' name.

979. My health and finances shall not be exchanged or caged, in Jesus' name.

980. Satanic legislation to stop me from achieving what I have set out to achieve, scatter, in Jesus' name.

981. Any evil prayer that my enemy prayed on any evil altar, O God, do not answer them, Jesus' name.

982. O Lord, deliver me from every set up on my way to the top, in Jesus' name.

983. O Lord, move me forward and upward by fire and thunder, in Jesus' name.

984. I reject the spirit of error, mistake and miscalculation, in Jesus' name.

985. Because Jesus never fails, I shall not fail, in Jesus' name.

986. Every curse in my family line that will work against me, break and be cancelled, in Jesus' name.

987. I will not lose my life or the life of any member of my family, in Jesus' name.

988. David saw the end of Goliath, I will see the end of all my competitors, in Jesus' name.

989. After all said and done, my head, you must wear your

crown, in Jesus' name.

990. The weapon the enemy intends to use against me shall turn against the enemy, in Jesus' name.

WITCHCRAFT COBWEBS MUST DIE

991. The activities of witchcraft cobwebs blocking my path to greatness, catch fire, in Jesus' name.

992. Owners of evil load, carry your load now, in Jesus' name.

993. The negative effect of parental idol worship on my life and destiny, be destroyed, in Jesus' name.

994. Every inherited mark of failure, be cut off from me, in Jesus' name.

995. Dirty and filthy hands of witchcraft troubling my life, wither, in Jesus' name.

996. Every dark presence magnetizing problems into my life, be destroyed, in Jesus' name.

997. Every organized warfare to strip me naked physically and spiritually, die, in Jesus' name.

998. Whoever used my pictures to programme poverty into my life shall fail, in Jesus' name.

999. Thou power of the emptier upon my life, break, in Jesus' name.

1000. Witchcraft umbrella blocking favour from flowing to me, catch fire, in Jesus' name.

1001. Witchcraft animals swallowing my wealth, die, in Jesus' name.

1002. Let the arrows of witchcraft organized for my sake, backfire, in Jesus' name.

1003. I shall not be forgotten where I am supposed to be remembered, in Jesus' name.

1004. The serpent of the magician swallowing my breakthroughs, I kill you with the sword of fire, in Jesus' name.

1005. Every evil veil covering my eyes from seeing what I am supposed to see, catch fire, in Jesus' name.

1006. Every pot of enchantment against me, break to pieces, in Jesus' name.

1007. My blessing, come out of the cage of witchcraft, in Jesus' name.

1008. Satanic priests operating any dark altar against me, fall down and die, in Jesus' name.

1009. Every power of witchcraft cooking my flesh, break to pieces, in Jesus' name.

1010. Agenda of envious witchcraft targeted against me, die, in Jesus' name.

1011. The crying blood against my success and progress, be silenced, in Jesus' name.

1012. Every household witch employing fetish power against me, die, in Jesus' name.

1013. My spirit, soul and body shall not be bewitched, in Jesus' name.

1014. Every witchcraft food I have eaten that is bringing problems into my life, come out and die, in Jesus' name.

1015. My life, possess your possessions by fire, in Jesus' name.

HIDDEN AND UNPROFITABLE COVENANT MUST TERMINATE

1016. Covenant of suffering, break and release me, in Jesus' name.

1017. Covenants and curses that render glory useless and irrelevant, die, in Jesus' name.

1018. Curses and evil covenants shall not cage my success this year, in Jesus' name.

1019. Every blessing that the enemy has chased away, come back to me, in Jesus' name.

1020. My destiny, reject the voice of death, in Jesus' name.

1021. I withdraw my name from every evil register, in Jesus' name.

1022. Thou wasting power of my father's house, lose your

hold in my life, in Jesus' name.

1023. Thou power of collective captivity in my foundation, break, in Jesus' name.

1024. My life, refuse to follow any evil pattern. Satanic collective umbrella, catch fire, in Jesus' name.

1025. Powers that want collective captivity to be repeated in my life, die, in Jesus' name.

1026. Powers ganging up against my joy and celebration, hear the word of the Lord, scatter, in Jesus' name.

1027. The wicked trade of suffering, blood of Jesus, blot them out, in Jesus' name.

1028. Activities of eaters of flesh and drinkers of blood in my bloodline, be destroyed, in Jesus' name.

1029. Spiritual robbers, return every good thing you have stolen from me, in Jesus' name.

1030. This year shall cooperate with my destiny, in Jesus' name.

1031. The light of the glory of the Lord of host shall shine upon me, in Jesus' name.

1032. This year, people shall come to know that I am serving a living God, in Jesus' name.

1033. Stubborn and cruel bondage, break, in Jesus' name.

1034. Anointing to do exploits this year, fall upon me, in Jesus' name.

1035. O God of mercy, let mercy speak life, favour and

health for me, in Jesus' name.

1036. The mention of my name shall cause the enemy to flee in terror, in Jesus' name.

1037. By the power of the Holy Ghost, I shall sing my song and dance my dance, in Jesus' name.

1038. The weapons that the enemy is planning to use against me shall turn against them, in Jesus' name.

1039. This year, I shall not fail, I shall not miscalculate and I shall not beg for bread, in Jesus' name.

1040. Anyone using a demonic mirror to cast spell on me, die with your spell, in Jesus' name.

1041. All satanic intelligent network of killer altars erected against me, catch fire, in Jesus' name.

1042. Every altar erected to delay and deny me my place in destiny, catch fire, in Jesus' name.

1043. Arrow of denial of rights and benefits, backfire, in Jesus' name.

1044. Arrow of intimidation, isolation and manipulation, backfire, in Jesus' name.

1045. Arrow of loss of personal identity and glory, scatter, in Jesus' name.

1046. Witchcraft transfer of affliction to my body through inflicting injury upon any object bearing my name, die, in Jesus' name.

DELETING EVIL DAYS FROM THE CALENDAR

1047. I cover my life and family with the blood of Jesus, in Jesus' name.

1048. Thou power of spell, charms and sorcery over my destiny, be broken, in Jesus' name.

1049. Chains of darkness binding my finances, career and health, break, in Jesus' name.

1050. Anti-success and anti-breakthrough forces, lose your hold upon my life, in Jesus' name.

1051. O Lord, bless me and increase my greatness this month, in Jesus' name.

1052. Every gang up on my way to the top, scatter, in Jesus' name.

1053. Powers that want me to begin but not finish, die, in Jesus' name.

1054. Powers tying me down to the wrong location, where I do not belong, catch fire, in Jesus' name.

1055. O Lord, give me the testimony that will advertise your name and power in my life, in Jesus' name.

1056. Powers that have vowed that my battles will not come to an end soon, die, in Jesus' name.

1057. Any negative word, spoken or written, fighting my success and greatness, wither, in Jesus' name.

1058. Anything in my foundation that is subjecting my life to unending battles, die, in Jesus' name.

1059. Powers that want failure to be my identity, your end

423

has come, perish, in Jesus' name.

1060. I plug my life to the divine socket. Let the current of favour flow into my life continually, in Jesus' name.

1061. Every arrow of intimidation, frustration and limitation programmed into the work of my hands, backfire, in Jesus' name.

1062. Anywhere my name is mentioned, let the mercy and favour of God answer for me, in Jesus' name.

1063. In the race of life, I shall not be a latecomer, in Jesus' name.

1064. Arrow of fruitless labour, die, in Jesus' name.

1065. Powers working hard to quench the fire of God in my life in order to attack me, you are failures, die, in Jesus' name.

1066. The fire of God must increase in me and the work of the flesh must decrease in me, in Jesus' name.

1067. Fire of God, empower my spirit man to reject satanic commands in my dreams, in Jesus' name.

1068. O Lord, this year, my expectation shall not be cut off, in Jesus' name.

1069. This month, I shall see all my desire come to pass in my life, in Jesus' name.

1070. I receive the baptism of the Holy Ghost fire and I drink the blood of Jesus, in Jesus' name.

1071. Powers that want my portion in life to be a leftover, you are liars, die, in Jesus' name.

1072. Jesus Christ, the Man of war, arise and trouble the Herod assigned against me, in Jesus' name.

1073. Powers hijacking my breakthroughs on the way, fall down and die, in Jesus' name.

1074. My personal Jericho, hear the word of the Lord, collapse, in Jesus' name.

1075. Satanic dog barking against me, be wasted, die, in Jesus' name.

1076. Witchcraft rat that is stylishly stealing my money, fire of God, suffocate it, in Jesus' name.

1077. Every prayer that any sorcerer is praying against me, turn against them, in Jesus' name.

1078. By the power of the Holy Ghost, I delete evil days from the calendar of my destiny, in Jesus' name.

1079. Blood of Jesus, remove the marks that identify me with darkness, in Jesus' name.

1080. Holy Ghost, guide me, lead me and order my steps to my place of blessings, in Jesus' name.

1081. Every collective and personal captivity, break and release me, in Jesus' name.

1082. Every altar of foundational strongman blocking my path to greatness, catch fire, in Jesus' name.

1083. Heavenly bulldozer, unseat anyone sitting where I am supposed to sit, in Jesus' name.

1084. By the power of the Holy Ghost, I shall sing my song and dance my dance, in Jesus' name.

1085. The weapons the enemy is planning to use against me, shall turn against them, in Jesus' name.

1086. This year, I shall not fail, I shall not miscalculate and I shall not beg for bread, in Jesus' name.

1087. Anyone using a demonic mirror to cast spell on me, die with your spell, in Jesus' name.

1088. I cancel every appointment with sudden death by the power in the blood of Jesus, in Jesus' name.

1089. Strange voices assigned to stop my breakthrough from manifesting, die, in Jesus' name.

1090. I receive power to pursue, overtake and recover all my portions, in Jesus' name.

1091. O Lord, promote me above all my enemies round about me, in Jesus' name.

1092. My brain and other organs of my body shall not be donated by domestic witchcraft, in Jesus' name.

1093. Isaac survived the period of famine, I will see the end of all my troubles, in Jesus' name.

1094. Every good thing I have been looking for shall begin to look for me, in Jesus' name.

1095. My leg, carry me to my place of honour, in Jesus' name.

1096. My life shall not be established in frustration, confusion and shame, in Jesus' name.

1097. All my blessings captured or stolen, be restored to me sevenfold, in Jesus' name.

426

1098. O God, by what makes you Almighty, answer your name in my life, in Jesus' name.

1099. By the finger of God, let all my obstacles clear away by fire, in Jesus' name.

1100. O Lord, I decree that my blessings shall not be given to another, in Jesus' name.

1101. In the remaining days of this year, no evil shall befall me, in Jesus' name.

1102. O Lord, make haste to bless me, in Jesus' name.

1103. Powers using my dreams to monitor my prospects, receive blindness, in Jesus' name.

1104. Everything that has to die for my miracle to manifest, die, in Jesus' name.

1105. Messenger of death assigned against my glorious destiny, perish, in Jesus' name.

I RECEIVE THE POWER OF THE HOLY GHOST FROM ON HIGH

1106. Holy Spirit of God, by your creative power, manifest in my life, in Jesus' name.

1107. I frustrate the token of diviners and enchanters, in Jesus' name.

1108. Powers protecting my enemy, be paralyzed, in Jesus' name.

1109. Fire of God, destroy every cobweb of stagnation and limitation working against me, in Jesus' name.

1110. Powers and spirits that are gathered to fight me, wither, in Jesus' name.

1111. God of new beginning, open a new chapter of ceaseless favour in my life, in Jesus' name.

1112. Anywhere my spirit, soul and body have been bound, fire of God, set me free, in Jesus' name.

1113. Delegated strongman standing and waiting at the edge of my breakthrough, be paralyzed, in Jesus' name.

1114. Let the shrines of ancient gods and goddesses assigned to my family, catch fire, in Jesus' name.

1115. Every visible and invisible chain holding me down, break, in Jesus' name.

1116. Holy Spirit, break every yoke of marine spirit troubling me, in Jesus' name.

1117. Every material and article of ancestral powers in my life, burn to ashes, in Jesus' name.

1118. Sicknesses and diseases of Egypt, my life is not your candidate, in Jesus' name.

1119. Every pot of darkness cooking my destiny, break, in Jesus' name.

1120. Witchcraft bullet of oppression fired at me, backfire, in Jesus' name.

1121. Anti-prosperity yoke of marine, break and release me, in Jesus' name.

428

1122. Covenant of suffering in the midst of abundance, break, in Jesus' name.

1123. O God, arise and bless me beyond my expectations, in Jesus' name.

1124. Arrow of blood bondage, come out of your hiding place, in Jesus' name.

1125. Powers that want me to serve and not be served, die, in Jesus' name.

1126. Spirit of emptiness, wither, in Jesus' name.

1127. Thou power of the night behind my problems, expire, in Jesus' name.

1128. Every demonic presence around my life and destiny, I chase you out, in Jesus' name.

1129. The gate of my breakthroughs under lock and key, open, in Jesus' name.

1130. Thou chain of evil cycles controlling my life, break, in Jesus' name.

1131. Satanic worms devouring my finances, be suffocated, in Jesus' name.

1132. My destiny shall not be meat at the dining table of darkness, in Jesus' name.

1133. Power that wants the error of my parents to be repeated in my life, I cut you off, in Jesus' name.

1134. Apostolic power of the Holy Ghost, break every yoke in my life, in Jesus' name.

429

1135. Possibility power of God, be made manifest in my life now, in Jesus' name.

1136. After all said and done, my head shall wear my crown, in Jesus' name.

1137. Every altar of darkness killing good things in my life, catch fire, in Jesus' name.

CURSES IN MY FOUNDATION MUST TERMINATE

1138. The curse of 'thou shall not excel' in my foundation, break, in Jesus' name.

1139. The curse of 'thou shall not be greater than this' in my life, break, in Jesus' name.

1140. The curse of suffering for what I do know nothing about, break, in Jesus' name.

1141. Any organ of my body in trouble as a result of hidden curses, be delivered, in Jesus' name.

1142. I withdraw my prosperity from the ancient altar of my father's house, in Jesus' name.

1143. I refuse to accept failure as part of my destiny, in Jesus' name.

1144. Anything representing me on any wicked and destructive altar, catch fire, in Jesus' name.

1145. The priest of darkness ministering against me for evil, somersault and perish, in Jesus' name.

1146. O Lord, let your consuming fire consume every spiritual rubbish in my life and destiny, in Jesus'

name.

1147. Every curse of the head becoming the tail, break and release me, in Jesus' name.

1148. Hammer of the Lord, break to pieces the head of leviathan rising up against me, in Jesus' name.

1149. Every yoke swallowing my blessing, break, in Jesus' name.

1150. By the redemptive power of the blood of Jesus, curses and covenants in my life, break, in Jesus' name.

1151. Every evil hand pointing at me for evil, wither and function no more, in Jesus' name.

1152. O God, arise and answer your name in my life, in Jesus' name.

1153. The enemy that has vowed not to let me go, woe to you, die, in Jesus' name.

1154. Associations that are gathered together to destroy me, die, in Jesus' name.

1155. I release myself from the bondage of evil altars, in Jesus' name.

1156. I vomit every satanic poison that I have swallowed, in Jesus' name.

1157. I cancel every demonic dedication, in the name of Jesus. Be repeating, "I cancel you, in Jesus' name."

1158. (Place your hand on your head and say) I break the yoke of every evil authority over my life, in Jesus' name. Pray it for five minutes.

1159. Mention the under listed authority and say, "Break, in Jesus' name."

Authority of demons.

Authority of familiar spirits.

Authority of spiritual spouse.

Authority of satanic priest.

Authority of diviners.

Authority of ancestral powers.

Authority of sorcerers.

Authority of the strongman.

1160. Every evil hand collecting what is due to me, wither, in Jesus' name.

1161. Every hired undertaker assigned to bury my star, you are a liar, fail, in Jesus' name.

1162. Every funeral song composed for me and all the participants, scatter, in Jesus' name.

1163. Every sacrifice and ritual carried out at the waterside against me, become impotent, in Jesus' name.

1164. O Lord, by your mercy and power, scatter the aggression of the enemies against me, in Jesus' name.

1165. Angels of my breakthrough, wherever you are, receive reinforcement and succeed, in Jesus' name.

1166. Every pit of death, destruction and failure dug for me by my foundation, be closed, in Jesus' name.

PRAYER S TO BREAK FREE FROM FAMILY CAPTIVITY

1167. O God, arise and scatter the table of darkness assigned to feed me with poison, in Jesus' name.

1168. Every evil dedication speaking 'thou shall not be great' speak no more, in Jesus' name.

1169. O Lord, release to me the key to unlock my hidden greatness, in Jesus' name.

1170. O Lord, by your name, 'Almighty,' manifest your power in my life now, in Jesus' name.

1171. All negative words that are spoken against my success, expire today, in Jesus' name.

1172. Every inherited hidden limitation working against me, break and let me go, in Jesus' name.

1173. I delete evil days from my calendar this year, in Jesus' name.

1174. O God, arise and uproot any evil seed in me that you did not plant, in Jesus' name.

1175. Every spirit of lukewarmness in spiritual matters, get out of my life, in Jesus' name.

1176. I claim back every spiritual ground I have lost to the enemy, in Jesus' name.

1177. My angels of blessing shall not depart without releasing my blessings, in Jesus' name.

1178. I trample upon every spirit behind spiritual emptiness and vagabond anointing, in Jesus' name.

1179. Disappointment and frustration shall not be my portion in the New Year, Jesus' name.

1180. Curses and evil covenants shall not cage my success this year, in Jesus' name.

1181. This year, O God, anoint me to pray without ceasing, in Jesus' name.

1182. Every spiritual sickness fashioned to pull me down, be cut off, in Jesus' name.

1183. O God, connect me to people that will move my life forward spiritually and materially this year, in Jesus' name.

1184. Every root of failure in my life, be cut off, in Jesus' name.

1185. This year, I shall not reap satanic harvest in any area of my life, in Jesus' name.

1186. All my imprisoned spiritual gifts, come forth, in Jesus' name.

1187. Whatever hindered my spiritual life last year shall cooperate with me this year, in Jesus' name.

1188. This year, I have appointment with destiny, I shall be remembered and celebrated, in Jesus' name.

1189. Holy Ghost fire, consume every spiritual rag and rubbish blocking me from greatness, in Jesus' name.

1190. Every evil ladder projected into my spiritual life to hinder my spiritual growth, I break you to pieces, in

Jesus' name.

1191. Holy Ghost fire, consume every coffin of darkness assigned against me, in Jesus' name.

1192. Any mouth commanding me to appear where I ought not to appear, perish without remedy, in Jesus' name.

1193. O God, arise and give me back, sevenfold of everything the enemy stole from me, in Jesus' name.

1194. O heaven, arise and execute the judgement of death upon my persecutors, in Jesus' name.

1195. O God, arise and frustrate the counsel of the wicked, in Jesus' name.

PRAYERS AGAINST EVIL DEDICATION

1196. Every problem associated with evil dedication, receive solution, in Jesus' name.

1197. Every affliction programmed to my dwelling place, expire, in Jesus' name.

1198. My virtue trapped inside the water, come forth and locate me, in Jesus' name.

1199. Serpentine powers promoting affliction in my life, wither and die, in Jesus' name.

1200. I break the head of leviathan assigned against me, in Jesus' name.

1201. The priest of darkness ministering against me for evil, somersault and perish, in Jesus' name.

1202. O Lord, let your consuming fire consume every spiritual rubbish in my life and destiny, in Jesus' name.

1203. Every curse of the head becoming the tail, break and release me, in Jesus' name.

1204. Hammer of the Lord, break to pieces the head of leviathan rising up against me, in Jesus' name.

1205. Every yoke swallowing my blessing, break, in Jesus' name.

1206. By the redemptive power of the blood of Jesus, curses and covenants in my life, break, in Jesus' name.

1207. Every evil hand pointing to me for evil, wither and function no more, in Jesus' name.

1208. O God, arise and answer your name in my life, in Jesus' name.

1209. I release myself from the bondage of evil altars, in Jesus' name.

1210. Powers boasting that I will move from battle to battle this year, be wasted, in Jesus' name.

1211. Every bloodline battle of my father's house that wants to swallow my star, die, in Jesus' name.

1212. Sicknesses that came as a result of generational curses, break, in Jesus' name.

1213. Commander of the army of darkness assigned against me, die, in Jesus' name.

1214. I break the yoke of stagnation by the power in the blood of Jesus, in Jesus' name.

1215. Powers that have vowed that my hands will not feed me, I cut you off, in Jesus' name.

1216. Possibility power of our Lord and Saviour Jesus Christ, work miracles in my life today, in Jesus' name.

1217. I am not going down. I am going upward. I am not going backward. I am going forward, in Jesus' name.

1218. Every effect of evil hands that have touched me, clear away by fire, in Jesus' name.

1219. Difficult and complex yokes, break, in Jesus' name.

1220. By the covenant of the blood of Jesus, hidden and clever yokes, break, in Jesus' name.

1221. Whatever must die for my miracle to manifest, what are you waiting for? Die, in Jesus' name.

1222. O God, by your eyes that do not sleep nor slumber, watch over me at all times, in Jesus' name.

1223. Every spiritual sickness fashioned to pull me down, be cut off, in Jesus' name.

1224. O God, connect me to people that will move my life forward spiritually and materially this year, in Jesus' name.

1225. Every root of failure in my life, be cut off, in Jesus' name.

1226. This year, I shall not reap satanic harvest in any area of my life, in Jesus' name.

1227. All my imprisoned spiritual gifts, come forth, in Jesus' name.

1228. Whatever hindered my spiritual life last year shall cooperate with me this year, in Jesus' name.

PRAYERS TO SET YOURSELF FREE FROM BESETTING SINS

1229. The power and the hold of sin over my life, be broken, in Jesus' name.

1230. O mighty hands of the Lord, break every chain of darkness holding me in a particular bondage, in Jesus' name.

1231. Christ has delivered me from the curse of the law by the shed blood at Calvary, therefore, let no demon trouble me again, in Jesus' name.

1232. Any problem in my life that is due to a particular sin in my life, O God, arise in your mercy and forgive me, in Jesus' name.

1233. The rod of the wicked sponsoring affliction in my life, be broken, in Jesus' name.

1234. My complete and total deliverance, manifest by fire, in Jesus' name.

1235. Sword of the Lord, enter into my foundation and cut off every link with any strange power, in Jesus' name.

1236. Every effect of evil hands that have touched me, clear away by fire, in Jesus' name.

1237. Difficult and complex yokes, break, in Jesus' name.

1238. By the covenant of the blood of Jesus, hidden and clever yokes, break, in Jesus' name.

1239. Whatever must die for my miracle to manifest, what are you waiting for? Die, in Jesus' name.

1240. Doors of limitation opened into my life, I shut you up by fire, in Jesus' name.

1241. Evil debts of my ancestors; I reject and disinherit you by fire, in Jesus' name.

1242. My glory that has been swallowed by evil powers, arise and locate me, in Jesus' name.

1243. Every evil conspiracy against my destiny, be exposed and nullified, in Jesus' name.

1244. Every strongman of my father's house, die, in Jesus' name.

1245. Let the backbone of the stubborn pursuer and strongman break, in the name of Jesus.

1246. I clear my goods from the warehouse of the strongman, in Jesus' name.

1247. I bind the strongman behind my spiritual blindness and deafness and paralyze his operations in my life, in Jesus' name.

1248. Strange powers troubling my head, wither, in Jesus' name.

1249. Arrows of intimidation, isolation and manipulation, backfire, in Jesus' name.

1250. Arrows of loss of personal identity and glory, backfire, in Jesus' name.

1251. Witchcraft transfer of affliction to my body through inflicting injury upon any object bearing my name, die, in Jesus' name.

1252. My brain and other organs of my body shall not be donated by domestic witchcraft, in Jesus' name.

1253. Isaac survived the period of famine, I will see the end of all my troubles, in Jesus' name.

1254. David saw the end of Goliath, I will see the end of my stubborn enemies, in Jesus' name.

PRAYERS TO OPEN CLOSED DOORS

1255. Door of double recovery of everything I have lost, open, in Jesus' name.

1256. Power of resurrection, work miracles in my life today, in Jesus' name.

1257. Strongman standing at the door of my breakthrough, fall down and die, in Jesus' name.

1258. I cover my life and family with the blood of Jesus, in Jesus' name.

1259. Thou power of spell, charms and sorcery over my destiny, be broken, in Jesus' name.

1260. I break the chain of darkness binding my finances, career and health, break, in Jesus' name.

1261. Anti-success forces, lose your hold upon my life, in Jesus' name.

1262. O Lord, bless me and increase my greatness this month, in Jesus' name.

1263. Every gang up on my way to the top, scatter, in Jesus' name.

1264. Powers that want me to begin but not finish, die, in Jesus' name.

1265. Powers that says even if I gather, they will scatter it, you are failures, die, in Jesus' name.

1266. Any negative word spoken or written, fighting my success and greatness, wither, in Jesus' name.

1267. Anything in my foundation that is subjecting my life to unending battles, die, in Jesus' name.

1268. Powers that want failure to be my identity, your end has come, perish, in Jesus' name.

1269. Every arrow of intimidation, frustration and limitation programmed into the work of my hands, be broken, in Jesus' name.

1270. The fire of God must increase in me and the work of the flesh must decrease in me, in Jesus' name.

1271. Fire of God, empower my spirit man to reject satanic commands in my dreams, in Jesus' name.

1272. O Lord, this year, my expectation shall not be cut off, in Jesus' name.

1273. This month, I shall see all my desire come to pass in my life, in Jesus' name.

1274. I receive the baptism of the Holy Ghost fire and I drink the blood of Jesus, in Jesus' name.

1275. Powers that want my portion in life to be leftover, you are liars, die, in Jesus' name.

1276. Jesus Christ, the Man of war, arise and trouble the Herod assigned against me, in Jesus' name.

1277. Powers hijacking my breakthroughs on the way, fall down and die, in Jesus' name.

1278. My door of success and progress under lock and key, open by fire, in Jesus' name.

1279. Door of miracles, signs and wonders, I command you to open for me, in Jesus' name.

1280. Door of opportunity that the enemy has closed against me, right now, open, in Jesus' name.

1281. Every door of joy and celebration that should have opened but it is not yet open, hear the word of the Lord, open, in Jesus' name.

REMOVING ROADBLOCKS AND HINDRANCES TO YOUR PROGRESS

1282. Let the thunder of God smite every evil priest working against me at the evil altar and burn him to ashes, in Jesus' name.

1283. Let every satanic priest ministering against me at evil altars fall down and die, in Jesus' name.

1284. Any hand that wants to retaliate or arrest me because of all these prayers I am praying, wither, in Jesus' name.

1285. Every stubborn evil altar priest, drink your own blood, in Jesus' name.

1286. I possess my possession stolen by the evil altar, in Jesus' name.

1287. I withdraw my name from every evil altar, in Jesus' name.

1288. I withdraw my blessings from every evil altar, in Jesus' name.

1289. I withdraw my breakthroughs from every evil altar, in Jesus' name.

1290. I receive the anointing to break forth and break through, in Jesus' name.

1291. The wall Jericho standing between me and my breakthrough, fall, Jesus' name.

1292. Failure and defeat shall not be my portion, in Jesus' name.

1293. Witchcraft burial conducted to bury good things in my life, die, in Jesus' name.

1294. Witchcraft cage fashioned against me, break, in Jesus'

name.

1295. Witchcraft warehouse, release my wealth, in Jesus' name.

1296. Witchcraft garment of demotion, I set you ablaze, in Jesus' name.

1297. This year, I shall not be engaged in useless battles, the enemy will not waste my strength, in Jesus' name.

1298. If the enemy has stolen my dominion, I recover it by fire, in Jesus' name.

1299. Anointing that breaks the yoke of delay, shame and disgrace, fall upon me, in Jesus' name.

1300. No matter how strong my enemies may be, this year, I shall be anointed to finish them, in Jesus' name.

1301. Powers preparing spiritual rags for me to wear, I am not your candidate, die, in Jesus' name.

1302. This year, men and women shall chase me about with blessings, in Jesus' name.

1303. My eagle shall not be caged in the pit of irrelevance; my eagle arise and shine, in Jesus' name.

1304. Powers, whose duty it is to close my opened door, die, in Jesus' name.

1305. Whether the enemy likes it or not, I shall see the goodness of the Lord in the land of the living, in Jesus' name.

1306. O God, arise and beautify me with your glory, in Jesus'

name.

1307. The heaven of my signs and wonders, open, in Jesus' name.

1308. I move forward by fire towards my divine assignment, in Jesus' name.

1309. Plantation of shame, failure and reproach, be uprooted, in Jesus' name.

1310. I refuse to carry the evil load of the enemy on my head, in Jesus' name.

1311. Yoke of marine dedication, break, in Jesus' name.

1312. Yoke of witchcraft initiation, break, in Jesus' name.

1313. Yoke of delay and frustration, break, in Jesus' name.

PRAYER TO TERMINATE INFIRMITY

1314. Holy Ghost fire, kill every disease and infirmity in my body, in Jesus' name.

1315. Sickness and disease originating from marine spirits, come out of my body, in Jesus' name.

1316. At the name of Jesus, every knee must bow, therefore every sickness that has a name in my body, disappear, in Jesus' name.

1317. My body, soul and spirit shall not be a habitation of devils, in Jesus' name.

1318. Stubborn root of infirmity and disease, be cut off now, in Jesus' name.

1319. Arrows that entered into my life during the hour of the night, come out and enter no more, in Jesus' name.

1320. I break the stronghold of sickness and disease and set it on fire, in Jesus' name.

1321. Every tree that God has not planted in my body, be cut down, in Jesus' name.

1322. My life, henceforth you shall not obey satanic instructions by the power in the blood of Jesus, in Jesus' name.

1323. Evil cloud preventing my rain of favour, clear away now, in Jesus' name.

1324. My life shall not be a disappointment to God and to my generation, in Jesus' name.

1325. My breakthroughs in coma, wake up by fire, in Jesus' name.

1326. Powers assigned to cage my prayer life through night feeding, die, in Jesus' name.

1327. Powers transforming to satanic creatures in order to attack me, die, in Jesus' name.

1328. Thou power of the grave and coffin assigned against me, bury your owners, in Jesus' name.

1329. Strange and contaminated anointing, dry up from my head, in Jesus' name.

1330. My virtues locked in a strange location, be released by fire, in Jesus' name.

1331. Every satanic decree of death passed against me, return to the head of those who passed it, in Jesus' name.

1332. Powers that do not want me to reach my ordained maximum for me, die, in Jesus' name.

1333. Powers that want me to serve those that I am better than, you are failures, die, in Jesus' name.

1334. Decision of sorcerers against me, backfire on them, in Jesus' name.

1335. Every door opened to the enemy to invade my life, close, in Jesus' name.

1336. Powers that want me to sleep and not wake up, my life is not your candidate, expire, in Jesus' name.

1337. Powers that want me to sleep and wake up with problems, die, in Jesus' name.

1338. Marks of miserable existence, clear away from me, in Jesus' name.

1339. The hidden marks of familiar spirits in my body, clear away, in Jesus' name.

1340. Every soul tie with spirits from the waters troubling my life, break, in Jesus' name.

1341. Holy Ghost, guide me and order my steps to my place of blessings, in Jesus' name.

1342. With the sword of fire, I cut off the hands of the wicked from the affairs of my life, in Jesus' name.

1343. Every ancestral power that wants me to suffer the affliction of my parents, you are a liar, die, in Jesus' name.

1344. Serpent and scorpion of incurable sickness, I cut off your heads, in Jesus' name.

1345. Powers that want to put me on sickbed, you are liars, die, in Jesus' name.

1346. I receive healing from every genetic affliction by the power in the blood of Jesus, in Jesus' name.

1347. Holy Ghost, destroy every sickness and disease hiding in my body, in Jesus' name.

1348. Whatever the Lord has not planted in my body, come out with all your roots, in Jesus' name.

1349. Poison of serpentine power, come out of my life by fire, in Jesus' name.

1350. My personal Jericho, hear the word of the Lord, collapse, in Jesus' name.

1351. Satanic dog barking at me, be wasted, in Jesus' name.

1352. Witchcraft rats stylishly stealing my money, fire of God, suffocate them, in Jesus' name.

1353. Arrow of spiritual slumber and rising and falling in my life, come out and die, in Jesus' name.

1354. Powers poisoning my food before I eat it, wither, in Jesus' name.

1355. Activities of destiny polluters at the hours of the

night, die, in Jesus' name.

1356. Marine powers of the night hour, release me and let me go, in Jesus' name.

1357. I command the weapons of my enemies to turn against them, in Jesus' name.

1358. I render the aggressive altar of familiar spirits impotent, in Jesus' name.

1359. The hammer of the Almighty, dismantle the altar of familiar spirits in my body, in Jesus' name.

1360. Wind of the Holy Ghost, blow away the poison of familiar spirits from my body, in Jesus' name.

1361. Powers using my dreams to control the affairs of my destiny, wither, in Jesus' name.

1362. I withdraw my prosperity from the hands of familiar spirits, in Jesus' name.

1363. I destroy any image representing me on the altar of familiar spirits, in Jesus' name.

1364. I am created to solve problems. I am not the problem, therefore any problem planted in my life by familiar spirits, die, in Jesus' name.

1365. Powers that abort glory at night, be suffocated unto death, in Jesus' name.

1366. Every battle limiting my progress and success, scatter and die, in Jesus' name.

1367. The internal coffins planted by familiar spirits, catch fire, in Jesus' name.

1368. Strangers living with me in my house, the fire of God is against you, die, in Jesus' name.

1369. Every inherited evil plantation in my life, catch fire, in Jesus' name.

1370. Stubborn obstacles of familiar spirits preventing me from being great, burn to ashes, in Jesus' name.

1371. Stubborn obstacles of career failure, catch fire, in Jesus' name.

1372. Every agent of familiar spirits blocking my way to the top, die, in Jesus' name.

1373. Every yoke of familiar spirits that has refused to break, right now, break, in Jesus' name.

1374. Breakthrough swallowers at the hours of the night, run mad and die, in Jesus' name.

1375. Every veil of familiar spirits shielding me from my miracle, burn to ashes, in Jesus' name.

1376. I shall not die but live to declare the wonders of God in the land of the living, in Jesus' name.

1377. Witchcraft powers projecting rubbish into my life at night, die, in Jesus' name.

1378. Glory of the Living God, overshadow my life for miracles, signs and wonders, in Jesus' name.

1379. Possibility power of the Lord, manifest in my life today, in Jesus' name.

PRAYERS OF DELIVERANCE FROM MARINE SPIRITS

1380. Serpents and mermaid spirits from the water troubling my life, die violently, in Jesus' name.

1381. Marine spirits, I reject your evil marks upon my life, in Jesus' name.

1382. Marine spirits interfering with my destiny in my dream, I destroy you, in Jesus' name.

1383. Blood of Jesus, erase evil marks, covenants and curses hindering my progress, in Jesus' name.

1384. Poison of serpents, come out of your hiding place, in Jesus' name.

1385. Every spirit spouse and the demonic children claiming me, catch fire and die, in Jesus' name.

1386. Wicked marine chains binding me, break, in Jesus' name.

1387. Image or picture representing me in the body of water, catch fire, in Jesus' name.

1388. Spell and ordination of marine powers, break, in Jesus' name.

1389. Every influence and handwriting of marine powers, break and release me, in Jesus' name.

1390. Wedding rings and clothes of marine powers, burn to ashes, in Jesus' name.

1391. Holy Ghost fire, burn the properties of marine powers in my custody, in Jesus' name.

1392. Blood of Jesus, separate me from every marine dedication working against me, in Jesus' name.

1393. Holy Ghost fire, consume the certificate of marriage with any marine agent, in Jesus' name.

1394. O Lord, repair any damage done to my life by any marine power, now, in Jesus' name.

1395. Every connection or covenant I have with any idol, break, in Jesus' name.

1396. From henceforth, let no marine spirit harass me, in Jesus' name.

1397. I overthrow the seat of marine powers working against me, catch fire, in Jesus' name.

1398. This year, the world will know that I am serving a living God, in Jesus' name.

1399. O Lord, thou art a shield for me and the lifter of my head. O God, arise and lift my head, in Jesus' name.

1400. I pull down every stronghold of marine bewitchment, in Jesus' name.

1401. Jesus Christ, the wonder working God, glorify your name in my situation, in Jesus' name.

1402. O God arise by your possibility power, let my story change, in Jesus' name.

1403. The eagle of my life, collect your wings back, arise and fly, in Jesus' name.

1404. Powers fighting me because they know that I am a

star, die, in Jesus' name.

1405. Powers fighting me because of the glory of God upon me, die, in Jesus' name.

1406. Powers removing my name from greatness, you have failed, die, in Jesus' name.

1407. Powers that have vowed that until I come to serve them, I will not prosper, you are not God, die, in Jesus' name.

1408. O God, arise and let the labour of the enemy over my life end in failure, in Jesus' name.

1409. O Lord, I am not satisfied with my present level, promote me by fire, in Jesus' name.

1410. I am an eagle, I am not a chicken therefore, I shall arise and shine, in Jesus' name.

1411. Anyone stealing from me through enchantment and spell, give me back what you stole from me, in Jesus' name.

1412. The garment of the failure of my father's house will not size me, in Jesus' name.

FOUNDATIONAL DELIVERANCE FROM MARINE BONDAGE

1413. Marine spirits interfering with my destiny in the dream, I destroy you, in Jesus' name.

1414. Marine stronghold working against my success and progress, break to pieces, in Jesus' name.

1415. Blood of Jesus, erase evil marks, covenants and curses hindering my progress, in Jesus' name.

1416. Poison of serpents, come out of your hiding place, in Jesus' name.

1417. Wicked marine chains binding me, break, in Jesus' name.

1418. The image or picture representing me in the body of water, catch fire, in Jesus' name.

1419. Spell and ordination of marine powers, break, in Jesus' name.

1420. Every influence and handwriting of marine powers, break and release me, in Jesus' name.

1421. Wedding rings and clothes of marine powers, burn to ashes, in Jesus' name.

1422. Holy Ghost fire, burn the properties of marine powers in my custody, in Jesus' name.

1423. Blood of Jesus, separate me from every marine dedication working against me, in Jesus' name.

1424. O Lord, repair any damage done to my life by any marine power now, in Jesus' name.

1425. I overthrow the seat of marine powers working against me, in Jesus' name.

1426. Stubborn obstacles of familiar spirits preventing me

from being great, burn to ashes, in Jesus' name.

1427. Stubborn obstacles to success in my career, catch fire, in Jesus' name.

1428. Every agent of familiar spirits blocking my way to the top, die, in Jesus' name.

1429. Every yoke of familiar spirits that has refused to break, right now, break, in Jesus' name.

1430. I receive deliverance from long term bondage of familiar spirits, in Jesus' name.

1431. Witchcraft powers afflicting my marriage, career and destiny, be buried, in Jesus' name.

1432. The cage of familiar spirits, release me now, in Jesus' name.

1433. I smash the head of the strongman on the wall of fire, in Jesus' name.

1434. Strongman manipulating my head, leave my head alone, die, in Jesus' name.

1435. Serpent of the strongman swallowing my prosperity, die, in Jesus' name.

1436. The garment of sickness planted by the strongman in my body, catch fire, in Jesus' name.

1437. In Jesus' name, my life shall not be food for the strongman.

1438. Masquerade of the strongman pursuing me at night, die, in Jesus' name.

1439. I bind the spirit of divination and sorcery working against me, in Jesus' name.

1440. My ears shall hear good news this month, in Jesus' name.

1441. Every internal disorder working against me, clear away, in Jesus' name.

1442. Demonic supernatural powers monitoring my life at night, die, in Jesus' name.

1443. The mark of strongman, clear away from me, in Jesus' name.

1444. Strongman of death pursuing my life, die, in Jesus' name.

1445. Strongman devouring my harvest, I bury you today, in Jesus' name.

1446. Strongman planning to hand me over to the domestic witchcraft of my father's house, die, in Jesus' name.

PRAYERS OF DELIVERANCE FROM FAMILIAR SPIRITS

1447. Any spell cast on me by familiar spirits, expire, in Jesus' name.

1448. I refuse to be a slave of familiar spirits, in Jesus' name.

1449. Spiritual strongman diverting my blessings, shoot yourself, in Jesus' name.

1450. I take the sword of the Lord and cut off the head of the strongman assigned against me, in Jesus' name.

1451. Strongman of poverty, die, in Jesus' name.

1452. Strongman of failure at the edge of success, die, in Jesus' name.

1453. The wind of the Holy Ghost blow away the poison of familiar spirit from my body, in Jesus' name.

1454. I withdraw my prosperity from the hands of familiar spirits, in Jesus' name.

1455. I destroy any image representing me on the altar of familiar spirits, in Jesus' name.

1456. I am created to solve problems, I am not the problem, therefore, any problem planted in my life by familiar spirits, die, in Jesus' name.

1457. Every battle limiting my progress and success, scatter and die, in Jesus' name.

1458. The internal coffins planted by familiar spirits, catch fire, in Jesus' name.

1459. Strangers living with me in my house, the fire of God is against you, die, in Jesus' name.

1460. Every inherited evil plantation in my life, catch fire, in Jesus' name.

1461. Stubborn obstacles of familiar spirits, preventing me from being great, burn to ashes, in Jesus' name.

1462. O God, arise and let the evil plan and programme of familiar spirits for my life scatter, in Jesus' name.

1463. Familiar spirits assigned to destroy my faith in God and make God a liar in my life, die, in Jesus' name.

1464. Every man or woman flying in any basket against my life, crash land, in Jesus' name.

1465. I shoot down every wicked army of familiar spirits shooting at me, in Jesus' name.

1466. Let the hidden secret of familiar spirits in my household be exposed and disgraced, in Jesus' name.

1467. Satanic animals programmed against me in my dreams, destroy yourselves, in Jesus' name.

1468. The familiar spirits that pursued my parents and now want to pursue me, die, in Jesus' name.

1469. I command the familiar spirit stronghold in my family to crumble, in Jesus' name.

1470. Familiar spirit bird flying at night against me, burn to ashes, in Jesus' name.

1471. I release myself from every familiar spirit manipulation and control, in Jesus' name.

1472. Familiar spirits using dogs and cats to terrorize me, die, in Jesus' name.

1473. Any demonic point of contact of familiar spirits, clear away, in Jesus' name.

1474. Holy Ghost, erase, cancel and nullify the marks of familiar spirits in my life, in Jesus' name.

1475. Any spell cast on me by familiar spirits, expire, in Jesus' name.

1476. I take the sword of the Lord and cut off the head of the strongman assigned against me, in Jesus' name.

1477. Powers exchanging my favour with disfavour, die, in Jesus' name.

1478. Powers increasing my warfare, I bury you in hot sand, in Jesus' name.

1479. My life, hear the word of the Lord, rise above the reproach of my father's house, in Jesus' name.

1480. Powers frustrating me at the edge of my breakthrough, I pull you down, die, in Jesus' name.

1481. Powers assigned to revenge the shedding of innocent blood in my father's house, shut up by the power in the blood of Jesus, in Jesus' name.

1482. Powers chasing away prosperity, honour and joy from me, die, in Jesus' name.

1483. Environmental strongman that is fully armed against my progress, be bound, in Jesus' name.

1484. Powers replacing my beauty with ashes, be disgraced, in Jesus' name.

BREAKING THE STRONGHOLD OF MARINE POWERS

1485. By the power in the blood of Jesus, I break the stronghold of marine powers in my life, in Jesus' name.

1486. Lord Jesus, by your never failing power, arise and fight for me, in Jesus' name.

1487. Every stubborn problem in my life, I cry against you, die, in Jesus' name.

1488. Battles assigned to follow me till my old age, expire and die, in Jesus' name.

1489. O God, arise and put on me the crown of double honour, in Jesus' name.

1490. Every enemy of my next level, before I open my eyes, expire, in Jesus' name.

1491. Organized battles against my star, somersault and die, in Jesus' name.

1492. O God, arise by your strong and mighty hands, pull me out of all ancient prisons, in Jesus' name.

1493. Powers diverting answers to my prayers, O God, arise and bury them, in Jesus' name.

1494. The wall of Jericho standing before me, before I open my eyes, fall, fall, fall, in Jesus' name.

1495. Every material of poverty in my life that is hindering my prosperity, catch fire, in Jesus' name.

1496. Breakthrough must meet breakthrough in my life, and favour must meet favour in my life now, in Jesus' name.

1497. I decree multiple celebrations and promotions by the power of the Lord Jesus Christ, in Jesus' name.

1498. Power to make national and global impact, fall upon me now, in Jesus' name.

1499. O God, arise and advertise me for uncommon favour, in Jesus' name.

1500. Every door that should open for me this year, that is closed, open now, in Jesus' name.

1501. Holy Ghost fire, fill my spirit, soul and life, in Jesus' name.

1502. All my blessings that are due, manifest by fire, in Jesus' name.

1503. Every yoke of this is how far you will go and no further, die, in Jesus' name

1507. By the power of the Lord Jesus, I cross over every mountain of impossibility, in Jesus' name.

1505. Magnet of bondage that is attracting problems to me, break, in Jesus' name.

1506. Powers cutting me off when it is my turn to get favour, I cut you off, in Jesus' name.

1507. Altars of affliction raised against my land, catch fire, in Jesus' name.

1508. The root and foundation of cruel affliction in my body, release me, catch fire, in Jesus' name.

1509. Powers drinking the blood of my success, I cut you off, die, in Jesus' name.

1510. Every congregation of the wicked assigned against

me, be bound, in Jesus' name.

1511. Horn of the wicked rising up against my star, I crush you, in Jesus' name.

1512. Powers speaking death to my favour, perish, in Jesus' name.

1513. My glory, reject the garment of Ichabod, in Jesus' name.

1514. Powers assigned to waste my labour this year, Rock of Ages, destroy them, in Jesus' name.

1515. Powers boasting that I will move from battle to battle this year, be wasted, in Jesus' name.

1516. Every bloodline battle of my father's house that wants to swallow my star, die, in Jesus' name.

1517. Sicknesses that came as a result of generational curses, break, in Jesus' name.

1518. Commander of the army of darkness assigned against me, die, in Jesus' name.

1519. I break the yoke of stagnation by the power in the blood of Jesus, in Jesus' name.

1520. Powers that have vowed that my hands will not feed me, I cut you off, in Jesus' name.

1521. Possibility power of our Lord and Saviour Jesus Christ, work miracle in my life today, in Jesus' name.

1522. I am not going down, I am going upward. I am not going backward, I am going forward, in Jesus' name.

1523. Let God be God in every area of my life, in Jesus' name.

1524. Yoke of labour without reward, break, in Jesus' name.

1525. Yoke of starting and not finishing, break, in Jesus' name.

1526. Yoke of suffering for what I know nothing about, break, in Jesus' name.

1527. Yoke of disappearance of helpers, break, in Jesus' name.

1528. Yoke of becoming the tail, break, in Jesus' name.

1529. Every garment of poverty and lack in my hands, I set you ablaze, in Jesus' name.

1530. I kill the affliction projected into my life by satanic programming, burn to ashes, in Jesus' name.

1531. Failure and shame shall not be my portion, in Jesus' name.

1532. Every good thing that I have started, I shall complete by the power in the blood of Jesus, in Jesus' name.

1533. Owners of evil load, carry your load of financial embarrassment and shame, in Jesus' name.

1534. I fire back every arrow of frustration, intimidation and confusion fired at me, in Jesus' name.

1535. I shall not die but live to declare the great things the Lord has done in my life, in Jesus' name.

1536. I curse every local altar fashioned against me, in Jesus' name.

1537. Let the hammer of the Almighty God smash every evil altar erected against me, in Jesus' name.

1538. O Lord, send your fire to destroy every evil altar fashioned against me, in Jesus' name.

1539. Every evil priest ministering against me at the evil altar, receive the sword of God, in Jesus' name.

1540. Let the thunder of God smite every evil priest working against me at the evil altar and burn him to ashes, in Jesus' name.

1541. Let every satanic priest ministering against me at evil altars fall down and die, in Jesus' name.

BREAKING THE YOKE OF POVERTY

1542. Yoke of poverty working against me spiritually and physically, break, in Jesus' name.

1543. Any power that wants me to suffer what my parents suffered, die, in Jesus' name.

1544. Any evil womb that has swallowed my blessings, vomit them now, in Jesus' name.

1545. Evil personality attacking my financial life in the dream, be disgraced forever, in Jesus' name.

1546. Let every wicked personality that has vowed to disgrace me financially die by fire, in Jesus' name.

1547. I reject counterfeit blessings assigned to waste my financial life, in Jesus' name.

464

1548. Any power manipulating my financial life and destiny, die, in Jesus' name.

1549. Any strange money causing financial crisis for me, catch fire and be burnt to ashes, in Jesus' name.

1550. Any power assigned to waste my effort this month, die shamefully, in Jesus' name.

1551. Let powers from my parent's houses expanding my problems die now, in Jesus' name.

1552. Spirit of death and hell living in my body, come out and die, in Jesus' name.

1553. Any witchcraft pot cooking my financial destiny, break by fire, in Jesus' name.

1554. Any power delaying the angels of my blessings from reaching me, wither, in Jesus' name.

1555. O God, arise and deliver me from every financial trouble right now, in Jesus' name.

1556. Any evil power that has hijacked my finances, release them now and die, in Jesus' name.

1557. Every problem that has refused to leave me alone, die suddenly, in Jesus' name.

1558. Let all dangers ahead of me this month be removed by the power in the blood of Jesus, in Jesus' name.

1559. Any area of my life under satanic attack, receive immediate deliverance, in Jesus' name.

1560. Any evil hand planting financial difficulties in the

garden of my life, wither and dry up by fire, in Jesus' name.

1561. Any arrow of death fired against my life, I fire you back, locate your senders and kill them, in Jesus' name.

1562. Let the blood of Jesus crush and conquer any evil sacrifice ever offered against me, in Jesus' name.

1563. Any evil summon going on against me from any evil altar, satanic covens, demonic forest or witchcraft gathering, I reject you completely, backfire, in Jesus' name.

1564. I break the backbone of poverty and failure in my life, by the power in the blood of Jesus, in Jesus' name.

1565. Arrows of affliction fired against my spirit, soul and body, come out and die, in Jesus' name.

1566. I challenge my life with the fire of God, in Jesus' name.

1567. The yoke of rising and falling in my life, be broken, in Jesus' name.

1568. The hands of terror laid upon me in the spirit realm, catch fire, in Jesus' name.

1569. I refuse be used as a sacrificial object at the altar of witchcraft, in Jesus' name.

1570. The evil seed of infirmity, be uprooted out of my systems, in Jesus' name.

1571. Infirmity sponsored by enchantment, wither, in Jesus'

name.

1572. Every cycle of repeated affliction programmed against me, wither, in Jesus' name.

1573. Arrow of infirmity fired into my body, wither, in Jesus' name.

1574. Every money and time wasting sickness assigned against me, wither, in Jesus' name.

1575. You the strong root of infirmity, be uprooted by fire, in Jesus' name.

1576. O God, arise and perfect everything that concerns my health, in Jesus' name.

1577. O axe of fire, cut down the evil tree of infirmity in my family line, in Jesus' name.

1578. I wage war against the serpents and scorpions of infirmity with the sword of fire, in Jesus' name.

1579. Dark plantations in any part of my body, wither by fire, in Jesus' name.

1580. Holy Ghost, immunize my body system against sudden attacks, in Jesus' name.

1581. Thou strongman of infirmity assigned against me, be paralyzed, in Jesus' name.

1582. Marks of infirmity, be removed from me, in Jesus' name.

1583. Every prosperity paralysis from household wickedness, come out with all your roots by fire, in Jesus' name.

1584. Every clever devourer, come out with all your roots, in Jesus' name.

1585. Every spirit of fragmented life, come out with all your roots, in Jesus' name.

1586. Every spirit of debt, come out with all your roots, in Jesus' name.

1587. Every handshake of poverty, come out with all your roots, in Jesus' name.

1588. Every financial paralysis by witchcraft, come out with all your roots, in Jesus' name.

1589. Every satanic insect prepared against me, begin to bite your senders, in Jesus' name.

1590. I challenge my body with the Holy Ghost fire, in Jesus' name.

1591. O God, arise and let me experience open heavens in every area of my life, in Jesus' name.

1592. I speak destruction to every evil growth, in Jesus' name.

1593. Covenant and curses behind any sickness, break and release me, in Jesus' name.

1594. Every good thing the Lord has promised me shall come to pass, in Jesus' name.

1595. I speak life and health to every part of my body, in Jesus' name.

1596. Sing and give thanks to God for answered prayers.

PRAYERS AGAINST YOUR STAFF OF BREAD

1597. Powers assigned to attack my source of income, be paralyzed, in Jesus' name.

1598. The backdoor through which the enemy is siphoning my money, be closed, in Jesus' name.

1599. Agenda of spiritual robbers assigned to steal what will make me great, be frustrated, in Jesus' name.

1600. Owners of evil load, appear and carry your load, in Jesus' name.

1601. I must succeed in everything I lay my hands upon, in Jesus' name.

1602. Powers that are spending my money in the spirit realm, collapse and die, in Jesus' name.

1603. Every dark rope tying down my money, break, in Jesus' name.

1604. O Lord, send your fire to destroy every evil altar fashioned against me, in Jesus' name.

1605. Every evil priest ministering against me at the evil altar, receive the sword of God, in Jesus' name.

1606. Let the thunder of God smite every evil priest working against me at the evil altar and burn him to ashes, in Jesus' name.

1607. Let every satanic priest ministering against me at evil altars fall down and die, in Jesus' name.

1608. Any hand that wants to retaliate or arrest me because

of all the prayers I am praying, dry up and wither, in Jesus' name.

1609. Every stubborn evil altar priest, drink your own blood, in Jesus' name.

1610. Let God be God in every area of my life, in Jesus' name.

1611. Powers that have vowed that I will beg for bread, you are liars, die, in Jesus' name.

1612. All my money in the hands of spiritual robbers, be released, in Jesus' name.

1613. Every register containing my name for poverty, catch fire, in Jesus' name.

1614. Witchcraft attacks promoting poverty in my life, burn to ashes, in Jesus' name.

1615. I fire back every arrow of infirmity fired at me, in Jesus' name.

1616. Spiritual termites devouring my wealth, die, in Jesus' name.

1617. Evil hands stealing from me, be cut off, in Jesus' name.

1618. Every pot of darkness cooking my health, break, in Jesus' name.

1619. Every demonic archive holding what belongs to me, release it and catch fire, in Jesus' name.

1620. The sun will not smite me by day nor the moon by night, in Jesus' name.

1621. My harvest of ten years, gather together and locate

me, in Jesus' name.

1622. Any secret battle blocking the fulfilment of my destiny prophecy, catch fire, in Jesus' name.

1623. This month, long life, good health and divine favour shall be my portion, in Jesus' name.

1624. Every backdoor through which my blessings are carted away, I close you, in Jesus' name.

1625. O Lion of Judah, arise and roar against my mountain, in Jesus' name.

1626. O God, arise and convert my waste land to wealth land, in Jesus' name.

1627. Every veil of darkness blocking my exploits, be roasted, in Jesus' name.

1628. My house, become too hot for the enemy to operate in easily, in Jesus' name.

1629. I shall arise and break new grounds by the power in the blood of Jesus, in Jesus' name.

1630. Wrong people planted around me to steal from me, be exposed, in Jesus' name.

PRAYERS TO SCATTER SATANIC CONSPIRACY

1631. Anywhere there is a demonic gang up against me, angels of fire, scatter them, in Jesus' name.

1632. I pursue, overtake and recover my portion by fire, in Jesus' name.

1633. Masquerades of darkness scaring my helpers away, be roasted, in Jesus' name.

1634. O God, arise and let the enemy make mistakes that will promote my destiny, in Jesus' name.

1635. I will not struggle to be recognized, in Jesus' name.

1636. Those who trust in charms and wicked devices, I render them useless and powerless, in Jesus' name.

1637. The hands of darkness placed on my blessing, catch fire, in Jesus' name.

1638. I am a star, whether the enemy likes it or not, and I must shine, in Jesus' name.

1639. O God, arise and answer my prayers, in Jesus' name.

1640. I tear off every satanic covering preventing me from seeing opportunities, in Jesus' name.

1641. I will laugh last over my enemy, in Jesus' name.

1642. Miracles that will advertise the wonders of God in my life, manifest, in Jesus' name.

1643. I will succeed in every endeavour that I lay my hands upon, in Jesus' name.

1644. The wickedness of the wicked in my life, expire, in Jesus' name.

1645. Powers that are drinking the blood of my spiritual life, die, in Jesus' name.

1646. Every horn of darkness fashioned to harm me this year, be broken to pieces, in Jesus' name.

1647. O God, arise and destroy every shrine harbouring evil prophets against me, in Jesus' name.

1648. This year, I shall not be engaged in useless battles. The enemy will not waste my strength, in Jesus' name.

1649. If the enemy has stolen my dominion, I recover it by fire, in Jesus' name.

1650. Anointing that breaks the yoke of delay, shame and disgrace, fall upon me, in Jesus' name.

1651. No matter how strong my enemies are, this year, I shall be anointed to finish them, in Jesus' name.

1652. Powers that are preparing spiritual rags for me to wear, I am not your candidate, die, in Jesus' name.

1653. Powers boasting that I will move from battle to battle this year, be wasted, Jesus' name.

1654. Every bloodline battle of my father's house waiting to swallow my star, die, in Jesus' name.

1655. Sicknesses that came as a result of generational curses, break, in Jesus' name.

1656. Commander of the army of darkness assigned against me, die, in Jesus' name.

1657. I break the yoke of stagnation by the power in the blood of Jesus, in Jesus' name

1658. Powers that have vowed that my hands will not feed me, I cut you off, in Jesus' name.

1659. Possibility power of our Lord and Saviour Jesus Christ, work miracles in my life today, in Jesus' name.

473

PRAYERS FOR SUCCESS IN CAREER

1660. Power to succeed where others have failed, fall upon me, in Jesus' name.

1661. I recover sevenfold of what the enemy has stolen from me, in Jesus' name.

1662. My destiny, don't just watch others succeed, succeed too, in Jesus' name.

1663. I shall not be a spectator in the field of life, in Jesus' name.

1664. Spirit of death and hell, lose your hold upon my life, in Jesus' name.

1665. Failure and shame shall not be my portion, in Jesus' name.

1666. I shall complete every good thing I have started by the power in the blood of Jesus, in Jesus' name.

1667. Owners of evil load, carry your load of financial embarrassment and shame, in Jesus' name.

1668. I fire back every arrow of frustration, intimidation and confusion fired at me, in Jesus' name.

1669. I shall not die but live to declare the great things the Lord has done in my life, in Jesus' name.

1670. I curse every local altar fashioned against me, in Jesus' name.

1671. Let the hammer of the Almighty God smash every evil altar erected against me, in Jesus' name.

1672. O Lord, send your fire to destroy every evil altar

474

fashioned against me, in Jesus' name.

1673. Every evil priest ministering against me at the evil altar, receive the sword of God, in Jesus' name.

1674. Lord, repair any damage done to my life by any marine power now, in Jesus' name.

1675. Every connection or covenant I have with any idol, break, in Jesus' name.

1676. From henceforth, let no marine spirit harass me, in Jesus' name.

1677. I overthrow the seat of marine powers working against me and I command it to catch fire, in Jesus' name.

1678. Stubborn obstacles of familiar spirits, preventing me from being great, burn to ashes, in Jesus' name.

1679. Stubborn obstacles of career failure, catch fire, in Jesus' name.

1680. Every agent of familiar spirits blocking my way to the top, die, in Jesus' name.

1681. Every yoke of familiar spirits that has refused to break, right now, break, in Jesus' name.

1682. Every veil of familiar spirits shielding me from my miracle, burn to ashes, in Jesus' name.

1683. I receive deliverance from long standing bondage of familiar spirits, in Jesus' name.

1684. Agenda of spiritual robbers assigned to steal what will make me great, be frustrated, in Jesus' name.

1685. Owners of evil load, appear and carry your load, in Jesus' name.

1686. I must succeed in everything I lay my hands upon, in Jesus' name.

1687. Powers that are spending my money in the spirit realm, collapse and die, in Jesus' name.

1688. Every dark rope tying down my money, break, in Jesus' name.

1689. O Lord, send your fire to destroy every evil altar fashioned against me, in Jesus' name.

1690. Every evil priest ministering against me at the evil altar, receive the sword of God, in Jesus' name.

PRAYERS OF SUCCESS IN EXAMINATION

1691. Power of excellence in examination, fall upon me, in Jesus' name.

1692. I shall be ten times better than my colleagues, in Jesus' name.

1693. Spirit of wisdom, knowledge and understanding, fall upon me, in Jesus' name.

1694. I shall not fail any examination again, in Jesus' name.

1695. Power of retentive ability, fall upon me, in Jesus' name.

1696. You the demon of loss of memory, I destroy you in my life today, in Jesus' name.

1697. Every yoke of bewitchment fired against me, backfire, in Jesus' name.

1698. Holy Ghost, anoint me with wisdom to beat my competitors and give them a wide margin, in Jesus' name.

1699. Every evil nocturnal meeting being held for my sake, scatter, in Jesus' name.

1700. Satanic resistance to the emergence of my candidacy, wither and scatter, in Jesus' name.

1701. All external and internal saboteurs, be exposed and disgraced, in Jesus' name.

1702. Fresh fire to outshine others, fall upon me, in Jesus' name.

1703. Holy Ghost, journey with me, guide and instruct me in the path of righteousness for your sake, in Jesus' name.

1704. Because of Jesus, I shall not fail, in Jesus' name.

1705. I connect to mysterious breakthroughs by fire, in Jesus' name.

1706. I recover all my stolen blessings, in Jesus' name.

1707. The spirit of get and lose, depart from me right now, in Jesus' name.

1708. My life, I prophesy to you, move forward right now, in Jesus' name.

1709. From now, I shall be in the right place at the right time,

in Jesus' name.

1710. O God, arise and raise a voice for me in unlikely places this year, in Jesus' name.

1711. Every dark market, where what belongs to me are being sold, scatter, in Jesus' name.

1712. Evil hands collecting what is due to me in the spirit realm, wither, in Jesus' name.

1713. Evil umbrella preventing the flow of my blessing, catch fire, in Jesus' name.

1714. My life shall not obey evil commands this year, in Jesus' name.

1715. The spirit of rising and falling, depart from me, in Jesus' name.

1716. The spirit of delay, break and release me, in Jesus' name.

1717. Every dream defilement affecting my academics, catch fire, in Jesus' name.

1718. I refuse to be tied down, evil chain break off me, in Jesus' name.

1719. My breakthroughs, what are you waiting for? Manifest, in Jesus' name.

1720. No one shall say sorry to me again concerning my academics, in Jesus' name.

1721. Glory of the living God, overshadow me, in Jesus' name.

1722. Blood of Jesus, remove every mark of failure at the edge of success from me, in Jesus' name.

1723. Spirit of death and hell, break your power over me, in Jesus' name.

PRAYERS TO DESTROY THE ATTACKS OF THE SPIRIT DEATH

1724. Spirit of sudden death assigned against me, be suffocated, in Jesus' name.

1725. Arrows of disgrace, my life is not your candidate, lose your hold over my life, in Jesus' name.

1726. Evil bird flying for my sake, crash land and disintegrate, in Jesus' name.

1727. Every spell of darkness assigned against my health, expire, in Jesus' name.

1728. My Father, My Father, no devourer is permitted to waste my life, in Jesus' name.

1729. Anything in me that is cooperating with the spirit of devourers to fight against my life, come out and die, in Jesus' name.

1730. Any ignorance that is preventing me from seeing the glory of God, be consumed by the Holy Ghost fire, in Jesus' name.

1731. Any spirit of the devourer assigned to scatter things in my life, I bind you, in Jesus' name.

1732. Any negative dream attacking my life, I bind you, in Jesus' name.

1733. The spirit of dryness and the spirit of famine shall not prosper in my life, in Jesus' name.

1734. Every covenant of profitless hard work in my foundation, be destroyed, in Jesus' name.

1735. Every power seating on my harvest, be unseated by fire, in Jesus' name.

1736. Wasters, devourers, emptiers, and spoilers assigned against my life, I bind you, in Jesus' name.

1737. Any power assigned to withhold my harvest and celebration this year, you are a failure; fire of God, consume them, in Jesus' name.

1738. I take authority over family devourers, financial devourers, marriage devourers, health devourers and employment devourers, in Jesus' name.

1739. Every power assigned to embarrass and disgrace me, die by fire, in Jesus' name.

1740. Powers militating against my fulfilment and uplifting, the blood of Jesus is against you, in Jesus' name.

1741. O God, after the order of Joseph, arise and use me to rewrite my family's history, in Jesus' name.

1742. I decree and declare that wasters shall not waste my life, emptiers shall not empty my life and destroyers shall not destroy my life, in Jesus' name.

1743. Holy Ghost fire, kill every disease and infirmity in my body, in Jesus' name.

1744. Sickness and disease originating from marine spirit, come out of my body, in Jesus' name.

1745. At the name of Jesus, every knee must bow. Therefore, every sickness that has a name in my body, disappear, in Jesus' name.

1746. My body, soul and spirit shall not be the habitation of devils, in Jesus' name.

1747. Stubborn root of infirmity and disease, be cut off now, in Jesus' name.

1748. Arrows that entered into my life during the hour of the night, come out and enter no more, in Jesus' name.

1749. I break the stronghold of sickness and disease and set it on fire, in Jesus' name.

1750. Every tree that God has not planted in my body, be cut down, in Jesus' name.

1751. My life, henceforth, you shall not obey satanic instructions by the power in the blood of Jesus, in Jesus' name.

1752. Evil cloud preventing my rain of favour from falling, clear away now, in Jesus' name.

1753. My life shall not be a disappointment to God and to my generation, in Jesus' name.

1754. My breakthroughs in coma, wake up by fire, in Jesus' name.

1755. Powers assigned to cage my prayer life through night

feeding, die, in Jesus' name.

PRAYING OUT EVIL ARROWS FROM YOUR BODY

1756. Yoke manufacturers of the idol of my father's house, I damage your power, in Jesus' name.

1757. Arrows fired into my destiny by the idol of my foundation, die, in Jesus' name.

1758. Anger of heaven provoked by my family idol, be cancelled by the blood of Jesus, in Jesus' name.

1759. Every evil dedication speaking against my moving forward, I dash you to pieces, in Jesus' name.

1760. Powers mentioning my name on an evil altar, be silenced and die, in Jesus' name.

1761. Arrow of failure, lose your hold upon my life, in Jesus' name.

1762. Every chain of limitation and frustration, break to pieces, in Jesus' name.

1763. Every idol chain holding me down, break, in Jesus' name.

1764. Negative anointing of my family idols, clear away from my blood, in Jesus' name.

1765. Idol of my father's house crying against my destiny, be silenced, in Jesus' name.

1766. Every evil covenant in my life, break now, in Jesus' name.

1767. I retrieve my destiny from the hand of Judas, in Jesus' name.

1768. I take over the wealth of the sinner, in Jesus' name.

1769. I recover the steering wheel of my wealth from the hands of evil drivers, in Jesus' name.

1770. Holy Ghost fire, revive my blessings, in Jesus' name.

1771. Holy Ghost fire, return my stolen blessings, in Jesus' name.

1772. O Lord, send your angels to bring my blessings, in Jesus' name.

1773. I shall not die the death of another person, in Jesus' name.

1774. Father, reveal to me the key to my prosperity, in Jesus' name.

1775. Every power sitting on my wealth, fall down and die, in Jesus' name.

1776. Every power of failure at the edge of success, die, in Jesus' name.

1777. Thou power of poor finishing, die, in Jesus' name.

1778. Heavenly fire, attack the power of poverty in my life, in Jesus' name.

1770. I overthrow the strongman that troubled me this year, in Jesus' name.

1780. Every habitation of wickedness around me, be desolate, in Jesus' name.

1781. Crystal ball and mirror of darkness working against me, break, in Jesus' name.

1782. All round success, pursue and locate me, in Jesus' name.

1783. Father Lord, make my life a success story, in Jesus' name.

1784. Every satanic decree against my life, die, in Jesus' name.

1785. I throw confusion into the camp of my enemy, in Jesus' name.

1786. I shall get to my destiny at the appointed time, in Jesus' name.

1787. I refuse to rotate, roam and circulate on the same spot, in Jesus' name.

1788. Every idol power barking against my full scale laughter, shut up and die, in Jesus' name.

1789. Every battle provoked against my life by family idols, scatter unto desolation, in Jesus' name.

1790. Agenda of idol powers to paralyze my breakthroughs, die, in Jesus' name.

1791. Tormenting powers fashioned against me by idol powers, release me and die, in Jesus' name.

1792. Wasters and emptiers assigned by idol powers to waste my life, die by fire, in Jesus' name.

1793. Every conscious and unconscious covenant with any idol, break by fire, in Jesus' name.

BREAKING COLLECTIVE YOKES AND CAPTIVITY

1794. I break the mysterious power of spell and enchantment, in Jesus' name.

1795. Invisible barriers that will not let me go, break, in Jesus' name.

1796. Witchcraft object programmed into my life, come out and dry up, in Jesus' name.

1797. Cover up of darkness preventing me from moving forward, catch fire, in Jesus' name.

1798. The rod of the wicked that is risen up against me, break in pieces, in Jesus' name.

1799. Arrow of rising and falling projected into my life, come out and die, in Jesus' name.

1800. Wherever my finances, career and destiny are tied down, I lose you, in Jesus' name.

1801. Powers conspiring and regrouping against me, break into pieces, in Jesus' name.

1802. My life, reject the arrow of confusion, frustration and limitation, in Jesus' name.

1803. The voice of the strongman asking me to come down, I am not coming down, die, in Jesus' name.

1804. I wage holy war against unexplainable difficulty in my life, in Jesus' name.

1805. Thou power of spiritual dryness and emptiness, lose your hold upon my life, in Jesus' name.

1806. Slumber and filthy thoughts holding me down, break, in Jesus' name.

1807. I release myself from fear of the unknown that cage men, in Jesus' name.

1808. I break the yoke of continued suffering in my life, in Jesus' name.

1809. Negative predictions and wishes against my destiny, fail, in Jesus' name.

1810. Yoke manufacturers of the idol of my father's house, I damage your power, in Jesus' name.

1811. Arrows fired into my destiny by the idol of my foundation, die, in Jesus' name.

1812. Anger of heaven provoked by my family idol, be cancelled by the blood of Jesus, in Jesus' name.

1813. Every evil dedication that speaks against my moving forward, I dash you to pieces, in Jesus' name.

1814. Powers mentioning my name on evil altars, be silenced and die, in Jesus' name.

1815. Every crooked line drawn into my journey by idol powers, be wiped off by the blood of Jesus, in Jesus' name.

1816. Any generational disgrace sponsored by family idol, clear away by the power in the blood of Jesus, in Jesus' name.

1817. Troubles assigned against my life by idol powers,

486

clear away by fire, in Jesus' name.

1818. Every shrine mentioning my name, clear away by the power in the blood of Jesus, in Jesus' name.

1819. Every destiny miscalculation provoked by idol powers, be reversed, in Jesus' name.

1820. Pursuing powers of my father's house, turn back and be roasted, in Jesus' name.

1821. I recover all my divine opportunities wasted by family idols, in Jesus' name.

1822. Lord, let the imagination of the wicked against our country be neutralized, in Jesus' name.

1823. Every secret I need to know about my mother's lineage, be revealed, in Jesus' name.

1824. Every secret I need to know about my hometown, be revealed, in Jesus' name.

1825. Every secret I need to know about the work I am doing, be revealed, in Jesus' name.

1826. O Lord, give me the spirit of revelation and wisdom in the knowledge of yourself, in Jesus' name.

1827. O Lord, make your way plain before my face on this issue, in Jesus' name.

1828. O Lord, remove spiritual cataract from my eyes, in Jesus' name.

1829. Every organised worker of iniquity, depart from me, in Jesus' name.

1830. O Lord, let all my enemies be ashamed and sore vexed, in Jesus' name.

1831. My Father, let sudden shame be the lot of all my oppressors, in Jesus' name.

1832. Every power planning to tear my soul like a lion tears a lamb, be dismantled, in Jesus' name.

1833. God shall destroy the camp of the enemy and their camp shall never be built up, in Jesus' name.

1834. O Lord, according to the deeds of the wicked, reward the work of their hands, in Jesus' name.

1835. O Lord, put off my sackcloth and clothe me with gladness, in Jesus' name.

1836. O Lord, cast out my enemies in the multitude of their transgressions, in Jesus' name.

1837. My Father, let sudden shame be the lot of all my oppressors, in Jesus' name.

1838. I withdraw my name from the register of frustration, in Jesus' name.

1839. I prophesy to my spiritual legs, begin to move me forward, in Jesus' name.

1840. I receive power to operate three levels of movement: I shall walk, I shall run and I shall fly as an eagle, in Jesus' name.

1841. O Lord, lift me to a higher ground, in Jesus' name.

1842. I become unstoppable as the wind, in the name of

Jesus' name.

1843. As from today, my middle name becomes excellence and advancement, in Jesus' name.

1844. Uncompleted projects in my life, receive the touch of God, in Jesus' name.

1845. I subdue and overthrow all anti-progress forces, in Jesus' name.

1846. Evil strangers, flee and never appear again, in Jesus' name.

1847. Every wicked advice against my life, be frustrated, in Jesus' name.

1848. Every cloth of disgrace, I tear you to pieces, in Jesus' name.

1849. O God that disgraced Ahitophel, bring the counsel of my enemies to nothing, in Jesus' name.

1850. You are the God of performance, perform wonders in my life, in Jesus' name.

1851. O Lord, make me a positive wonder, in Jesus' name.

1852. By the power of God, dark places shall not oppress me, in Jesus' name.

1853. I cancel every satanic appointment with death, in Jesus' name.

1854. I bury every shrine conjuring my image, in Jesus' name.

1855. I am hot coals of fire, therefore any witchdoctor that tampers with my destiny shall be roasted, in Jesus' name.

1856. Every witchcraft power touching my life, die, in Jesus' name.

1857. I refuse that my life shall be used as a sacrifice material to the devil, in Jesus' name.

1858. Anything planted in my life to disgrace me, come out with all your roots, in Jesus' name.

1859. I reject every demonic stagnation of my blessings, in Jesus' name.

1860. I reject weak financial breakthroughs and I claim big financial breakthroughs, in Jesus' name.

1861. Hidden and clever devourers, be bound, in Jesus' name.

1862. I release myself from every evil family pattern of poverty, in Jesus' name.

1863. I refuse to allow my wealth to die on any evil altar, in Jesus' name.

1864. I reject prosperity paralysis, in Jesus' name.

1865. I possess all my foreign benefits, in Jesus' name.

1866. I dash every poverty dream to the ground, in Jesus' name.

1867. My hands have started to build and will finish it, in Jesus' name.

1868. I refuse to become the foot mat of amputators, in

Jesus' name.

1869. God of providence, raise divine capital for me, in Jesus' name.

1870. I occupy my rightful position, in Jesus' name.

1871. Every delayed and denied prosperity, manifest by fire, in Jesus' name.

1872. Every bewitchment on my account, receive deliverance, in Jesus' name.

1873. Every snail anointing on my blessings, fall down and die, in Jesus' name.

1874. Every power broadcasting my life for evil, be silenced, in Jesus' name.

1875. I refuse to lock the door of blessings against myself, in Jesus' name.

1876. I release myself from every spirit of poverty, in Jesus' name.

1877. I curse the spirit of poverty, in Jesus' name.

1878. I release myself from every bondage of poverty, in Jesus' name.

1879. You evil personalities hiding in my head and causing it to fail, come out and die, in Jesus' name.

1880. Every contractor hired against my head, I terminate your contracts from the source by fire; die, in Jesus' name.

1881. You evil spirit hindering my head from being

crowned, release my head and die, in Jesus' name.

1882. You evil spirit hindering my head from attaining fame and promotion, release my head and die, in Jesus' name.

1883. You spirit preventing my head from acquiring its birthright, release my head and die, in Jesus' name.

1884. Foreign witchcraft powers cooperating with household witchcraft against my head, scatter by fire, in Jesus' name.

1885. Household witches gathering against my head, scatter and die, in Jesus' name.

1886. Household witchcraft verdict and conclusion against my head, be nullified by fire, in Jesus' name.

1887. Witchcraft covens linked to the problem of my head, catch fire and scatter, in Jesus' name.

1888. You evil objects being used to monitor my head for evil, be scattered and rendered invalid, in Jesus' name.

1889. You evil priests ministering against my head from any evil altar, fall down and die, in Jesus' name.

1890. You evil altar erected against the promotion and prominence of my head, be uprooted and scatter, in Jesus' name.

1891. I pursue, overtake and recover by fire, whatever the enemy has stolen from my head, in Jesus' name.

1892. My head, defy any spiritual summon to death or

failure, in Jesus' name.

1893. My head, refuse to cooperate with my enemy against me, in Jesus' name.

1894. My head, always prevail and excel, in Jesus' name.

1895. You powers manipulating my head, scatter and die by fire, in Jesus' name.

1896. Every household witchcraft power, fall down and die, in Jesus' name.

1897. Every waster of my prosperity, become impotent, in Jesus' name.

1898. Every known and unknown aggressor of my comfort, be paralyzed, in Jesus' name.

1899. Any power calling my head for evil, scatter, in Jesus' name.

1900. I fire back every arrow of witchcraft in my head, in Jesus' name.

1901. Every evil hand laid on my head when I was a little child, die, in Jesus' name.

1902. My head, reject every bewitchment, in Jesus' name.

1903. Arrows of darkness fired into my brain, die, in Jesus' name.

1904. Power of household wickedness upon my brain, die, in Jesus' name.

1905. My brain, wake up by fire, in Jesus' name.

1906. Holy Ghost fire, incubate my brain, in Jesus' name.

1907. Thou creative power of God, fall upon my brain now, in Jesus' name.

1908. Anything stolen from my brain, when I was a child, I repossess you now, in Jesus' name.

1909. You grave, holding my brain and its success captive, open up and vomit them to me by fire, in Jesus' name.

1910. You my head that has been rendered useless, begin to succeed by fire, in Jesus' name.

1911. You scorpions assigned against my head, release me and die by fire, in Jesus' name.

1912. Evil arrows fashioned against my head, I command you to go back to your senders, in Jesus' name.

1913. Spiritual worms assigned to devour my head, come out and die, in Jesus' name.

1914. Spiritual devourers assigned to devour my head, come out and die, in Jesus' name.

1915. Evil objects buried against the fruitfulness of my head, be uprooted and scatter by fire, in Jesus' name.

1916. Any power calling my head for evil, scatter, in Jesus' name.

1917. I fire back every arrow of witchcraft in my head, in Jesus' name.

1918. Every curse issued against my legs, break, in Jesus' name.

1919. Every agenda of darkness assigned to terrorise my

legs, scatter, in Jesus' name.

1920. Holy Ghost, overshadow my head, in Jesus' name.

1921. Holy Ghost, overshadow my feet, in Jesus' name.

1922. Holy Ghost, overshadow my hands, in Jesus' name.

1923. Holy Ghost, overshadow every part of my body, in Jesus' name.

1924. Father, by the power that breaks yokes, let every yoke upon my head, be broken, in Jesus' name.

1925. Father, by the power that breaks yokes, let every yoke upon my hands, break, in Jesus' name.

1926. Father, by the power that breaks yokes, let every yoke upon my legs, be broken, in Jesus' name.

1927. Every handwriting of darkness upon my head, I wipe you off by the power in the blood of Jesus, in Jesus' name.

1928. Every handwriting of darkness upon my hands, I wipe you off by the power in the blood of Jesus, in Jesus' name.

1929. Every handwriting of darkness upon my legs, I wipe you off by the power in the blood of Jesus, in Jesus' name.

1930. Holy Ghost fire, purge every poison out of my head, in Jesus' name.

1931. Holy Ghost fire, purge every poison out of my hands, in Jesus' name.

1932. Holy Ghost fire, purge every poison out of my feet, in Jesus' name.

1933. I soak my head, hands and feet in the blood of Jesus, in Jesus' name.

1934. Any problem that entered into my life through head attacks, die, in Jesus' name.

1935. Powers of my father's house, release my head by fire, in Jesus' name.

1936. Serpents and scorpions assigned against my head, die, in Jesus' name.

1937. I reject the spirit of the tail and I claim the spirit of the head, in Jesus' name.

1938. O God, arise and convert my hands to your weapons of war, in Jesus' name.

1939. Father, I decree that any good thing I lay my hands upon shall prosper by the power in the blood of Jesus, in Jesus' name.

1940. Every sluggishness upon my hands, l shake you off by the power in the blood of Jesus, in Jesus' name.

1941. My legs, receive the power of dominion, in Jesus' name.

1942. My feet, take me to my place of breakthrough by the power in the blood of Jesus, in Jesus' name.

1943. My feet, take me to my place of my divine assignment by the power in the blood of Jesus, in Jesus' name.

1944. Every arrow of bad luck fired at my feet, go back to your senders, in Jesus' name.

1945. Everywhere the soles of my feet shall tread, heaven will take dominion, in Jesus' name.

1946. Wherever I walk into, darkness will walk out, in Jesus' name.

1947. I receive the power to disgrace every leg pollution, in Jesus' name.

1948. Father, anoint my feet for uncommon speed, in Jesus' name.

1949. Father, anoint my feet for uncommon success, in Jesus' name.

1950. By the spirit of the prophet, I move forward by fire, in Jesus' name.

1951. By the spirit of the prophet, I take dominion over wickedness, in Jesus' name.

1952. Holy Ghost, anoint my legs for uncommon success, in Jesus' name.

1953. Holy Ghost, anoint my head, hands and legs for uncommon testimonies, in Jesus' name.

1954. Father, I fire back every arrow of sluggishness assigned to my feet, in Jesus' name.

1955. Anywhere I go, favour will be assigned to my feet, in Jesus' name.

1956. O Lord, let my feet be beautiful and bring glad tidings anywhere I go, in Jesus' name.

1957. Spirit of bad feet, backfire, in Jesus' name.

1958. Spirit of polluted feet, backfire, in Jesus' name.

1959. Every arrow fired into my head, go back to the sender, in Jesus' name.

1960. I decree that insanity is not my lot, so every arrow of insanity, go back to the sender, in Jesus' name.

1961. My head, be lifted up above my enemies around me, in Jesus' name.

1962. My head, be lifted up above the unbelievers around me, in Jesus' name.

1963. My head, hear the word of the Lord, arise, possess your possessions and possess your destiny, in Jesus' name.

1964. Every handwriting of darkness working against my head, backfire, in Jesus' name.

1965. I plug my head into the resurrection power of the Lord Jesus Christ, in Jesus' name.

1966. I plug my hands into the resurrection power of the Lord Jesus Christ, in Jesus' name.

1967. I plug my feet into the resurrection power of the Lord Jesus Christ, in Jesus' name.

1968. I plug my head into the socket of divine favour, in Jesus' name.

1969. I plug my hands into the socket of divine favour, in Jesus' name.

1970. I plug my feet into the socket of divine favour, in Jesus' name.

1971. Every curse assigned against my head, disappear, in Jesus' name.

1972. Every evil cap of my parents will not fit my head, in Jesus' name.

1973. My hands, receive fire to prosper, in Jesus' name.

PRAYERS OF RECOVERY

1974. Every good thing the enemies have stolen from me, I recover all, in Jesus' name.

1975. The years that devourers have devoured, be restored to me, in Jesus' name.

1976. The wall of Jericho resisting my moving forward, collapse, in Jesus' name.

1977. Evil hands anointed to waste my head, wither, in Jesus' name.

1978. Every arrow of untimely death fired into my brain, backfire, in Jesus' name.

1979. My head, hear the word of the Lord, arise and shine, in Jesus' name.

1980. Any dark invisible cover on my head, catch fire, in Jesus' name.

1981. Every curse operating against my hand, break by the power in the blood of Jesus, in Jesus' name.

1982. For my shame, I receive double breakthroughs, in Jesus' name.

1983. Every manipulation of my glory through my hair, scatter now, in Jesus' name.

1984. Every hand of the strongman upon my head, dry up, in Jesus' name.

1985. You the owners of evil load of shame and embarrassment, carry your load, in Jesus' name.

1986. Limiting powers of my father's house, leave me alone and die, in Jesus' name.

1987. Every power of death assigned against my head, die, in Jesus' name.

1988. Chains of stagnancy upon my head, break, in Jesus' name.

1989. Shrines that have swallowed my money, vomit it now, in Jesus' name.

1990. Every evil river stealing from me, dry up, in Jesus' name.

1991. Covenant of affliction in my life, break, in Jesus' name.

1992. Every grave dug for me, bury your digger, in Jesus' name.

1993. The dark padlock of the enemy shall not hold my glory down, in Jesus' name.

1994. The wickedness of the wicked assigned against me, terminate, in Jesus' name.

1995. Holy Ghost fire, arise and kill every satanic deposit in my head, in Jesus' name.

1996. My head, receive deliverance by fire, in Jesus' name.

1997. Every power summoning my finances to the grave, die, in Jesus' name.

1998. Thou power of God, arise and attack all covens assigned against my prosperity, in Jesus' name.

1999. Every ordinance invoked by the power of darkness into the heavens against the work of my hands, I wipe you off, in Jesus' name.

2000. My door of progress under lock and key, open, in Jesus' name.

2001. Blockage to my moving forward, clear away, in Jesus' name.

2002. Strongman in my foundation, be bound, in Jesus' name.

2003. Multiple testimonies that glorify the name of the Lord, manifest in my life, in Jesus' name.

PRAYERS OF DELIVERANCE OF THE HEAD

2004. Rain of wisdom, knowledge and favour, fall upon my head, in Jesus' name.

2005. Voices of strangers casting spells against my head, die, in Jesus' name.

2006. Blood of Jesus, water of life and fire of God, wash my head, in the name of Jesus.

2007 I shake off bullets of darkness from my head, in Jesus' name.

2008. My head shall not be bewitched, in Jesus' name.

2009. Every power using my hair against me, die, in Jesus' name.

2010. Invisible load of darkness upon my head, catch fire, in Jesus' name.

2011. My head, my head, receive the touch of the resurrection power of the Lord Jesus Christ, in Jesus' name.

2012. Though war should rise against me, in this will I be confident, in Jesus' name.

2013. And now shall my head be lifted up above my enemies round about me, in Jesus' name.

2014. Curses of thou shall not excel placed on my head, break, in Jesus' name.

2015. O Lord, deliver me not unto the will of my enemies, in Jesus' name.

2016. Divine raging storms, locate any coven assigned to bury the destiny of this country, in Jesus' name.

2017. O God, release your wrath upon every power of witchcraft troubling my destiny, in Jesus' name.

2018. O God, arise and root them out of their land in your anger, in Jesus' name.

2019. O God, arise and cast your fury upon the agents of affliction troubling my star, in Jesus' name.

2020. O Lord, let the way of my oppressors be dark and

slippery and let the angel of the Lord persecute them, in Jesus' name.

2021. O Lord, let destruction come upon my enemies unaware and the net they have hidden catch them, in Jesus' name.

2022. O Lord, let the enemy fall into the destruction he has created, in Jesus' name.

2023. O Lord, let not my enemies wrongfully rejoice over me, in Jesus' name.

2024. Father, let my enemies be ashamed and brought to confusion together with those who rejoice at my hurt, in Jesus' name.

2025. O Lord, let my enemies be clothed with shame, in Jesus' name.

2026. Stir up Thyself, O Lord and fight for me, in Jesus' name.

2027. Every evil altar erected for me and my family, be disgraced, in Jesus' name.

2028. O Lord, let the thunder of God smite every priest working against our country at the evil altar and burn them to ashes, in Jesus' name.

2029. Every ancestral secret retarding my progress, be revealed, in Jesus' name.

2030. Evil secret activities currently affecting my life, be exposed and disgraced, in Jesus' name.

2031. Every secret I need to know to excel spiritually and financially, be revealed, in Jesus' name.

2032. Every secret hidden in the marine kingdom affecting my elevation, be exposed and disgraced, in Jesus' name.

2033. Every secret hidden in satanic archives crippling my elevation, be exposed and disgraced, in Jesus' name.

PRAYERS OF HEALING OF BEWITCHED HANDS

2034. Thou power of bewitchment operating in my life, expire, in Jesus' name.

2035. Every barrier planted to stagnate me, break, in Jesus' name.

2036. Blood of Jesus, neutralize the satanic spell operating against me, in Jesus' name.

2037. Every parental curse of thou shall not excel, break, in Jesus' name.

2038. Power to pursue and recover what the enemies have stolen from me, fall upon me, in Jesus' name.

2039. Spiritual robbers stealing the prosperity of my family, die, in Jesus' name.

2040. Powers assigned to make me to be forgotten by my helpers, die, in Jesus' name.

2041. Every coded spell and incantation of limitation, be destroyed, in Jesus' name.

2042. Every fetish power assigned to fight me from the

504

cradle to the grave, die, in Jesus' name.

2043. O God, arise and make a way for me by your wonder working power, in Jesus' name.

2044. Evil hands strengthening my yoke, wither, in Jesus' name.

2045. My buried blessings, hear the word of the Lord, come out and manifest, in Jesus' name.

2046. Witchcraft battles assigned to disgrace me, die, in Jesus' name.

2047. Resurrection power of the Lord Jesus, break my yoke, in Jesus' name.

2048. Every battle assigned to make me naked, be buried, in Jesus' name.

2049. Yoke of hardship and poverty, break and release me, in Jesus' name.

2050. Thou horn of my star, continue to rise and shine, in Jesus' name.

2051. Hidden chains of darkness binding me to rags of poverty, catch fire, in Jesus' name.

2052. Power of the grave holding me down, break and let me go, in Jesus' name.

2053. Satanic undertakers assigned against me, you shall not succeed over my life, in Jesus' name.

2054. My Joseph, your season of showing forth has come, appear in your palace, in Jesus' name.

2055. Vulture of death flying against me, die, in Jesus' name.

2056. Every congregation of the dead appearing in my dream, perish, in Jesus' name.

2057. Holy Ghost power, arise and break my yoke, in Jesus' name.

2058. Every trigger of the chains of calamity, break and let me go, in Jesus' name.

2059. Generator of evil things in my life, be cut off, in Jesus' name.

2060. Powers chasing good things away from me, perish, in Jesus' name.

2061. O God, arise and wipe away my tears and replace it with joy, in Jesus' name.

2062. My life and destiny are not for sale in the market of darkness, in Jesus' name.

2063. Eaters of flesh and drinkers of blood, the hammer of fire shall break your mouths, in Jesus' name.

2064. Every pot of darkness cooking my star, catch fire, in Jesus' name.

2065. Blood of Jesus, erase the marks of the enemies from my forehead, in Jesus' name.

2066. Powers assigned to donate me for sacrifice, be suffocated, in Jesus' name.

PRAYERS OF PROMOTION

2067. O God, arise and let my miracle manifest by fire, in Jesus' name.

2068. Evil hands anointed to waste my head, wither, in Jesus' name.

2069. Every arrow of untimely death fired into my life, backfire, in Jesus' name.

2070. My head, hear the word of the Lord, arise and shine, in Jesus' name.

2071. Any dark invisible cover on my head, catch fire, in Jesus' name.

2072. Every curse operating against my head, die by the power in the blood of Jesus, in Jesus' name.

2073. Every manipulation of my glory through my hair, scatter now, in Jesus' name.

2074. Every hand of the strongman upon my head, dry up, in Jesus' name.

2075. Every power of death assigned against my head, die, in Jesus' name.

2076. Chains upon my head, break, in Jesus' name.

2077. Holy Ghost fire, arise and kill every satanic deposit in my head, in Jesus' name.

2078. My head, receive deliverance by fire, in Jesus' name.

2079. Every power summoning my head from the gate of the grave, die, in Jesus' name.

2080. Thou power of God, arise and attack all covens assigned against my head, in Jesus' name.

2081. Every ordinance invoked by the powers of darkness into the heavens against my head, I wipe you off, in Jesus' name.

2082. Rain of wisdom, knowledge and favour, fall upon my head, in Jesus' name.

2083. Voices of strangers casting spells against my head, die, in Jesus' name.

2084. Blood of Jesus, water of life and fire of God, wash my head, in Jesus' name.

2085. I shake off bullets of darkness from my head, in Jesus' name.

2086. Every power using my hair against me, die, in Jesus' name.

2087. Invisible load of darkness upon my head, catch fire, in Jesus' name.

2088. My head, my head, receive the touch of the resurrection power of the Lord Jesus Christ, in Jesus' name.

2089. And now shall my head be lifted up above my enemies round about me, in Jesus' name.

2090. Divine raging storms, locate any coven assigned to bury the destiny of this country, in Jesus' name.

2091. O God, release your wrath upon every power of

witchcraft troubling my destiny, in Jesus' name.

2092. O God, arise and root them out of their land in your anger, in Jesus' name.

2093. O God, arise and cast your fury upon the agents of affliction troubling my star, in Jesus' name.

2094. O Lord, let the way of the oppressor be dark and slippery and let the angel of the Lord persecute them, in Jesus' name.

2095. O Lord, let the enemy fall into the destruction he has created, in Jesus' name.

PRAYERS OF BREAKTHROUGH

2096. Foundation of my destiny, receive total and complete deliverance from ancestral pollution, in Jesus' name.

2097. I break the yoke of rising and falling working against my breakthrough, in Jesus' name.

2098. I am unstoppable by the power in the blood of Jesus, in Jesus' name.

2099. Every curse that does not want me to shine, break, in Jesus' name.

2100. I release my blessings from the cage of familiar spirits, in Jesus' name.

2101. I walk out of the cage of domestic witchcraft by the power in the blood of Jesus, in Jesus' name.

2102. Poison of serpents and scorpions, come out of my life, in Jesus' name.

2103. Stubborn and wicked tormentors assigned against me, wither, in Jesus' name.

2104. The anointing of the Lord that breaks every yoke, arise and break my yokes, in Jesus' name.

2105. Battles assigned to prolong my bondage, die, in Jesus' name.

2106. Powers drinking the blood of my breakthrough, wither and die, in Jesus' name.

2107. Enemies that are united to wage war against me, die, in Jesus' name.

2108. Powers sending evil birds to steal from me, die, in Jesus' name.

2109. Balaam and Balak conspiring to stop my breakthrough, perish, in Jesus' name.

2110. Powers diverting my blessings to a wrong location, wither, in Jesus' name.

2111. Battles assigned to kill my helpers, I judge you, die, in Jesus' name.

2112. Powers mocking me at the edge of my success, expire, in Jesus' name.

2113. My spirit man, reject defilement, in Jesus' name.

2114. O God, arise and let my breakthrough manifest, in Jesus' name.

2115. Arrow that steals good things fired into my life, backfire, in Jesus' name.

2116. My destiny, you shall not be a cloud without rain, in Jesus' name.

2117. Whether the enemies like it or not, I must sing my song and dance my dance, in Jesus' name.

2118. Every rag of suffering and chronic poverty, burn to ashes, in Jesus' name.

2119. Witchcraft projection into my dream to hijack my blessings, roast by fire, in Jesus' name.

2120. Powers delaying answers to my prayers, fall down and die, in Jesus' name.

2121. My glory, what are you doing in witchcraft prison? Come out and shine, in Jesus' name.

2122. Every vulture of death assigned against me, die, in Jesus' name.

2123. Graveyard clothes assigned against my breakthrough, catch fire, in Jesus' name.

2124. My life, hear the word of the Lord, receive fresh fire, in Jesus' name.

2125. Every Judas assigned to hand me over to buyers and sellers of glory, die, in Jesus' name.

2126. O God, arise and glorify your name in my life, in Jesus' name.

2127. Anointing to pursue, overtake and recover my blessings, fall upon me, in Jesus' name.

2128. Poison of darkness in my life, come out, in Jesus' name.

PRAYERS TO RELEASE YOUR STAR FROM STAR HUNTERS

2129. My star, my star, my star, reject bewitchment, in Jesus' name.

2130. Powers assigned to reduce the effectiveness of my star, die, in Jesus' name.

2131. Powers assigned to make my star attract pollution, die, in Jesus' name.

2132. Battles increasing my battles on daily basis, wither, in Jesus' name.

2133. Garment of affliction, my life is not your candidate, in Jesus' name.

2134. Powers assigned to make my gifts and potential useless, die, in Jesus' name.

2135. My head, receive deliverance from satanic loads, in Jesus' name.

2136. Rope of domestic witchcraft tying me down, break, in Jesus' name.

2137. Holy Ghost fire, incubate my life, in Jesus' name.

2138. Evil prayers killing my good news, die, in Jesus' name.

2139. Witchcraft bird flying against me, fall down and die, in Jesus' name.

2140. Evil tree harbouring my breakthrough, catch fire, in Jesus' name.

2141. Agenda of destiny hijackers against me, be wasted, in Jesus' name.

2142. Lion of Judah, roar against my mountain, in Jesus' name.

2143. Powers assigned to exchange my glory for shame, die, in Jesus' name.

2144. My prosperity in the belly of serpents, be released, in Jesus' name.

2145. Army of darkness blocking the angel of my breakthrough, perish, in Jesus' name.

2146. Dark angels, release my blessings in your custody, in Jesus' name.

2147. Tongues of the wicked cursing my breakthrough, dry up, in Jesus' name.

2148. My hands, hear the word of the Lord, possess your possessions, in Jesus' name.

2149. I delete evil days from my calendar this year, in Jesus' name.

2150. Where is the Lord of Elijah? Arise and let my story change, in Jesus' name.

2151. Satanic arrows fired at the work of my hands, catch fire, in Jesus' name.

2152. Every gate of hell holding what belongs to me, release it and burn to ashes, in Jesus' name.

2153. Foundation of my destiny, attract divine favour, in Jesus' name.

2154. No matter how far the enemy has gone, O God, arise and let me have victory over them, in Jesus' name.

2155. My project of prosperity, become successful, in Jesus' name.

2156. O Lord, let my enemies be clothed with shame, in Jesus' name.
2157. Stir up thyself, O Lord, and fight for me, in Jesus' name.
2158. Every evil altar erected for me and my family, be dismantled, in Jesus' name.
2159. Let the thunder of God smite every evil priest working against our country at the evil altar and burn them to ashes, in Jesus' name.
2160. Every ancestral secret retarding my progress, be revealed, in Jesus' name.
2161. Evil secret activities currently affecting my life, be exposed and disgraced, in Jesus' name.

PRAYERS OF DELIVERANCE FROM DREAM DEFILEMENT
2162. Arrows of dream pollution, come out of my life, in Jesus' name.
2163. I paralyze the forces on assignment to make me unfit for blessing, in Jesus' name.
2164. Let all my adversaries be clothed with shame and embarrassment continually, in Jesus' name.
2165. My hands, reject every pollution, in Jesus' name.
2166. Every arrow fired to downgrade my hands, I send you back to the senders, in Jesus' name.
2167. Authority of darkness assigned to paralyze my hands, die, in Jesus' name.
2168. My hands, reject the arrow of weakness and sadness, in Jesus' name.

2169. My hands, become the weapons of war, in Jesus' name.

2170. O God, arise and convert my hands to your battle axe, in Jesus' name.

2171. Arrow of delay fired at my glory, backfire, in Jesus' name.

2172. Thou power of slippery breakthroughs, lose your hold upon my life, in Jesus' name.

2173. Dream defilement to render my spiritual life empty, die, in Jesus' name.

2174. Evil plantation, come out of my life and destiny, in Jesus' name.

2175. Every sacrifice offered to Mother Earth against me, be reversed, in Jesus' name.

2176. Every coded curse issued against me, be cancelled, in Jesus' name.

2177. Anyone dancing to cut off my head, you shall dance no more, in Jesus' name.

2178. Power chasing me at night to abort my testimony, be arrested, in Jesus' name.

2179. Blood of Jesus, remove my name from the register of those marked for sudden death, in Jesus' name.

2180. Buyers and sellers of souls, my soul is not for sale, in Jesus' name.

2181. Every blood defilement, clear away by the blood of Jesus, in Jesus' name.

2182. Satanic nurses and doctors injecting poison into my system, be paralyzed, in Jesus' name.

2183. Anyone turning into strange creatures to attack me at night, die, in Jesus' name.

2184. Every blood of sacrifice speaking against me, be silenced forever, in Jesus' name.

2185. Family bondage, break, in Jesus' name.

2186. Witchcraft padlocks holding my breakthrough, break, in Jesus' name.

2187. O God, arise and my let my mouth be larger than that of my enemy, in Jesus' name.

2188. Messengers of bad news, my family is not your candidate, in Jesus' name.

2189. Wherever my spirit is locked down, Holy Ghost fire, set me free, in Jesus' name.

2190. By the key of the household of David, I open the door of my unending laughter, in Jesus' name.

2191. Anointing of all round success, fall upon me, in Jesus' name.

2192. Water of pollution, dry up from my body, in Jesus' name.

2193. Sickness, sorrow and pain are not my portion, in Jesus' name.

516

PRAYERS TO PARALYZE CAREER STRONGMAN

2194. Powers behind frustration at the edge of success, fail, in Jesus' name.

2195. My eagle, collect your wings back, arise and fly, in Jesus' name.

2196. O God, arise and make me a mysterious wonder this year, in Jesus' name.

2197. Curses delaying my celebration, break, in Jesus' name.

2198. Angels of my breakthrough, where are you? Appear, in Jesus' name.

2199. The crown of shame shall not fit my head, in Jesus' name.

2200. Powers of demonic sacrifice blocking my blessings, clear away, in Jesus' name.

2201. Powers waiting to feed me with the bread of sorrow and water of affliction, die, in Jesus' name.

2202. Witchcraft animals chasing blessings away from me, die, in Jesus' name.

2203. Powers putting evil legs on my breakthroughs, I cut off your legs with the sword of fire, in Jesus' name.

2204. Arrows denying me my harvest, die, in Jesus' name.

2205. Every spiritual burial done against me at the bank of any ancient river, be nullified, in Jesus' name.

2206. Where others have failed, I shall succeed, in Jesus' name.

2207. Powers assigned to shorten my hands in the spirit realm, wither, in Jesus' name.

2208. Strongman of my career success, be paralyzed, in Jesus' name.

2209. My hands, drop every rag of poverty, in Jesus' name.

2210. Masquerade of darkness, chasing helpers away from me, die, in Jesus' name.

2211. I collect back what the enemy has stolen from me sevenfold, in Jesus' name.

2212. Powers assigned to prolong my pain, die, in Jesus' name.

2213. I am unstoppable by the power in the blood of Jesus, in Jesus' name.

2214. Every curse hindering me from shining, break, in Jesus' name.

2215. I release my blessings from the cage of familiar spirits, in Jesus' name.

2216. I walk out of the cage of domestic witchcraft by the power in the blood of Jesus, in Jesus' name.

2217. Poison of serpents and scorpions, come out of my life, in Jesus' name.

2218. Stubborn and wicked tormentors assigned against me, wither, in Jesus' name.

2219. By the anointing of the Lord that breaks every yoke, I arise and break my yokes, in Jesus' name.

2220. Witchcraft worms assigned to eat up my success, die, in Jesus' name.

2221. Powers that want my problems to swallow me, die, in Jesus' name.

2222. Satanic expectation for my life, fail, in Jesus' name.

2223. Chain of bad luck, break and release me, in Jesus' name.

2224. My future shall not be buried in shame, in Jesus' name.

2225. Powers caging me from within, die, in Jesus' name.

PRAYERS AGAINST SATANIC ALTARS AND PRIESTS

2226. My destiny, I prophesy upon you, you shall be great, in Jesus' name.

2227. All my destiny helpers, I command you to appear, in Jesus' name.

2228. Every trap set to catch me, catch your owners, in Jesus' name.

2229. Spoilers and robbers of my glorious destiny, my destiny is not your candidate, die, in Jesus' name.

2230. All my enemies that are gathered against me, before I open my eyes, scatter, in Jesus' name.

2231. My blessings traded out by dark powers through demonic exchange, locate me, in Jesus' name.

2232. The evil legs roaming around strange places to harm me, wither, in Jesus' name.

2233. The satanic chapter opened against me, close by fire, in Jesus' name.

2234. Woe unto every vessel that the enemy is using against me, in Jesus' name.

2235. Arrows of darkness fired at me, go back to your sender, in Jesus' name.

2236. Satanic elders sitting on what belongs to me, I push you down from my blessing, in Jesus' name.

2237. I bind every spirit giving support to my enemy to harm me, in Jesus' name.

2238. Witchcraft snares purposely made to cage my finances, be broken, in Jesus' name.

2239. I destroy the timetable of the enemy for my life this year, in Jesus' name.

2240. Let God be God in every area of my life and in the lives of my children, in Jesus' name.

2241. I break the inherited cycle of failure operating in my life, in Jesus' name.

2242. Through these prayers, I receive deliverance, in Jesus' name.

2243. Words of the enchanters fighting my destiny, die, in Jesus' name.

2244. The satanically empowered word that is caging my eagle, wither, in Jesus' name.

2245. The wickedness of the wicked over my present and

future, expire, in Jesus' name.

2246. Every evil name the enemy is calling me, which is not my God-given name, wither, in Jesus' name.

2247. The enemy that has vowed not to let me go, woe to you, die, in Jesus' name.

2248. Associations that are gathered to destroy me, scatter and die, in Jesus' name.

2249. I release myself from the bondage of evil altars, in Jesus' name.

2250. I vomit every satanic poison that I have swallowed, in Jesus' name.

2251. I cancel every demonic dedication, in the name of Jesus.

2252. Every evil authority of family shrine or idol upon my destiny, crash, in Jesus' name.

2253. Every evil authority of witchcraft powers over my life and destiny, die, in Jesus' name.

2254. Every evil authority of satanic altars over my life and destiny, scatter, in Jesus' name.

2255. Every evil authority of the strongman over my life and destiny, perish, in Jesus' name.

2256. Every owner of evil load, carry your load, in Jesus' name.

2257. I render every aggressive altar impotent, in Jesus' name.

2258. Every evil altar erected against me, be disgraced, in Jesus' name.

2259. Anything done against my life under demonic anointing, be nullified, in Jesus' name.

2260. I curse every local altar fashioned against me, in Jesus' name.

2261. Let the hammer of the Almighty God smash to pieces every evil altar erected against me, in Jesus' name.

2262. O Lord, send your fire to destroy every evil altar fashioned against me, in Jesus' name.

PRAYERS TO TERMINATE DELAY

2263. Spirit of delay, lose you hold upon my life, in Jesus' name.

2264. Every evil priest ministering against me at an evil altar, receive the sword of God, in Jesus' name.

2265. Let the thunder of God smite every evil priest working against me at an evil altar and burn him to ashes, in Jesus' name.

2266. Let every satanic priest ministering against me at evil altars fall down and die, in Jesus' name.

2267. Any hand that wants to retaliate or arrest me because of all these prayers I am praying, dry up and wither, in Jesus' name.

2268. Every stubborn evil altar priest, drink your own blood, in Jesus' name.

2269. I possess my possession stolen through an evil altar, in Jesus' name.

2270. I withdraw my name from every evil altar, in Jesus' name.

2271. I withdraw my blessings from every evil altar, in Jesus' name.

2272. I withdraw my breakthroughs from every evil altar, in Jesus' name.

2273. I withdraw my glory from every evil altar, in Jesus' name.

2274. I withdraw my prosperity from every evil altar, in Jesus' name.

2275. I withdraw anything representing me at any evil altar, in Jesus' name.

2276. Powers assigned to make my star attract pollution, die, in Jesus' name.

2277. Battles increasing my battles on daily basis, wither, in Jesus' name.

2278. Garment of affliction, my life is not your candidate, catch fire, in Jesus' name.

2279. Powers assigned to make my gifts and potential useless, die, in Jesus' name.

2280. My head, receive deliverance from satanic loads, in Jesus' name.

2281. Rope of domestic witchcraft tying me down, break, in

Jesus' name.

2282. Holy Ghost fire, incubate my life, in Jesus' name.

2283. Evil prayers killing my good news, die, in Jesus' name.

2284. Evil gang up against my progress, scatter, in Jesus' name.

2285. Every yoke of rejection at my season of celebration, break, in Jesus' name.

2286. My life, move forward and upward, in Jesus' name.

2287. Enemies making dark consultations to waste my life, be buried, in Jesus' name.

2288. Powers using demonic marks to control my life negatively, be paralyzed and run mad, in Jesus' name.

2289. Strange marks assigned to make me sorrow this year, be wiped off, in Jesus' name.

2290. Satanic marks assigned to make me restless this year, clear away, in Jesus' name.

2291. Marks of darkness that want poverty to be my identity, clear away, in Jesus' name.

2292. Witchcraft marks that terminate joy and laughter, my life is not your candidate, in Jesus' name.

2293. Evil marks that make one to labour and sweat without favour, die, in Jesus' name.

2294. Demonic marks promoting emptiness and trading off my virtues, clear away, in Jesus' name.

PRAYERS FOR VICTORY IN THE COURT OF LAW

2295. O God, I plead for mercy (mention your name....). O God, be merciful unto me, in Jesus' name.

2296. Every curse of the vagabond and uselessness operating in my life, I break it, in Jesus' name.

2297. The powers that have conspired to keep me in obscurity in order to waste me shall die, in Jesus' name.

2298. Every tongue speaking against my getting justice, I silence you, in Jesus' name.

2299. I decree that I shall have favour before God and before the men that will lead me to victory, in Jesus' name.

2300. Every satanic gang up against my life, be broken, in Jesus' name.

2301. Powers holding my destiny in captivity, break, in Jesus' name.

2302. My life shall not be a workshop for the enemy of my soul, in Jesus' name.

2303. Let the power of redemption of the Lord Jesus intervene for my victory, in Jesus' name.

2304. The prison cell assigned to keep me out of circulation, release me now, in Jesus' name.

2305. All state prosecutors handling my case shall begin to show me favour, in Jesus' name.

2306. I break the yoke of incarceration holding me in captivity, in Jesus' name.

525

2307. Every spirit of wastage assigned to me by the enemy of my glory, die, in Jesus' name.

2308. (Mention your name) I command you to move from bondage to liberty, in Jesus' name.

2309. (Mention your name) I command the prison gate to release me, in Jesus' name.

2310. By the key of the household of David, let the prison door be opened for me, in Jesus' name.

2311. I break the hold of any evil power and authority over my life, in Jesus' name.

2312. I tear down the stronghold of satan working against me, in Jesus' name.

2313. Every voice of accusation against my victory, be silenced, in Jesus' name.

2314. I command my case to be revisited again. This time, the mercy of God shall intervene for me, in Jesus' name.

2315. Evil voice speaking against my deliverance, wither, in Jesus' name.

2316. O God, by your power, bring (mention your name) out of every valley of working without results, in Jesus' name.

2317. Invisible chains of environmental witchcraft that want to prolong my stay in captivity, break, in Jesus' name.

2318. Satanic legislation working against me, I nullify it now, in Jesus' name.

2319. The concluded work of darkness against my destiny, scatter, in Jesus' name.

2320. The key of my victory in the hands of spiritual robbers, be released now, in Jesus' name.

2321. Ancestral witchcraft embargo holding me down, break, in Jesus' name.

2322. The wind of positive change shall blow in my favour, in Jesus' name.

2323. Wickedness of the wicked, expire today, in Jesus' name.

2324. Every satanic set-up to frustrate me, be dismantled, in Jesus' name.

2325. Lord Jesus, by your mercy, pull (mention your name) out of the valley of hopelessness, in Jesus' name.

2326. Every evil chain tying down my greatness, break, in Jesus' name.

2327. I give thanks to God for His intervention in my case, in Jesus' name.

PRAYERS AGAINST PROJECT ABANDONMENT

2328. Powers assigned to make my helpers turn their backs on me, be buried, in Jesus' name.

2329. Anyone placing curses on any object representing me,

fall down and die, in Jesus' name.

2330. Any evil personality wearing rags to represent me in the demonic realm, die, in Jesus' name.

2331. Satanic priests using my pictures to project evil things into my destiny, die, in Jesus' name.

2332. Powers that say my prosperity will be for a while, you are liars, die, in Jesus' name.

2333. Darkness from the pit of hell assigned to suffocate my glory, expire, in Jesus' name.

2334. Satanic current flowing into my life for evil, I cut you off, in Jesus' name.

2335. Dead waters troubling the peace of my life, dry up, in Jesus' name.

2336. All my enemies shall prostate themselves to serve me, in Jesus' name.

2337. I shall not be used as a sacrificial animal on the table of darkness, in Jesus' name.

2338. Powers that say if I rise up, I will crash suddenly, you are liars, die, in Jesus' name.

2339. Wind of fire, release confusion into the camp of my enemy, in Jesus' name.

2340. Strangers of darkness, flee from the garden of my life and die, in Jesus' name.

2341. This year, I shall not struggle to be recognized for honour, in Jesus' name.

2342. I shall not use my hands to empower my enemies

against me, in Jesus' name.

2343. My season of celebration shall not be postponed or delayed, in Jesus' name.

2344. I speak to every mountain standing before me, move out of my way by fire, in Jesus' name.

2345. Generational curses assigned to make me serve people I am better than, break, in Jesus' name.

2346. O God, arise and provoke unending favour for me, in Jesus' name.

2347. Every graveyard cloth of death, catch fire, in Jesus' name.

2348. My head, reject the crown of shame and wear the crown of honour, in Jesus' name.

2349. My miracle of 'come and see what great thing God has done for me', appear by fire, in Jesus' name.

2350. I shall not eat the bread of sorrow nor drink the water of affliction, in Jesus' name.

2351. Powers assigned to steal my glory, my glory is not available to be stolen, in Jesus' name.

2352. Arrow that kills good things, fired at me, die, in Jesus' name.

2353. Any battle that has vowed to die with me, you are a liar, die, in Jesus' name.

2354. Battles that are older or stronger than me, die, in Jesus' name.

2355. My glory hidden in any ancient pot, come out and shine, in Jesus' name.

2356. Power of repeated problems, break and release me, in Jesus' name.

2357. Evil tongue licking my blessing, dry up, in Jesus' name.

2358. Powers that want to offer me as a sacrifice, be buried, in Jesus' name.

2359. O God, arise and bring honey out of the rock for me this month, in Jesus' name.

2360. All my imprisoned benefits, come out and locate me, in Jesus' name.

2361. Covenant of suffering, break and release me, in Jesus' name.

2362. O God, arise and add flavour to my favour, in Jesus' name.

2363. My destiny shall not be buried in shame, in Jesus' name.

PRAYERS TO TERMINATE SPIRITUAL BLINDNESS

2364. Arrows of spiritual sickness and dryness, come out of my life, in Jesus' name.

2365. Every tongue mocking me, be silenced, in Jesus' name.

2366. Powers assigned to make me live below my divine

destiny, die, in Jesus' name.

2367. Satanic lions blocking my way of success and progress, die, in Jesus' name.

2368. Congregation of the wicked gathered against me, scatter, in Jesus' name.

2369. Destiny Judas assigned to exchange my destiny for silver and gold, die, in Jesus' name.

2370. Hammer of fire, break barriers on my way to greatness, in Jesus' name.

2371. Every fasting of the wicked to sabotage my destiny, fail, in Jesus' name.

2372. Any evil thing done with dust or sand against me, expire, in Jesus' name.

2373. Every invisible wedding ring of darkness, catch fire, in Jesus' name.

2374. I receive power to shine and continue to shine in the midst of my enemies, in Jesus' name.

2375. Ungodly soul tie, break and release me, in Jesus' name.

2376. Every spell and prayer of darkness against me, expire, in Jesus' name.

2377. Powers that have vowed that I will suffer for what I did not do, you are liars, die, in Jesus' name.

2378. My head, you shall not be covered in shame, in Jesus' name.

2379. Evil plantation of the enemy in my head, come out

with all your roots, in Jesus' name.

2380. Battles that want my children to hate me, die, in Jesus' name.

2381. Evil hands assigned to feed me with poison, wither, in Jesus' name.

2382. Anywhere my destiny has been tied down, O God, arise and loose me, in Jesus' name.

2383. Jesus Christ, the yoke breaker, arise and break my yoke, in Jesus' name.

2384. The spirit behind rejection and failure, die, in Jesus' name.

2385. Chains of delay holding me down year in year out, break, in Jesus' name.

2386. Thou power of rising and falling, break and release me, in Jesus' name.

2387. All my wasted years and opportunities, be restored, in Jesus' name.

2388. The satanic panel forcing me to appear where I am not supposed to appear, die, in Jesus' name.

2389. No matter the strength of my pursuers, I break their powers by the hammer of fire, in Jesus' name.

2390. Principalities blocking my heavens, I pull you down, in Jesus' name.

2391. I cry to God for His mercies; let my heaven open by fire, in Jesus' name.

2392. Every contender with my angels of blessings, die, in

Jesus' name.

2393. Wandering spirits at night, you shall not prosper against me, in Jesus' name.

2394. Territorial strongman delegated against me, fall down and die, in Jesus' name.

2395. Demonic reinforcement against my breakthroughs, scatter, in Jesus' name.

2396. Let God be God in every area of my life, in Jesus' name.

2397. Bullets of death, my life is not your candidate, backfire, in Jesus' name.

2398. My heaven shall not be brass and my earth shall not be iron, in Jesus' name.

PRAYERS AGAINST SLIPPERY BREAKTHROUGHS

2399. Problems with the agenda to disgrace me, expire suddenly, in Jesus' name.

2400. Frustration and disappointment shall not be my portion, in Jesus' name.

2401. Battles ordained to demote my destiny, wither, in Jesus' name.

2402. My head, jump out of the altar of slaughter, in Jesus' name.

2403. The hiding place of the enemy in my life, become desolate, in Jesus' name.

2404. No evil power shall weigh me down, in Jesus' name.

2405. My celebration shall not become tribulation, in Jesus'

name.

2406. Every battle assigned to take my health, die, in Jesus' name.

2407. Every battle assigned to take my peace, die, in Jesus' name.

2408. Battles following me from my mother's womb, die, in Jesus' name.

2409. Battles that want me to grow old without any achievement, die, in Jesus' name.

2410. Battles that want me to labour without gain, die, in Jesus' name.

2411. Jesus Christ, you are the Man of battle, fight for me, in Jesus' name.

2412. O Lord, wherever I have been tied down, arise and set me free, in Jesus' name.

2413. Spirits behind rejection and failure at the edge of success, die, in Jesus' name

2414. Chains of delay holding me down, break, in Jesus' name.

2415. Satanic padlocks holding my breakthroughs down, break, in Jesus' name.

2416. All my wasted years, be restored to me with great blessings, in Jesus' name.

2417. Yoke of failure planted in my life during sleep, be uprooted and catch fire, in Jesus' name.

2418. No matter the strength of my oppressors, O God, arise and break it, in Jesus' name.

2419. The register of failure bearing my name, catch fire, in Jesus' name.

2420. Powers making progress difficult for me, die, in Jesus' name.

2421. Powers assigned to make me move around in cycles, break and release me, in Jesus' name.

2422. Powers hiding my breakthroughs in the rock, release them and perish, in Jesus' name.

2423. Powers assigned to make me live below my standard, fail and expire, in Jesus' name.

2424. Personality of darkness pushing me backwards in the race of life, die, in Jesus' name.

2425. Destiny-demoting dreams, my life shall not cooperate with you, in Jesus' name.

2426. Powers blocking me from entering my land of breakthrough, die, in Jesus' name.

2427. Every demonic panel set up against my destiny, expire, in Jesus' name.

2428. Forces of darkness suffocating me financially, die, in Jesus' name.

2429. Battle axe of God, arise and break the head of my stubborn enemies, in Jesus' name.

2430. Power hijacking my blessing before it gets to me, die, in Jesus' name.

2431. Spirit of stagnation programmed to stop me, wither, in Jesus' name.

2432. Witchcraft powers sponsoring delay in my life, be destroyed, in Jesus' name.

2433. Sickness assigned to tie me down, break and release me, in Jesus' name.

2434. I stop the enemy before they stop me, in Jesus' name.

2435. Battle of shame and embarrassment, my life is not your candidate, in Jesus' name.

2436. Thou power of slow progress, break and release me, in Jesus' name.

2437. My legs, depart from every evil bus stop, in Jesus' name.

2438. Powers registering me in the school of failure, die, in Jesus' name.

PRAYERS AGAINST DREAM HARASSMENT

2439. Dreams of oppression projected against my life, be destroyed, in Jesus' name.

2440. Witchcraft dreams programmed to make me fail, scatter, in Jesus' name.

2441. Dreams programmed to set my life backward, expire, in Jesus' name.

2442. Anti-favour dreams, cease, in Jesus' name.

2443. Wicked hands assigned to feed me at night, wither, in

Jesus' name.

2444. Anything tied or buried, hindering my progress, catch fire, in Jesus' name.

2445. I challenge my life with the fire of God, in Jesus' name.

2446. Strange animals projected into my dream to introduce stagnation, I cut you off, in Jesus' name.

2447. Glory terminators appearing in my dreams, be suffocated, in Jesus' name.

2448. Spiritual vampires appearing in my dreams, be destroyed, in Jesus' name.

2449. Success terminators assigned to trigger frustration through dreams, die, in Jesus' name.

2450. I place my hand on my head and destroy every evil mark of the enemy, in Jesus' name.

2451. Hidden blood covenant troubling my life, break, in Jesus' name.

2452. Night dreams aborting my breakthroughs in the day, be destroyed, in Jesus' name.

2453. All my enemies gathered against me, before I open my eyes, scatter, in Jesus' name.

2454. My blessings traded out by powers of darkness through demonic exchanges, be restored, in Jesus' name.

2455. The evil legs roaming around strange places to harm me, wither, in Jesus' name.

2456. Satanic chapters opened against me, close by fire, in Jesus' name.

OTHER BOOKS BY PASTOR LADEJOLA ABIODUN

- *Commanding supernatural blessings*
- *Deliverance from captivity*
- *Provoke your deliverance*
- *Our God is a big God*
- *Power to defeat satanic agents*
- *Power to move from poverty to prosperity*
- *Eagle believer*
- *Lord, I need a miracle*
- *A successful home*
- *The mystery of angelic intervention*
- *The mystery of power*
- *When your battle is from home*
- *The lost signs*
- *The power of prophetic destiny*
- *Power to make maximum impact*
- *Power against stubborn death*
- *I reject satanic embarrassment*
- *Power against environmental limitation*
- *Your season of promotion*
- *No more dryness*
- *Who is to be blamed?*
- *War against environmental poverty*
- *The mystery of divine favor*
- *Power to trouble your trouble*
- *Converting your pain to gain*

Printed in Poland
by Amazon Fulfillment
Poland Sp. z o.o., Wrocław
09 June 2023

8b5a4bf6-f7db-400f-8790-3175d1c9b9aeR01